Creating Successful Learning Environments for African American Learners With Exceptionalities

Creating Successful Learning Environments for African American Learners With Exceptionalities

Edited by Festus E. Obiakor and
Bridgie Alexis Ford

For information:

Corwin Press, Inc.
A Sage Publications Company
2455 Teller Road
Thousand Oaks, California 91320
www.corwinpress.com

Sage Publications Ltd.
6 Bonhill Street
London EC2A 4PU
United Kingdom

Sage Publications India Pvt. Ltd.
M-32 Market
Greater Kailash I
New Delhi 110 048 India

Printed in the United States of America

Library of Congress Cataloging-in-Publication Data

Creating successful learning environments for African American learners with exceptionalities / Festus Obiakor, Bridgie Alexis Ford, editors.
    p. cm.
Includes bibliographical references and index.
  ISBN 0-7619-4556-3 (cloth) — ISBN 0-7619-4557-1 (pbk.)
 1. African Americans—Education. 2. Special education—United States. 3. Discrimination in education—United States. 4. Educational equalization—United States. I. Obiakor, Festus E. II. Ford, Bridgie Alexis.
  LC2731 .C74 2002
  371.9´089´96073—dc21   2002005178

This book is printed on acid-free paper.

02   03   04   05   10   9   8   7   6   5   4   3   2   1

Acquisitions Editor:	Robb Clouse
Editorial Assistant:	Erin Clow
Copy Editor:	Hawley Roddick
Production Editor:	Diane S. Foster
Typesetter:	Siva Math Setters, Chennai, India
Proofreader:	Scott Oney
Indexer:	Molly Hall
Cover Designer:	Michael Dubowe
Production Designer:	Michelle Lee

Contents

Foreword

Teaching African American students successfully continues to be a challenging dilemma for far too many general and special educators. And it makes little difference where these students are located in the educational enterprise. Whether in PreK-12 grades or college, general or special education programs, public or private schools, or in urban or suburban settings, African American students are not performing as well as they should and can. Their performance is disproportionately low across all indicators, including academic achievement, program placements, attendance and persistence rates, and disciplinary referrals. These patterns are too consistent and persistent across time, location, and social class to be happenstance or merely the result of the motivation and abilities of individuals. Something is systematically amiss in the quality of general and special educational services deigned for African Americans and how they are delivered. Ironically, most efforts to change these trends have been driven by pathological orientations and techniques that emphasize what these children don't have and can't do. For example, the poor reading skills of African Americans are attributed to the lack of books and reading in their homes. They are at risk of school failure because of high incidences of poverty, single-parent homes, and residence in high-crime areas. Thus many reform initiatives to compensate for or correct these deficiencies attempt to build success on a foundation of failures, or social shortcomings. In reality, it is success that breeds success.

In this book, Obiakor and Ford expose many success-oriented avenues, which, when followed diligently, will create more successes. No doubt, achieving more success for African American students requires a fundamental shift in the orientations and obligations of general and special education leaders. Throughout most educational policies and practice to date, educators have placed the responsibility for failure on students and the onus of success on treating all students in the same categories the same. The problem with the first premise is it blames the victims, absolves educators of accountability, and makes the victims responsible for correcting their own problems. The second premise is flawed because it ignores the reality and relevance of diversity in humanity and education, as well as imposing European American standards of normalcy and rightness on all other ethnic groups. Consequently, when everybody is treated the same, students from other ethnic, racial, linguistic, social, and cultural groups are treated as if they were imitations of middle-class, English dominant, European Americans.

It is common knowledge that natal cultural socialization is always a critical variable in teaching and learning in general and special education. Is it any wonder, then, that African Americans and other students of color do not perform as well in school as they might, when they are always judged by, and have to learn according to, cultural rules and expectations that are not their own?

These impositions are unfair, unjust, and pedagogically unsound. African American students, like members of other ethnic groups, have the right to receive educational opportunities that validate and empower them through maximizing their learning opportunities. This can be done best by making their cultures and background experiences the sources and centers of their teaching and learning, or teaching them through who they are. By this, I totally agree with Obiakor and Ford in this book that teachers and other educators should design, implement, and assess instructional programs based on accurate knowledge about the lives, cultures, experiences, and perspectives of African American children and how they learn best.

To make this book successful, Obiakor and Ford invited many experienced scholars and educators to share their ideas on what works for African American learners. And it appears, they all agree that culturally insensitive education affects virtually all African American students but some to a greater extent than others. Those affected most negatively are poor, live in urban centers, and are assigned to special education. They are placed in double jeopardy by being African American and by having special education needs. Each of these identities is problematic for conventional educational sense making; together they cast a dismal shadow over the educational opportunities and outcomes of African Americans. These students receive the poorest quality education relative to intellectually stimulating programs, teachers' effectiveness, stability, physical and fiscal resources, and curriculum and instructional relevance. African American males in special education are the most marginalized of all students. They are highly disproportionately represented, especially in those categories of special education that are the most nebulous to define, the least financed, and the most isolating. In addition, they are the most susceptible to being misdiagnosed and the least likely of all students to move out of special education once placed there. Most of these situations apply to general as well as special education. Clearly, circumstances facing African American learners occur because too many educators do not understand—or confuse African American cultural values, behaviors, and nuances with social pathologies and educational impediments that need to be mediated or eradicated. For example, what some teachers consider to be indicators of attention deficiency may be nothing more than African American cultural proclivities toward motion and movement, dramatic presentation of self, and what Boykin (1986) calls *verve,* which can be understood as energetic, exuberant, and vivacious performance of expressions and engagements. Some speech behavior and reading habits are not language errors but characteristics of African American Ebonics. The tendency of some children to seek out the companionship of others and socialize while working on learning assignments may not be indicators of off-task behaviors, low attention span, and obstructive behaviors, but of cultural patterns of cooperative learning and stage- or context-setting prior to task performance. Diagnostic, achievement, aptitude, and attitude test scores of African American students are as much a function of having to negotiate incongruences between two significantly different cultural systems (mainstream school and African American) and their performance formats as individual capabilities. Consequently, many African American students are categorized as disturbed, with socially maladaptive and behavior disorders and language deficiency (and are undereducated or miseducated) because of cultural ignorance and disrespect on the part of some general and special educators and other school leaders.

Fortunately, there are other educators like Obiakor and Ford and the contributing authors to *Creating Successful Learning Environments for African American Learners With Exceptionalities* who are standing up and speaking out about the injustices these educational practices foist on African American students. They also are proposing different interpretations of, and alternative strategies for, meeting the challenges of educating African American students. They suggest that teaching for these students is more accurate, relevant, and effective when it is centered in their culture and ethnicity. To do this, general and special educators must have a thorough knowledge of the culture, experiences, and contributions of African Americans, and then use this knowledge to guide their educational decision making and instruction. Revising the content taught in all school subjects (including special education) to reflect this cultural knowledge is imperative. But it is not enough. All other dimensions of the educational enterprise have to be changed to be culturally responsive as well, including instruction, classroom and school climates, counseling and guidance, administration, discipline, performance assessment, and extracurricular activities.

Embedded within these proposals is the idea that African American students should have similar kinds and qualities of educational rights and opportunities as European Americans. This, however, does not mean that they should be treated identically. Rather, the new knowledge, attitudes, values, and skills African Americans are expected to learn should be initially filtered through their *own* cultural frames of reference. This proposal is not really radical or unorthodox. It already exists in generally accepted notions of what constitutes good teaching for mainstream students in the form of such ideas as building on prior knowledge, using students' established cognitive schemas, and scaffolding. These techniques must be applied to teaching African American students in special education as well. But they need to be translated from general, abstract principles to the specific, practical, and experiential realities of their cultural socialization and lives. The essence of these recommendations is articulated in this book as an appeal for using culturally responsive teaching with African American students in special education in order to dignify their humanity and improve their intellectual, academic, social, personal, and economic development. Knowing, respecting, and using their cultural frames of reference are prerequisites for determining and responding appropriately to their educational needs. In taking this stance, Obiakor and Ford stand up and step out for African American children to be taught through who they are culturally as well as developmentally; they are unequivocal advocates of culturally responsive teaching.

If teachers, researchers, policymakers, and other educators acquire the necessary knowledge and heed the advice found in this book, African American students in special education will have a far better chance of receiving more relevant, equitable, and excellent learning opportunities and outcomes. Fewer inappropriate referrals and less disproportion in special education will occur. Classroom instruction will be more stimulating and challenging. This will entice students to spend more engaged time and focused efforts on instructional tasks, which, in turn, will lead to higher levels of achievement. Students will be culturally validated and develop greater ethnic pride as they are empowered through high levels of academic and social achievement. I firmly believe positive benefits of culturally responsive teaching for African American students are profound. They have the potential to reverse the present achievement trends. However, the only questions that remain to be answered are: Will educational power brokers and decision makers do what is reasonable and right? Will they ensure that African American students are taught from the vantage point of who they are culturally and ethnically before they are expected to learn through other cultural frames of reference? Will they hold teachers and themselves accountable for doing culturally responsive teaching with African American students without any equivocation? The ideas, explanations, and techniques presented in this book lay some solid foundations for how this educational agenda should proceed in the field of special education. What remains to be done now is transferring this guidance into action in classroom instruction, teacher preparation, and school leadership. Our children deserve nothing less!

Geneva Gay, PhD
Department of Curriculum and Instruction
University of Washington, Seattle

REFERENCE

Boykin, A. W. (1986). The triple quandary and the schooling of Afro-American children. In U. Neisser (Ed.), *The school achievement of minority children: New perspectives* (pp. 57-92). Hillsdale, NJ: Lawrence Erlbaum.

Preface

The critical question today continues to be, "How can African American learners with and without exceptionalities maximize their fullest potential in school programs?" Many well-meaning general and special educators find themselves in precarious positions as they attempt to answer this question—they want to assist African American learners through appropriate educational programming, but they are faced with the traditional embodiments of misidentification, misassessment, miscategorization, misplacement, and misinstruction. The National Research Council (2002), an arm of the National Academy of Sciences (NAS) in Washington, D.C., noted in its report that "from the enactment of the 1975 federal law [Public Law 94-142] requiring states to provide a free and appropriate education to all students with disabilities, children in some racial/ethnic groups have been identified for services in disproportionately large numbers" (p. ES-1). This Council further confirmed that "disproportion in special education persists" (p. ES-1), especially for African American learners who find themselves in classrooms taught by unprepared, underprepared, and culturally insensitive teachers.

We believe in the special education that works for African Americans with exceptionalities. Sadly, the race for school reform and accountability has failed to yield fruitful dividends. In our opinion, the focus ought to be on programs that tap into the energies, gifts, and talents of African American learners. In addition, the focus must be on programs that respond to differences as strengths and not as weaknesses. The National Research Council (2002) offered a vision, one

> in which general and special education services are more tightly integrated; one in which no child is judged by the school to have a learning or emotional disability or to lack exceptional talent until efforts to provide high-quality instructional and behavioral support in the general education context have been tried without success. (p. ES-5)

It is in the spirit of this vision that we write *Creating Successful Learning Environments for African American Learners With Exceptionalities*. We go beyond the rhetoric of the blame game to present innovative pedagogical techniques that work. To achieve this noble goal, we invited some leading African American scholars and practitioners to share methods that can best help African American learners to maximize their fullest potential from early childhood to adulthood.

Creating Successful Learning Environments for African American Learners With Exceptionalities is a unique book for this day and age. It is divided into three parts: Part I presents foundations for educating African American learners. Part II discusses how learning environments can be managed or manipulated to buttress success for African American learners. And Part III describes how the school environment can be complemented to provide a comprehensive educational program for African American learners. These divisions present opportunities for general and special educators to have the (a) concrete rationale, (b) innovative knowledge base, and (c) additional components that optimize learning. The 17 chapters of this book are distinct, yet their ideas are remarkably interrelated. While Chapters 1 through 4 deal with foundational issues (e.g., school accountability, legal implications, and assessment and categorization issues), Chapters 5 through 10 present conceptual frameworks, pedagogical implications, key points to remember, and discussion questions. To a large measure, Chapters 11 through 16 discuss service delivery for young children, parental partnership, community participation, teacher preparation, and culturally responsive leadership. Chapter 17 presents summary comments on all the chapters of this book.

Creating Successful Learning Environments for African American Learners With Exceptionalities, in more ways than one, responds to the critical issues of misidentification, misassessment, miscategorization, misplacement, and misinstruction. It challenges tradition, yet it fosters the beautiful tradition of good teaching. Our premise in this book is that truly good teachers can work with African American children and youth at all grade levels. But we must prepare these teachers to be *good*. We can no longer afford to pretend that all is well—we are optimistic that innovative ideas presented in this book will go a long way to create unparalleled pathways for constructive discourse in the fields of general and special education. We agree that:

> When children come to school from disadvantaged backgrounds, as a disproportionate number of minority students do, high-quality instruction that carefully puts the prerequisites for learning in place, combined with effective classroom management that minimizes chaos, can put students on a path to academic success. (National Research Council, 2002, p. ES-4)

Our book shamelessly exposes traditional problems in general and special education; however, it also presents innovative and proactive solutions for school reformers, leaders, and practitioners interested in maximizing the fullest potential of African American learners.

Creating Successful Learning Environments for African American Learners With Exceptionalities can be used as a required survey text for undergraduate and graduate courses in special education. It can also be used as a supplementary text in general and special education. Courses in urban education, multicultural education, intercultural education, African and African American studies, and Africology will find this book useful. In addition, researchers and scholars will find it useful resource material. The multidimensional perspectives presented by the contributors highlight the unique strength of this book. We thank them for their excellent vision, both in joining us for this book project and in succinctly presenting their ideas. Books of this nature will only be successful through the wonderful support of friends and well-wishers. We especially thank Geneva Gay for writing the Foreword and Edgar Epps for writing the summary comments. Our heartfelt thanks go to our family and extended family members for their patience and love throughout this process.

REFERENCE

National Research Council (2002). *Minority students in special and gifted education.* Washington, DC: National Academic Press.

About the Editors

Festus E. Obiakor, PhD, is a Professor in the Department of Exceptional Education, University of Wisconsin—Milwaukee. He is a teacher, scholar, and consultant with a national and international reputation. He has served as a Distinguished Visiting Professor/Scholar at Frostburg State University, Hendrix College, Indiana University of Pennsylvania, University of Georgia, Eastern Illinois University, Abilene Christian University, West Virginia University, Hampton University, Marquette University, Illinois State University, and Brigham Young University. He is the author or coauthor of more than 100 publications, including books, articles, and essays, and he has conducted workshops and presented papers at local, state, regional, national, and international levels.

Bridgie Alexis Ford, PhD, is a Professor in the Department of Curricular and Instructional Studies, University of Akron, Akron, OH. She is the author or coauthor of several works in special education and general education journals and books, and of state level inservice training materials. Her work focuses on effective service delivery for African American youth and productive school partnerships with African American communities. Through grant funding, she has organized community-based programming for African American youth with and without disabilities. She is the first editor of *Multiple Voices,* the refereed publication of the Division for Culturally and Linguistically Diverse Exceptional Learners, a division of The Council for Exceptional Children. She has conducted numerous professional workshops for school and medical personnel and has presented papers at local, state, regional, national, and international conferences.

About the Contributors

Lisa J. Bowman, PhD, is a Post Doctoral Research Associate at Juniper Gardens Children's Project at the University of Kansas, Kansas City, KS. Her research focus is the early identification of special education students at high risk for school dropout.

Helen Bessant Byrd, PhD, is Professor of Special Education at Norfolk State University, Norfolk, VA. She is the author of numerous scholarly publications.

Gwendolyn Cartledge, PhD, is a Professor in the School of Physical Activity and Educational Services and Special Education Programs at Ohio State University. She teaches courses that focus on the academic and social development of children with mild disabilities, emphasizing students with serious emotional disturbances. Her professional research and writings have centered on the development of social skills in children with and without disabilities, with a more recent focus on learners from culturally diverse backgrounds. She currently is investigating interventions to reduce disciplinary and special education referrals for African American males.

Bertina H. Combes, PhD, is Associate Professor of Special Education at the University of North Texas (UNT). She holds a master's degree in education in administration and supervision from Southern University and a PhD in special education from the University of Texas. She also serves as Associate Dean for Educator Preparation and Academic Affairs in the College of Education at UNT. Her areas of research interests include transition of students with learning disabilities, mentoring, and diversity issues in teacher education.

Vera I. Daniels, PhD, is a Professor in the Institute for the Study and Rehabilitation of Exceptional Children and Youth, and Department of Special Education, at Southern University and A & M College, Baton Rouge, LA. She received her PhD from the University of Michigan, Ann Arbor, and her MEd from Southeastern Louisiana University, Hammond, LA. She also holds a BS from Alcorn State University, Lorman, MS. She engaged in postdoctoral studies as a Postdoctoral Scholar with the Center for Minority Research in Special Education at the University of Virginia, Charlottesville. Her research interests are in the areas of inclusion, classroom management, discipline, effective classroom practices, and issues related to minority students in gifted and special education.

Elizabeth A. Dooley, PhD, is Chair of the Department of Educational Theory and Practice, and Associate Professor of Special

Education, at West Virginia University located in Morgantown, WV. She has over 14 years of teaching and administrative experience in higher education and 9 years of public school and clinical teaching experience. She holds permanent teacher licensure in elementary education and special education (learning disabilities and mental retardation). She is the Program Coordinator for a nationally known, campus-based enrichment program, the Health Sciences Technology Academy, where more than 45 teachers and 500 high school students from culturally diverse groups receive specialized instruction in math, technology, and science each year. She has published in areas that focus on preparing teachers for diversity in the classroom, educating exceptional African American students, and summer enrichment programs for underserved groups.

Katherine (Kitty) L. Dooley is an attorney practicing in Charleston, WV. A sole practitioner, she is the principal of the Dooley Law Firm, where she practices in the areas of personal injury, medical malpractice, consumer rights, and juvenile law. She has served as counsel to the West Virginia Department of Education. She is a 1990 graduate of the West Virginia University College of Law with a doctor of jurisprudence degree and is a 1980 graduate of Marshall University with a bachelor's degree in journalism. She practiced law privately in both Bluefield and Charleston, WV, before opening her own practice. She is also a former Senior Assistant Attorney General working in consumer protection and antitrust law. She previously served in the U.S. Army as an intelligence officer, obtaining the rank of captain prior to her honorable discharge.

Beth A. Durodoye, PhD, is Associate Professor of Counseling at the University of North Texas. She earned her master's degree in counseling from Marshall University, and her EdD in counselor education from the University of Virginia. Her specialization is multicultural counseling with particular interests in African American families, and cross-cultural advocacy and training in education.

Regina L. Enwefa, PhD, is an Assistant Professor in the Department of Communicative Disorders, School of Allied Health Sciences, at Jackson State University, Jackson, Mississipi. She received a bachelor's degree in special education, early childhood education, and elementary education from Grambling State University and a master of arts degree in speech language pathology from the University of Illinois at Urbana-Champaign. She has a PhD in communication sciences and disorders in children and adults from Howard University, Washington, DC. She also has written for various scholarly publications and has been a frequent presenter at workshops and conferences nationally and internationally.

Stephen C. Enwefa, PhD, is Associate Professor in the Department of Educational Foundations and Leadership and Communicative Disorders in the School of Education at Jackson State University, Jackson, Mississippi. He earned his PhD in communication sciences and disorders in children and adults from Howard University, Washington, DC; an MA in speech and hearing sciences from the University of Illinois, Urbana-Champaign; and a master of public administration degree and a BS in chemistry from Grambling State University, Grambling, LA. He has more than 10 years of professional experience in university and public school settings and has given presentations at numerous conferences at local, state, national, and international levels. He is also the author of various scholarly publications.

Edgar G. Epps, PhD, is Professor of Educational Policy and Community Studies at the University of Wisconsin–Milwaukee, and Marshall Field IV Professor of Urban Education Emeritus at the University of Chicago. He was educated at Talladega College, Alabama; Atlanta University; and Washington State University, where he earned his PhD in sociology. He publishes in various scholarly publications. His research interests include race and ethnic relations, minority access to higher education, faculty diversity in higher education, and educational reform in urban school districts.

Adell Fair is the Principal of John Muir Middle School in Milwaukee, WS. He is a graduate of Mississippi Valley State University and received his master's degree from the University of Wisconsin–Milwaukee as well as an administrative license from Concordia University in Mequon, WS. During the last 28 years, he has been a parent, teacher, coach, mentor, and administrator and has won numerous awards for his work in these various roles. He and his wife, Martha Wheeler-Fair, Principal of Starms Early Childhood Centers in Milwaukee, have two daughters and live in Milwaukee.

Christlyn Frederick-Stanley is a school administrator in the Milwaukee Public Schools District currently working as an Assistant Principal at Neeskara Elementary School. She holds a master of education degree from National-Louis University in Evanston, IL. She has worked in Milwaukee Public Schools as an elementary teacher in an inclusive, multiaged classroom, and as a program implementer managing schoolwide programs. She has had many opportunities to present workshops on curriculum and successful schoolwide programs. She is actively involved in her community through her church and other organizations. She works diligently to ensure that all children receive an opportunity for quality education.

Geneva Gay, PhD, is Professor of Education at the University of Washington, Seattle, where she teaches graduate courses in general curriculum theory and multicultural education. She is nationally and internationally known for her scholarship in multicultural teacher education, curriculum design, classroom instruction, and the intersections of culture, ethnicity,

teaching, and learning. Her writings include more than 135 articles and book chapters as well as the coeditorship of several books, one of which received the 2001 Outstanding Writing Award from the American Association of Colleges for Teacher Education.

Patrick A. Grant, EdD, is Professor in the Department of Special Education at Slippery Rock University of Pennsylvania. He obtained his BS from Lincoln University. He has an MS in both art, speech, and drama and in counseling, as well as an EdD in special education from the University of Oregon. He is also the author of scholarly books and articles.

Pauline B. Grant is a Reading Specialist and Tutor at West Side Primary School, New Castle, PA. She holds a bachelor of science degree in education—as well as a master's degree in education—from Slippery Rock University, Slippery Rock, PA. In addition, she is the author of some scholarly publications.

Cheryl Evans Green, MSW, PhD, is Associate Professor at the College of Health and Public Affairs, School of Social Work, University of Central Florida. She has presented papers at different professional levels.

Cathy D. Kea, PhD, is an Associate Professor at North Carolina Agricultural and Technical State University in Greensboro, NC. She is a teacher educator, researcher, and writer who studies effective teaching variables, multicultural education and special education, and faculty-student mentoring relationships.

Martha Scott Lue, PhD, is Professor in the College of Education at the University of Central Florida, Orlando. A graduate of Florida Agricultural and Mechanical University and the University of Missouri, Columbia, in speech and language pathology, she holds an educational specialist degree in learning disabilities from Georgia State University–Atlanta. She also has a degree in special education from the University of Florida–Gainesville. Her research interests include urban diversity;

culturally, linguistically, and ethnically diverse learners; and exceptional learners. She is a member of many national professional organizations including the Council for Exceptional Children and the National Association for Multicultural Education. She serves as the Faculty Liaison for the Urban Network to Improve Teacher Education. A member of the Christian Methodist Episcopal Church, she holds membership in the national Delta Sigma Theta sorority.

Angela Stephens McIntosh is an Assistant Professor in the Department of Special Education at San Diego State University in California. She studied minority issues in special education in the Center of Minority Research in Special Education at the University of Virginia and is completing her dissertation. She served on the faculty at Hampton University in Hampton, VA, and has been a special education teacher for students with autism in Virginia Beach, VA. She resides in San Diego with her husband, father, and three children.

Loretta P. Prater, PhD, is Chair of the School of Family and Consumer Sciences at Eastern Illinois University. In addition to her administrative role, she has teaching responsibilities that include undergraduate classes in an introduction to education, family relations, sex education, addictions and the family; and the graduate level evaluation class. She has published in the areas of adolescent pregnancy and parenting, single parenthood, and school and family interactions. She has served as a consultant for community agencies and has completed applied research projects through successful grant writing initiatives.

Shelia Yvette Smalley, PhD, is an Associate Professor in the Department of Child, Family, and Community Sciences, College of Education, at the University of Central Florida, Orlando. A graduate of Bethune Cookman College, Daytona Beach, Florida, with an undergraduate degree in psychology, she has a degree from the University of Florida, Gainesville, in special education and educational leadership. She has served as a principal in the Orange County, Florida, public school system, a classroom teacher, a trainer of trainers, and a teacher trainer in exceptional education at the University of Central Florida. Her research focus includes culturally and linguistically diverse exceptional students and their parents; inner-city, at-risk students, parents, and communities. She is a member of numerous professional organizations, including the Council for Exceptional Children and Kappa Delta Pi, International.

Stanley C. Trent, PhD, received his doctoral degree in special education from the University of Virginia. He served as an Assistant Professor of Special Education at Michigan State University from August 1992 to May 1997. Currently, he is an Associate Professor of Special Education at the University of Virginia and the Director and Coprincipal Investigator of the Center of Minority Research in Special Education. His work related to inclusive education and the education of minority students with disabilities has appeared in various scholarly publications. In addition, he has served as a guest editor for two journal issues focusing on the education of culturally and linguistically different exceptional learners. He has published several book chapters and papers that focus on issues related to the education of this group of students. His unique professional experiences as a special education teacher, administrator, teacher educator, and researcher provide him with both the practical and theoretical knowledge needed to examine educational reform, sustainability, and instruction that positively affect the achievement of children with disabilities from culturally and linguistically diverse backgrounds. In 2000, he was named the Alpha Phi Foundation's Professor of the Year, International.

Cheryl A. Utley, PhD, is an Associate Research Professor in the Schiefelbusch Institute for Life Span Studies, Juniper Gardens Children's Project, University of Kansas, Kansas City, KS. She is a Courtesy Assistant Professor in the Department of Special Education, University of Kansas. Her graduate degrees are from the University of Arizona and the University of Wisconsin–Madison. She is a researcher, teacher educator, and scholar. Her specific interests include multicultural education and special education, assessment, observational learning, effective instructional practices, and research-to-practice issues.

Darrell L. Williams is a doctoral student in the Department of Administrative Leadership, University of Wisconsin–Milwaukee. In addition, he is currently the principal of Whittier School of Excellence, Milwaukee, WS. He received his master of arts in administrative leadership from Marian College, Fond Du Lac, WS, and a bachelor of science in elementary education from Rust College, Holly Springs, MS. Over the past 10 years, he has served in both teaching and administrative roles. He has coauthored several publications and has presented at several conferences on state and local levels.

Part I

Foundations of Educational Change

Chapter One

School Accountability and Reform: Implications for African Americans With Exceptionalities

Festus E. Obiakor and Bridgie Alexis Ford

Every child can learn. Every school can ensure the success of every child. Statements to this effect appear in goals statements, curriculum reports, and school district offices. They are posted in school buildings and appear as mottoes on school stationery. But does our education system behave as if they are true? If we truly believed that every child could learn under proper circumstances, we would be relentless in the search of those circumstances. We would use well-validated instructional methods and materials known to be capable of ensuring the success of nearly all children if used with intelligence, flexibility, and fidelity. We would involve teachers in constant, collaborative, professional development activities to continually improve their abilities to reach every child. We would frequently assess children's performance to be sure that all students are on a path that leads to success, and to be able to respond immediately if children are not making adequate progress. If children are falling behind despite excellent instruction, we would try different instructional approaches, and, if necessary, we would provide them with tutors or other intensive assistance. We would involve parents in support of their children's school success; we would check to see whether vision, hearing, health, nutrition, or other nonacademic problems were holding children back, and then we would find a solution to those problems. If we truly believed that all children could learn, we would rarely, if ever, assign children to special education or long-term remedial programs that in effect lower expectations for children. If we truly believed that all schools could ensure the success of all children, then the failure of even a single child would be cause for great alarm and immediate, forceful intervention.

—Robert E. Slavin, Nancy A. Madden,
Lawrence J. Dolan, and Barbara A. Wasik (1996, p. xi)

These issues raised by Slavin and colleagues indicate the failure of general and special educators to address educational problems confronting today's children and youth, especially those who are at risk of school failure. Interestingly, every new day brings new reform or accountability programs, yet the more things change, the more they remain the same. Earlier, Cuban (1984, 1990) and Kauffman, Kameenui, Birman, and Danielson (1990) noted that educators have fallen prey to the kind of "hard-sell" mentality that often accompanies reform movements. According to Kauffman and colleagues, there is a constant search for easy solutions, rather than "hard thinking that brings about advances in theory, application, and practice" (p. 114). For African American learners, the question has been simple and consistent: that is, how can we provide equitable educational programs that help them to maximize their fullest potential? However, the responses have been inconsistent, disingenuous, and sometimes racist. Today, while the reform rhetoric continues, too many African American learners continue to be misidentified, misassessed, miscategorized, misplaced, and misinstructed (Obiakor, 2001). One is left to wonder if we are really interested in solving these problems or if we are interested in the politics of the problems. In this chapter, we examine historical and current special education contexts as they affect school accountability and reform programs for African American learners. In addition, we prescribe ways to create successful learning environments for African American children and youth with exceptionalities.

LESSONS FROM HISTORY: DEFERRED DREAMS

Historically, the struggle for equality has been at the forefront of most African Americans in the United States. Though there are pockets of restructuring and reform programs that have buttressed academic success of African American learners, the undergirding principle of equitable educational programming for these learners remains a problem. Consider the endemic predicaments confronting them in school programs. First, standardized instruments are consistently used to misjudge their intelligence or place them in restrictive special education programs (Hilliard, 1992, 1995; Obiakor, Algozzine, & Ford, 1994). Second, teacher expectations of them are frequently inaccurate and negative (Obiakor, 1999, 2000, 2001). Third, they are consistently perceived to have "low" or "negative" self-concept or self-worth (Obiakor, 1992, 1995). Fourth, they continue to lack realistic role models who understand their history, symbols, cultural values, and learning styles in school programs (Harvey & Scott-Jones, 1985; Ogbu, 1990). And fifth, schools in their neighborhoods are still viewed as "bad" or "poor" schools (Obiakor, 2001).

While the above multidimensional problems continue to manifest themselves in general and special education programs for African Americans, efforts to address them have been culturally one-dimensional and ill conceived. For instance, school reform programs have continued to place more emphasis on excellence through high stakes testing and less emphasis on common sense or practical perspectives that work. This quest for higher test scores legitimizes the monocultural mentality that landmark court actions (e.g., *Brown v. State Board of Education of Topeka,* 1954) have sought to combat. As Corder and Quisenberry (1987) concluded, "during the first half of the 20th century, courts were kept busy deciding the constitutionality of educational issues in regard to Black Americans" (p. 156). Earlier, Staples (1984) decried the plight of African Americans in school programs. He noted that "the ideology of equal opportunity masks the reality of a country stratified along racial, gender, and class lines" (p. 12). He also became saddened by what he called the *new racism* which (a) tends to deny the existence of racism or the responsibility for it, (b) defends phony meritocracy, and (c) relies on standardized tests that are not valid predictors of quality performance. A few years later, Jackson (1988) focused on the entrenched problems that are correlates of overrepresentation and underrepresentation of African Americans in special and gifted programs, respectively. They are

1. Loss of teaching and administrative jobs by Blacks through dismissals, demotions, or displacement

2. Loss of racial models, heroes, and authority figures for Black children

3. Loss of cherished school symbols, programs, and names of schools by Black children when their schools were closed and they were shifted to White schools

4. Subjection to segregated classes and buses and exclusion from extracurricular activities

5. Suspension and expulsion of disproportionate numbers of Black students

6. Exposure of Black children to hostile attitudes and behavior of White teachers and parents

7. Victimization by forced one-way busing policies and the uprooting of Black children for placement in hostile school environments

8. Victimization by misclassification in special education classes' tracking systems

9. Victimization by unfair discipline practices and arbitrary school rules and regulations

10. Victimization by ignorance of Black children's learning styles and cultural, social, educational, and psychological needs (p. 455)

The aforementioned problems have put an added pressure on school accountability and reform programs for African American learners. It is imperative that reformers acknowledge these traditional problems before initiating change policies. We cannot talk about equal education for all when, in reality, our traditional educational programs foster historical inequities. We must continue to ask what reform and restructuring lessons have been learned from history. What efforts must be made to design programs that foster quality and equity? How can general educators understand the relationship between what they do and what happens to students in special education? For African American learners, these questions must be answered to initiate and design equitable and quality programs at all educational levels.

HOW "SPECIAL" IS SPECIAL EDUCATION FOR AFRICAN AMERICAN LEARNERS?

Special education was intended to be individualized and tailor-made for each child with a special need. The Education of All Handicapped Children Act (1975) ensured that all children, despite their disability, would have the right to enter into the public education system and receive a free and appropriate education (Smith, 1998). For the past 26 years, many general and special educators have carried out only the letter, not the spirit, of this legislation. As a result, many scholars (e.g., Daniels, 1998; Russo & Talbert-Johnson, 1997) have questioned whether or not this was a form of resegregation under the guise of educational reform. Interestingly, special education was intended to buttress regular education (Shapiro, Loeb, Bowermaster, Wright, Headden, & Toch, 1993) and on the surface, it seemed to have great face validity. For example, consider that special education laws required (a) special education classrooms to maintain a lower teacher-to-pupil ratio than regular education classrooms, (b) special expenditures that are two to four times higher than those of general education, (c) specially tailored programs designed specifically for the child, and (d) special services to be delivered by well-prepared teachers (MacMillan & Reschly, 1998).

For more than 4 decades, the judicial system has been involved in the arena of special education on account of such unbalanced representation. Many landmark cases have demonstrated the unethical use of standardized measures in schools to place African American children into special education. The courts ruled in the above cases that IQ tests alone were not valid for placing children into inferior special education classrooms. In the *Larry P. v. Wilson Riles* (1979 & 1986) case, Judge Peckham put a moratorium on intelligence tests for Black children in California. These cases brought national attention to this issue. As MacMillan and Reschly (1998) stated, the outcry of the people was not merely because African Americans were disproportionately represented in special education classes but because they were also put in classes that were stigmatizing, degrading, and less effective than their previous regular education classes.

Apparently, the current selection process for special education has been labeled as inadequate, misleading, unethical, and dangerous (Obiakor & Johnson, 1997). The use of controversial methods (e.g., IQ tests) has been debated in courts over the past 4 decades. Sadly, these inadequate assessments and discriminatory tests are still employed with great regularity (Obiakor, Harris-Obiakor, Obi, & Eskay, 2000; Ysseldyke & Marston, 1999). It is no wonder that the disproportionate representation of African Americans in special education programs has attracted national attention (National Research Council, 2002; Obiakor & Utley, 2001; Patton, 1998). To effectively analyze how "special" special education has been for African American learners and fully create successful learning environments for those with exceptionalities, the intricate steps of special education (identification, assessment, categorization, placement, and instruction and intervention) must be briefly examined.

Identification

As early as the 1960s and 1970s, many concerned scholars and educators warned that special education would be disserving to certain students, and the manifestation of this prophecy still holds true in this new millennium for many students from diverse ethnic, socioeconomic, and linguistic backgrounds (Grossman, 1998). The identification of a student sets the stage for further legally mandated activities not routinely addressed in regular education classrooms. Once a child has been identified as having an educational disability, the laws (e.g., reauthorization of the Individuals With Disabilities Education Act of 1997) mandate that teachers employ several interventions before the next phase (i.e., testing) is set in motion. In a recent study, Sbarra and Pianta (2001) reported that kindergarten and first-grade teachers differ in perception for competence behaviors between African American and Caucasian students. Furthermore, they observed that the differences expressed were based on the cultural biases of teachers. Parents trust and rely on certified educators to detect various disabilities; however, some teachers play on the subjective nature of the current system and abuse this initial referral protocol as a means of getting rid of selected students they deem as incorrigible (Obiakor, 1999; Obiakor, Algozzine, et al., 2002).

Grossman (1998) acknowledged that most educators do not believe they are biased against those outside the mainstream society. These educators tend to forget that schools are a microcosm of the larger society. He further noted that people see what they expect to see and that the propaganda of the media has vilified those outside the mainstream culture. As a consequence, teachers judge ethnic minority and poor students' behaviors as more deviant than European children, even when they are exactly the same. In the same vein, these teachers are more likely to bequeath praise and congratulatory remarks and attentiveness to European students in comparison to African Americans (see Grossman, 1998; New, 1996; Sbarra & Pianta, 2001). Frequently, inappropriate identification is followed by inappropriate assessment, another gross injustice (Obiakor, 2001; Obiakor, Algozzine, et al., 2002).

Assessment

Educators have continued to use outdated materials and assessment instruments despite the decisions of the courts, outcry from parents, and failing schools. The current assessment procedure is based on a myopic strategy (Boykin, 2000), a one-size-fits-all paradigm (Obiakor, Algozzine, et al., 2002) despite the great heterogeneity inside and outside schools. An assessment measure is designed to present valuable information to the specialist to determine the needs of the child; however, assessment tools used in special education cases are designed to produce scores used to determine eligibility (Obiakor, Algozzine, et al., 2002).

The irony of the aforementioned process is that many creators of these same instruments (e.g., Alfred Binet) warned that a single number could not describe an individual's intelligence and could produce a brutal pessimism (Kwate, 2001; Onwuegbuzie & Daley, 2001). For instance, Kwate stated that IQ scores are inherently meaningless and misleading and have outlived the usefulness they once had. Moreover, these assessments cannot assess African American children's giftedness, and thus they do serious harm to them. Scholars (Allen & Graden, 1995; Obiakor, Algozzine, et al., 2002; Ysseldyke & Marston, 1999) have suggested that schools approach assessment from a developmental perspective and not from a deficit perspective. In a search for pathology, educators and psychometricians spend more time assessing African American children to declare them eligible for categorical labels and special education placements (Gardner, 1993).

Categorization

There is a great deal of ambiguity regarding the criteria for categorical labeling in special education. Very often, biased teachers predict an ominous cloud of doom for African American students who fail to conform to their individual standards. For instance, the etiology of learning disabilities (LD) is a psychological enigma. Many schools use an arbitrary IQ-achievement discrepancy, which is not empirically supported, to determine eligibility. Therefore, criteria for the same diagnosis can vary within the same city and state. Ysseldyke and Marston (1999) stated that psychometric measures could not reliably differentiate between students with LD and those who are low achievers (LA); furthermore, the LD criteria are inadequate in discriminating between LD and LA students (Graden, Casey, & Christenson, 1985). This ambiguity may be found in the lack of empirical evidence to differentiate between children with mild cognitive disability and those with academic difficulties (see Ysseldyke & Marston).

In his classic book, *The Futures of Children: Categories, Labels, and Their Consequences*, Hobbs (1975) noted that words and labels are needed to classify students but that they make victims out of students. As he pointed out:

> Categories and labels are powerful instruments for social regulation and control, and they are often employed for obscure, covert, or hurtful purposes: to degrade people, to deny their access to opportunity, to exclude "undesirables" whose presence in some way offends, disturbs familiar custom, or demands extraordinary effort. (p. 11)

Ysseldyke, Algozzine, and Thurlow (2000) later reiterated Hobbs's views when they wrote:

> Labeling students is not a benign activity nor is it a necessary evil, as school officers and others sometimes claim. Despite a presumed need for them, labels are an unfortunate by-product of a system that attaches money to acts, thus resulting in classifications and categories. Labels are often irrelevant to the instructional needs of students. Furthermore, labels become real attributes that prevent meaningful understanding of actual individual learning needs. By causing some to believe that students labeled as having mental retardation cannot perform certain tasks, the act of classifying condemns these students to a life of lesser expectations and performance. Labels require official sanction. Resources diverted to the process of identifying and classifying students are extensive. Time and money spent on labeling are time and money not spent on teaching. Time spent being labeled is time not spent being taught or learning. (p. 110)

Placement

It has been proven that special education has a disproportionate number of ethnic minorities diagnosed with various disabilities (Reschly & Ysseldyke, 1995; Sparks, 1999; Strickland & Ascher, 1992). Some scholars (e.g., Patton, 1998) have acknowledged that special education is structurally flawed and does not have the best interest of African American learners at heart. Between 1980 and 1990, special education as a whole increased among all racial groups: European Americans increased 6%, African Americans increased 13%, Hispanic Americans increased 53%, and Asian Americans/Pacific Islanders increased 107.8% (U.S. Department of Education, 2000). Earlier, in her investigation, Harry (1992) discovered that the national data can be a little misleading. For instance, it was reported that African Americans make up 16% of the general enrollment and 21% of special education enrollment. Yet, when probed deeper, the African American population, which constituted 16% of the general school population, made up 35% of the Educable Mentally Retarded (EMR) category, 27% of the Trainable Mentally Retarded (TMR) category, and 27% of the Seriously Emotionally Disturbed (SED) classification. In addition, while some categories of exceptionalities are objective (e.g., vision, hearing, and traumatic brain injury), some are not objective (e.g., learning disabilities and mental retardation); and some are even desirable (e.g., gifted and talented programs where African American learners are, unfortunately, underrepresented).

It is sad to note that the mandated laws in special education are seldom treated as laws. Frequently, they are treated as suggestions or proposals. It is no surprise that nonachieving African American learners are placed in special education classes before academic interventions are attempted. The paradox is that the intervention for these learners has been the actual placement into retrogressive special education classes. Obiakor (1999), Patton (1998), and Russo and Talbert-Johnson (1997) agreed that these learners are placed in educational structures that are not conducive to their academic success. In other words, African American learners are more likely to be tracked for punishment facilities, pathological labels, and subsequent placements in special education. Unfortunately, in these placement settings, they receive stigmatizing labels, isolation from peers, and patronizing teachers. In the end, many of these students grow up to experience low rates of employment, low income, and increased rates of incarceration.

Instruction and Intervention

It is logical to assume that misidentification leads to misassessment, misassessment leads to miscategorization, miscategorization leads to misplacement, and misplacement leads to misinstruction and misintervention (Obiakor, 1994, 1999, 2001; Obiakor & Johnson, 1997). In their classical work more than 3 decades ago, Henderson and Bibens (1970) asked reform-based questions that teachers interested in being accountable to their students must address. The questions include

1. Is the teacher able to put his [her] students at ease?

2. Is the teacher's voice pleasant, or is it harsh and irritating to the listener?

3. Is the teacher positive in his [her] classroom techniques or does he [she] have a negative approach to teaching?

4. Is the teacher able to present material in an interesting and meaningful way so that he [she] holds the attention of his [her] student?

5. Is the teacher sincere with members of his [her] class?

6. Does the teacher's classroom bearing suggest that he [she] enjoys teaching, or does it appear that to him [her] teaching is just a job?

7. Does the teacher exhibit a sense of humor, or is the entire learning situation a dry and boring process?

8. Does the teacher have a real concern for all of his [her] students? Does he [she] appear to want to help each student in the learning activity?

9. Does the teacher know and understand the material he [she] teaches, or does he [she] attempt to bluff his [her] way by pretending to know more than he [she] actually does? (p. 143)

The above questions are sometimes swept under the rug in many school reform quarters. There is almost a Band-Aid approach to good teaching. Obiakor (2001) and Orlich, Harder, Callahan, and Gibson (2001) argued that good teaching must incorporate

1. The school milieu

2. A holistic view of instruction

3. Equity as the big picture

4. Sequencing and organizing of instruction

5. Goals, standards, and outcomes for instruction

6. Managing of the classroom environment

7. The process of questioning

8. Inquiry, teaching, and higher-level thinking

9. Small-group discussions and cooperative learning

10. Monitoring of student success

Undoubtedly, the phony definition of "good" teaching and intervention has been very harmful to many African American learners. The school sometimes is not viewed as a learning community where individuals from different cultural, racial, and socioeconomic backgrounds come together (Ford, Obiakor, & Patton, 1995). *Goodness* is rarely used to define schools in African American neighborhoods even though the majority of the teachers who teach African American learners are Anglo Americans. Apparently, these teachers are culturally disconnected from these children whom they teach. The critical questions are these: How can African American children and youth perform to the optimal level when they confront these negative burdens in school programming? Why are educational interventions for African American learners not effective, proactive, and innovative? Why are school reform programs for African American students always political rather than realistic?

MAKING SCHOOL REFORM ACCOUNTABLE TO AFRICAN AMERICAN LEARNERS

We believe it is the responsibility of general and special educators to search beyond their five senses and delve into the realm that transcends what they think they see and what they think they know to discover the precious gifts and talents hidden inside the temples of African American learners. Apparently, some school reformers are unwilling to disrupt their equilibrium and accept the arduous task of maximizing the fullest potential of all their students, not just those they presume to be "good" students (Obiakor, 2001). To make this happen in our demographically changing society, it is essential to have an ecological model that supports the collaboration and consultation of all entities of our society. This ecological model is the comprehensive support model (CSM) which encourages collaboration of the student, family, school, community, and government in the teaching-learning process (Obiakor, 1994, 1999, 2001; Obiakor, Grant, & Dooley, 2002).

Based on the CSM, school accountability and reform must be everyone's business. It becomes imperative to inspire the student's self to try new things. To maximize the potential of the self, African American students must believe in themselves. In addition, their families must believe in them, the school must be a least-restrictive environment for them, the community must be creative in providing opportunities and choices for them, and the government must make laws and provide financial assistance that supports them. This can be particularly helpful to African Americans who have consistently endured racial discrimination, lowered expectations, and illusory generalizations in school programs. As a consequence, reform-minded scholars and educators must respond to the following critical questions:

1. How can African American learners be self-empowered and recognized as a part of the solution?

2. How can African American families be valued as equal partners in the educational programs for their children?

3. How can schools be nonrestrictive learning environments that foster multidimensional teaching-learning processes for African American students?

4. How can communities shift their paradigms to provide positive opportunities and choices for African American learners?

5. How can local, state, and federal governments protect and assist African American learners?

In this new millennium, we must make everyone accountable to the teaching-learning process of African American learners. All components of the CSM must listen to each other and communicate as they empower each other. The blame game must be over to allow positive forces to collaborate, consult, and cooperate for the common good of the whole village. To make school reform programs accountable to African American learners, the whole village must be at work (Obiakor, 1994, 1996, 2001). Not long ago, the Milwaukee Catalyst (1998) reiterated the whole-village concept of accountability that highlights five essential school-community relationships, namely:

1. Effective school leadership

2. Family-community partnerships

3. A school environment that supports learning

4. Effective staff development and collaboration

5. A quality instructional program (p. 1)

As the Milwaukee Catalyst concluded,

> Making practices like these a reality requires major changes—not only in the class-room but also in the way the entire school is run and in its ties with students, families, and the community. Making these changes allows the schools to focus their responses and attention on improving teaching, learning, and the student achievement for all children. (p. 2)

Simply put, general and special educators must do something innovative, creative, and visionary if they are going to assist African American learners with exceptionalities to survive the burdens of misidentification, misassessment, miscategorization, misplacement, and misinstruction and misintervention. School reformers can no longer afford to ignore any part of the whole village—they must begin and continue to listen to multiple voices.

CONCLUSION

In this chapter, we have examined historical and current special education contexts as they affect school accountability and reform programs for African American learners. In addition, we have prescribed ways to create successful learning environments for African American children and youth with exceptionalities. We strongly agree that as individuals are different, so must the teaching-learning process be. Ironically, this has not been the precedent in traditional educational programming for African American learners. It appears that we have consistently talked about responding to individual differences as we teach and interact, but, very often, regarding African Americans, these differences are viewed as deficits. Our experiences tell us that educational reform programs for African Americans have failed to yield measurable dividends—we are tempted to ask, "Where's the beef?"

As it appears, the more things change for African American learners, the more they remain the same. In fact, we wonder if general and special educators are interested in solving problems confronting African American learners or if they are interested only in the politics of the problems. This dangerous phenomenon leads us to ask two critical questions: How can we avoid the mistakes of the past in school accountability and reform programs for African American learners? How can we initiate and design visionary programs? We believe realistic special education programs are necessary for African American learners who truly have disabilities; however, we also believe many of these learners do not deserve to be in such segregated programs. The reason is simple—traditional educational programs are loaded with discriminatory practices, unrealistic expectations, disproportionate representations, and illusory conclusions. To minimize these complex problems and make reform programs accountable, we must adopt a CSM that incorporates powerful energies of the self, family, school, community, and government. In fact, the whole village must be at work if we must truly help African American learners to maximize their fullest potential. In the end, our paradigms must be shifted and our resolve must be stronger if we are to create successful learning environments for African American learners with exceptionalities.

REFERENCES

Allen, S. J., & Graden, J. L. (1995). Best practices in collaborative problem solving for intervention design. In A. Thomas & J. Grimes (Eds.), *Best practices in school psychology* (Vol. 3, pp. 667-678). Washington, DC: National Association of School Psychology.

Boykin, A. W. (2000). Talent development, cultural deep structure, and school reform: Implications for African immersion initiatives. In D. S. Pollard & C. S. Ajirotutu (Eds.), *African-centered schooling in theory and practice* (pp. 143-161). Westport, CT: Bergin & Garvey.

Brown v. Board of Education of Topeka, 347 U.S. 483 (1954).

Corder, L. J., & Quisenberry, M. L. (1987). Early education and Afro-Americans: History, assumptions and implications for the future. *Early Education: Journal of the Association for Childhood Education International, 63*, 154-166.

Cuban, L. (1984). School reform by remote control: SR 813 in California. *Phi Delta Kappan, 66*, 213-215.

Cuban, L. (1990). Reforming again, again, and again. *Educational Researcher, 19*(1), 3-13.

Daniels, V. I. (1998). Minority students in gifted and special education programs: The case for educational equity. *The Journal of Special Education, 32*(1), 41-43.

Education for All Handicapped Children Act (1975), Pub. L. No. 94-142, 20 U.S.C. § 1401 *et seq.*

Ford, B. A., Obiakor, F. E., & Patton, J. M. (Eds.). (1995). *Effective education of African American exceptional learners: New perspectives.* Austin, TX: Pro-Ed.

Gardner, H. (1993). *Multiple intelligences: The theory of practice.* New York: Basic Books.

Graden, J. L., Casey, A., & Christenson, S. L. (1985). Implementing a prereferral intervention system: Part II. The data. *Exceptional Children, 51*, 467-496.

Grossman, H. (1998). *Ending discrimination in special education.* Springfield, IL: Charles C Thomas.

Harry, B. (1992). *Cultural diversity, families, and the special education system.* New York: Teachers College Press.

Harvey, W. B., & Scott-Jones, D. (1985). We can't find any: The elusiveness of Black faculty members in American higher education. *Issues in Education, 3*(1), 68-76.

Henderson, G., & Bibens, R. F. (1970). *Teachers should care: Social perspectives of teaching.* New York: Harper & Row.

Hilliard, A. G. (1992). The pitfalls and promises of special education practice. *Exceptional Children, 59*, 168-172.

Hilliard, A. G. (1995). Culture, assessment, and valid teaching for the African American student. In B. A. Ford, F. E. Obiakor, & J. M. Patton (Eds.), *Effective education of African American exceptional learners: New perspectives* (pp. ix-xvi). Austin, TX: Pro-Ed.

Hobbs, N. (1975). *The futures of children: Categories, labels, and their consequences.* San Francisco: Jossey-Bass.

Individuals With Disabilities Education Act Amendments (1997), Pub. L. No. 105-17.

Jackson, J. L. (1988). In pursuit of equity, ethics, and excellence: The challenge to close the gap. In K. Ryan & J. M. Cooper (Eds.), *Kaleidoscope: Readings in education* (5th ed., pp. 44-448). Boston: Houghton-Mifflin.

Kauffman, M. P., Kameenui, E. J., Birman, B. P., & Danielson, L. (1990). Special education and the process of change: Victim or master of educational reform? *Exceptional Children, 57*, 109-115.

Kwate, N. A. O. (2001). Intelligence or misorientation? Eurocentrism in the WISC–III. *Journal of Black Psychology, 27*, 221-238.

Larry P. v. Wilson Riles (1979 & 1986). C-71-2270 FRP. Dist. Ct.

MacMillan, D. L., & Reschly, D. J. (1998). Overrepresentation of minority students: The case for greater specificity or reconsideration of the variables examined. *The Journal of Special Education, 32*(1), 15-24.

Milwaukee Catalyst. (1998). *Facts: A resource guide.* Milwaukee, WI: Author.

National Research Council. (2002). *Minority students in special and gifted education.* Washington, DC: National Academic Press.

New, C. A. (1996). Teacher thinking and perceptions of African American male achievement in the classroom. In F. A. Rios (Ed.), *Teacher thinking in cultural contexts* (pp. 85-103). Albany: State University of New York Press.

Obiakor, F. E. (1992). Self-concept of African American students: An operational model for special education. *Exceptional Children, 59*, 160-167.

Obiakor, F. E. (1994). *The eight-step multicultural approach: Learning and teaching with a smile.* Dubuque, IA: Kendall/Hunt.

Obiakor, F. E. (1995). Self-concept model for African American students in special education settings. In B. A. Ford, F. E. Obiakor, & J. M. Patton (Eds.), *Effective education of African American exceptional learners: New perspectives* (pp. 71-88). Austin, TX; Pro-Ed.

Obiakor, F. E. (1996). Collaboration, consultation, and cooperation: The "whole village at work." In N. Gregg, R. C. Curtis, & S. F. Schmidt (Eds.), *African American adolescents and adults: An overview of assessment issues* (pp. 77-91). Athens: University of Georgia; Roosevelt Warm Springs Institute for Rehabilitation, Learning Disabilities Research and Training Center.

Obiakor, F. E. (1999). Teacher expectations of minority exceptional learners: Impact on "accuracy" of self-concepts. *Exceptional Children, 66*, 39-53.

Obiakor, F. E. (2000, October). *Transforming teaching-learning to improve student achievement.* Position paper presented at the Best Practice conference, Institute for the Transformation of Learning, Marquette University, Milwaukee, WI.

Obiakor, F. E. (2001). *It even happens in "good" schools: Responding to cultural diversity in today's classroom.* Thousand Oaks, CA: Corwin.

Obiakor, F. E., Algozzine, B., & Ford, B. (1994). Education reform and service delivery to African American students. In S. G. Garcia (Ed.), *Addressing cultural and linguistic diversity in special education: Issues and trends* (pp. 1-9). Reston, VA: The Council for Exceptional Children.

Obiakor, F. E., Algozzine, B., Thurlow, M., Gwalla-Ogisi, N., Enwefa, S, Enwefa, R., & McIntosh, A. (2002). *Addressing the issue of disproportionate representation: Identification and assessment of culturally diverse students with emotional or behavioral disorders.* Arlington, VA: Council for Children With Behavioral Disorders, a Division of the Council for Exceptional Children.

Obiakor, F. E., Grant, P., & Dooley, E. (2002). *Educating all learners: Refocusing the comprehensive support model.* Springfield, IL: Charles C Thomas.

Obiakor, F. E., Harris-Obiakor, P., Obi, S. O., & Eskay, M. (2000). Urban learners in general and special education programs: Revisiting assessment and intervention issues. In F. E. Obiakor, S. A. Burkhardt, A. F. Rotatori, & T. Wahlberg (Eds.), *Advances in special education: Intervention techniques for individuals with exceptionalities in inclusive settings* (pp. 115-131). Stamford, CT: JAI Press.

Obiakor, F. E., & Johnson, M. J. (1997). Children and youth at risk: From understanding to intervention. *Emporia State Research, 40*(1), 1-15.

Obiakor, F. E., & Utley, C. A. (2001). Culturally responsive teacher preparation for programming for the twenty-first century. In C. A. Utley & F. E. Obiakor (Eds.), *Special education, multicultural education, and school reform: Components of quality education for learners with mild disabilities* (pp. 188-207). Springfield, IL: Charles C Thomas.

Ogbu, J. U. (1990). Understanding diversity: Summary statements. *Education and Urban Society, 22*, 425-429.

Onwuegbuzie, A. J., & Daley, C. E. (2001). Racial differences in IQ revisited: A synthesis of nearly a century of research. *Journal of Black Psychology, 27*, 209-220.

Orlich, D. C., Harder, R. J., Callahan, R. C., & Gibson, H. W. (2001). *Teaching strategies: A guide to better instruction* (6th ed.). Boston: Houghton Mifflin.

Patton, J. (1998). The disproportionate representation of African Americans in special education: Looking behind the curtain for understanding and solutions. *The Journal of Special Education, 32*(1), 25-31.

Reschly, D. J., & Ysseldyke, J. E. (1995). School psychology paradigm shift. In A. Thomas & J. Grimes (Eds.), *Best practices in school psychology* (Vol. 3, pp. 17-31). Washington, DC: National Association of School Psychology.

Russo, C. J., & Talbert-Johnson, C. (1997). The overrepresentation of African American children in special education: The resegregation of educational programming? *Education and Urban Society, 29,* 136-148.

Sbarra, D. A., & Pianta, R. C. (2001). Teacher ratings of behavior among African American and Caucasian children during the first two years of school. *Psychology in the Schools, 38,* 229-238.

Shapiro, J. P., Loeb, P., Bowermaster, D., Wright, A., Headden, S., & Toch, T. (1993, December 13). Separate and unequal. *U.S. News and World Reports,* pp. 1-8.

Slavin, R. E., Madden, N. A., Dolan, L. J., & Wasik, B. A. (1996). *Every child, every school: Success for all.* Thousand Oaks, CA: Corwin.

Smith, D. D. (1998). *Introduction to special education: Teaching in an age of challenge* (3rd ed.). Needham Heights, MA: Allyn & Baker.

Sparks, S. (1999). Educating the Native American learner. In F. E. Obiakor, J. O. Schwenn, & A. F. Rotatori (Eds.), *Advances in special education: Multicultural education for learners with exceptionalities* (pp. 73-90). Stamford, CT: JAI Press.

Staples, R. (1984, March/April). Racial ideology and intellectual racism: Blacks in academia. *The Black Scholar,* pp. 2-17.

Strickland, D. S., & Ascher, C. (1992). Low-income African American children and public schooling. In P. W. Jackson (Ed.), *Handbook of research on curriculum: A project of the American Educational Research Association* (pp. 609-625). New York: Macmillan.

U.S. Department of Education. (2000). *Twenty-second annual report to Congress on the implementation of the Individuals With Disabilities Act.* Washington, DC: U.S. Government Printing Office.

Ysseldyke, J., & Marston, D. (1999). Origins of categorical special education services in schools and a rationale for changing them. In D. J. Reschly, W. D. Tilly, & J. P. Grimes (Eds.), *Special education in transition: Functional assessment and noncategorical programming* (pp. 1-18). Longmont, CO: Sopris West.

Ysseldyke, J. E., Algozzine, B., & Thurlow, M. L. (2000). *Critical issues in special education* (3rd ed.). Boston: Houghton Mifflin.

Chapter Two

Legal Foundations of Special Education for African American Learners

Elizabeth A. Dooley and Katherine L. Dooley

The education of African American students and the education of children with disabilities have been historically exclusionary. Students with disabilities were not permitted to attend public schools, and the courts generally upheld exclusionary practices until the early 1970s (Alexander & Alexander, 1995; Osborne, 1996). Prior to 1868, the educational rights of African American children were not recognized as constitutional because many individuals did not believe children of color were worthy of an education. In fact, equal protection under the law was not considered until the Fourteenth Amendment was ratified in 1868. Even after the ratification of the Fourteenth Amendment, Jim Crow laws (i.e., state-sanctioned discrimination) did not allow for equal educational opportunities (Alexander & Alexander, 2001). The education of students with disabilities begins with an era consisting of discriminatory practices and exclusion and continues to this era when African American students are denied an education based on race and placed disproportionately in special education settings.

At a time when compulsory school attendance laws were imposed on parents in 1853, African American children and children with disabilities were denied an education. Governmental leaders believed education was key to the advancement of its citizens. Many states had compulsory attendance laws, yet many students were clearly denied access to a quality education. Alexander and Alexander (1995) reported that the government favored education for its citizens and viewed, as they indicated, compulsory attendance in the best interest of the United States:

> Mass education is not only the best and surest means of preservation of liberty, but it is also essential to the economic and social welfare of the people. Horace Mann (in 1848) probably expressed it best when he said that "for the creation of wealth, then—for the existence of a wealthy people and a wealthy nation—intelligence is the grand condition. . . . The greatest of all arts of political economy is to change a consumer into a producer; and the next greatest is to increase the producing power—an end to be directly attained, by increasing his intelligence." (p. 15)

It is important to note that in those days African American students were either denied an education or were provided an education in a separate, segregated environment with little to no resources. Separate and unequal schooling was the order of the day. However, the efforts of parents and some advocacy groups have led to some inroads for both groups. This chapter discusses the legal foundations of special education for African American learners. Embedded in this discussion are the relationship between the civil rights legislation and litigation and special education legislation and litigation.

CIVIL RIGHTS LEGISLATION AND LITIGATION

Over the years, civil rights legislation and disability legislation have made it possible for all children to be entitled to a free and appropriate education. Civil rights legislation was enacted to prohibit discrimination based on race, color, or national origin. Special education legislation was enacted to ensure that all students with disabilities are granted the opportunity to receive a free and appropriate education. Thus all children have educational rights.

The landmark case of *Brown v. Board of Education of Topeka* (1954) held that schools segregated based on race were inherently unequal and a violation of the Fourteenth Amendment to the Constitution guaranteeing equal protection of the law to all citizens of the United States. This case marked the first time that the guarantees of the Fourteenth Amendment were made applicable to public education. In this case, the Supreme Court concluded that in the field of public education, the doctrine of separate but equal had no place because separate educational facilities were inherently unequal. The Court held that the plaintiffs and others similarly were deprived of the equal protection of the laws guaranteed by the Fourteenth Amendment.

At the time when the Brown case was heard by the Supreme Court, there were actually four cases where plaintiffs were challenging separate but equal schooling practices. The four cases were each concerned with an aspect of de facto racial segregation, "governmentally promulgated and enforced discrimination in the South" (Alexander & Alexander, 2001, p. 507). Since the cases were similar, the Supreme Court consolidated the four cases into one.

After the Brown decision, blatant acts of discrimination continued to be of grave concern. As a result, the Civil Rights Act of 1964 was enacted to protect the rights of all people and to protect citizens against rampant injustices. The Civil Rights Act states that "No person in the United States shall, on the ground of race, color, or national origin, be excluded from participation in, be denied benefits of, or be subjected to discrimination under any program or activity receiving federal financial assistance" (Title VI, § 601). This act applied to all school districts receiving funding from federal programs. Districts found to be out of compliance with Title VI by engaging in practices that exclude students from educationally sound programs, or discriminating against students, or denying students services where a benefit or opportunity exists, will be in jeopardy of losing federal funding. Because of the civil rights legislation and because of the implications of the decision in the Brown case concerning other groups who were denied rights to an education, it was not long before others realized that the Court's application of the equal protection to public education could have wider application than just to race. The decision rendered in Brown held special promise to those students with disabilities.

SPECIAL EDUCATION LITIGATION AND LEGISLATION

Eighteen years after Brown, the special promise of the Brown decision to children with special needs began to get attention because parents of children with mental retardation and advocacy groups began to challenge exclusionary practices. As a result, two important court cases were litigated, bringing about favorable and major changes in the ways in which children with disabilities were treated. The first was the *Pennsylvania Association for Retarded Children v. Commonwealth of Pennsylvania* (PARC) case (1972). In this case, the plaintiffs (parents of 17 children with mental retardation) contended that students were not receiving the public education to which they were entitled. The court concluded that

> A retarded child should receive a free, public program of education and training appropriate to the child's capacity, within the context of a presumption that, among the alternative programs of education and training required by statue to be available, placement in a regular public school class is preferable to placement in a special public school class [i.e., a class for "handicapped" children] and placement in a special public school class is preferable to placement in any other type of program of education and training. (cited in Alexander & Alexander, 2001, p. 440)

The second major case was *Mills v. Board of Education of District of Columbia* (1972). Plaintiffs in this case charged that children with special needs (approximately 22,000 children with retardation, emotional disturbances, blindness, deafness, speech problems, and learning disabilities) were improperly excluded from public schools without due process of the law. The court ruled in favor of the plaintiffs. Alexander and Alexander (2001) reported that the courts enumerated 14 directives. The first directive stipulated the following:

> No child eligible for a publicly supported education in the District of Columbia public schools shall be excluded from regular public school assignment by a rule, policy, or practice of the Board of Education . . . or its agents unless such child is provided (a) adequate alternative educational services suited to the child's needs, which may include special education or tuition grants, and (b) a constitutionally adequate prior hearing and periodic review of the child's status, progress and the adequacy of any educational alternative. (cited in Alexander & Alexander, 2001, p. 442)

In addition to the court rendering the decision that no student shall be excluded from a public education, within those 14 directives, the court established guidelines for due process.

Soon after the PARC and Mills cases, federal legislation was introduced to Congress. Also, 46 right-to-education cases were filed in 28 states (Yell, 1998). Thereafter, federal statutes aimed at securing the rights of people with disabilities were enacted. Chief among these was the Education for All Handicapped Children Act (EAHCA; 1975). In the EAHCA, the principles of the least restrictive environment and individualized educational planning were joined with free, appropriate, and nondiscriminatory practices along with a federal commitment to financially supported state programs. When the law was later amended in 1990, it became the Individuals With Disabilities Education Act (IDEA), which continued to require public schools to (a) provide a free and appropriate education at public expense, (b) meet state standards from preschool through secondary school, and (c) conform with the demands of individualized education programs. These aforementioned cases and laws have impacted special education and equal educational opportunities for all students. As a result, issues related to the desegregation of education for African American students and the integration of students with disabilities into the public school system became major parts of school accountability and reform movements.

SPECIAL EDUCATION AND THE AFRICAN AMERICAN STUDENT

The public school system has had a major role to play in creating an environment conducive to and supportive of all students learning. Because of federal and state mandates, educational agencies are required to provide equal educational opportunities and cannot discriminate against any student. School personnel have a legal obligation to provide all children with equal access and equal educational opportunities. Ironically, while the early common law, developed through successful litigation in the area of civil rights, led to tremendous progress and strides in the area of special education, there continue to be concerns about inequitable educational practices for African American learners. There is evidence to suggest that even when the most sophisticated laws are in place, African American learners and students with disabilities continue to experience inequities in the educational system. Inequities for both populations are most often related to issues of access to special education services as evidenced in referral, evaluation, and placement. Inequities for the African American learner consist of issues of ability grouping, misidentification, and minority overrepresentation in special education (Grossman, 1995; Individuals With Disabilities Act, 1997; Markowitz, Garcia, & Eichelberger, 1997; Oswald, Coutinho, Best, & Nirbhay, 1999; Russo & Talbert-Johnson, 1977). For instance, in a study conducted by Oswald and colleagues, they found that African American students were 2.4 times more likely to be identified as mildly mentally retarded and 1.5 times more likely to be identified as seriously emotionally disturbed than their non-African American peers. Earlier, the U.S. Department of Education Department of Civil Rights (1995) reported that African American students constituted 21% of all students in special education classes in the United States and accounted for 16.8% of the public school population. The overrepresentation of African American students and ability grouping (tracking) of students have resulted in the resegregation of classrooms around the county. Dooley and Voltz (1999) stated that

> It's uncanny to note that while *Brown vs. the Board of Education* (1954, 1955), was the most significant school desegregation case, requiring that schools make a "good faith effort to desegregate schools with all deliberate speed," there continue to be practices

that perpetuate segregation in the educational system. Two examples of these practices are the disproportionate placement of African American children in special education and "tracking." (p. 19)

Information from annual and technical reports suggests that there are concerns over the education of children with disabilities and African American children. The U.S. Department of Education Department of Civil Rights (1999) reported that 6,628 discrimination complaints were filed during the fiscal year of 1999. Fifty-one percent of those complaints were filed against elementary and secondary schools; 43% were filed against postsecondary education institutions. Of the total number of complaints filed alleging discrimination, 57% were filed on the basis of disability; 25% were filed on the basis of race and national origin. Because of the disproportionate representation of minority youth in special education, the IDEA (1997) required each state receiving federal assistance to collect and report data on race and ethnicity in addition to disability. More specifically, states must report the following by race and ethnicity:

1. The number of children with disabilities who are receiving a free appropriate public education

2. The number of children with disabilities who are receiving early intervention services

3. The number of children with disabilities who are participating in regular education

4. The number of children with disabilities who are in separate classes, separate schools or facilities, or public or private residential facilities

5. The number of children with disabilities who, for each year of age from 14 to 21 years, stopped receiving special education and related services because of program completion or other reasons

6. The number of children with disabilities who are removed to an interim alternative educational setting

7. The number of infants and toddlers, by race and ethnicity, who are at risk of having substantial developmental delays and who are receiving early intervention services

In addition to reporting data, the IDEA (1997) specifically addressed the issue of disproportionality. States must make provisions to collect and examine data to determine if significant disproportionality based on race is occurring in the state with respect to the identification of children as children with disabilities, and with respect to the placement in certain educational settings. If a significant disproportionality exists in either of these cases, the state will be required to make provisions to review the policies, procedures, and practices used to identify children with disabilities and to make the necessary revisions to ensure compliance with the IDEA.

IMPLEMENTATION OF SPECIAL EDUCATION LAWS FOR AFRICAN AMERICANS

While federal laws are in place to ensure that all students receive an appropriate education, there continue to be inequalities in education, particularly for African American children. Perhaps teachers and administrators need more guidance when it comes to procedural safeguards

---

BOX 2.1   GOOD INTENTIONS BUT POOR IMPLEMENTATION OF IDEA

Demetria, a third grader, was referred for special education testing. She was an A-to-B student, and there was no apparent reason that she should have been referred for special education testing. When confronted, her teacher stated that she was concerned about Demetria's future success, particularly in middle school. The teacher continued by providing her opinion of her future success by stating that she was having difficulty processing information and that, in order for this student to grasp information, she (the teacher) had to repeat directions to this third grader. Furthermore, it was the teacher's opinion that future teachers (teachers in middle school, junior high, and high school) would not understand, and Demetria would have a devastating experience. Since the teacher was merely implementing effective teaching techniques (reteaching and questioning), the referral was unfounded and rejected. Demetria graduated with high honors and is a premedicine student at a large, reputable university.

---

concerning the referral, assessment, identification, and placement of African American students (see Box 2.1 for an example).

Governmental agencies, national organizations, and other formal structures recognize the fact that the laws, without specific guidelines or policy, do not bring about desirable outcomes for African American learners and other culturally and linguistically diverse students. Because of undesirable outcomes or discriminatory practices, federal agencies and other organizations are providing specific instructions, suggestions, or recommendations that may conceivably provide a remedy or alleviate unfavorable outcomes. The U.S. Department of Education, Department of Civil Rights (1998) issued a revision of the Civil Rights Act of 1964 and made some direct statements regarding equitable practices and, in some cases, provided examples of violations as indicated below:

1.   Assignment to Classes

School districts are not allowed to segregate students on the basis of race, color, or national origin in making classroom assignments. When schools offer courses of study that result in disproportionate numbers based on minority or nonminority status, schools must be able to demonstrate valid and nondiscriminatory reasons that such assignments occurred. The U.S. Department of Education Department of Civil Rights recognizes that valid educational reasons may exist when a class provides specialized instruction to assist limited-English-proficient students to acquire English language skills.

2.   Special Education Classes for Students With Disabilities

School districts must ensure that students are not misidentified as being disabled and that misclassification does not result in students being inappropriately labeled and placed in special education programs. School districts are required to educate students with disabilities in an integrated setting with nondisabled peers.

3.   Classes Designed for National Origin Minority Students With Limited English Proficiency

School districts must provide equal educational opportunity to national-origin minority students with limited English proficiency (LEP). Therefore students with limited English proficiency should participate in schools regardless of the individual student's ability to speak and understand English and should not be assigned to special education because of the individuals student's lack of English language skills; and schools should consider allowing enough time for English language acquisition. Many schools have responded to the needs of LEP students by developing special courses of instruction. The courses of instruction should allow for students to move into the regular classroom setting in a reasonable period of time.

4. Assignment to Ability Grouping and Tracking

Schools should not employ practices such as ability grouping or tracking that result in discrimination on the basis of race, color, or national origin. Ability grouping places students in classes or instructional groups based on the students' level of ability or achievement. Tracking places students in different courses of instruction. Ability grouping and tracking may result in disproportionate enrollments of minority or nonminority students in certain classes.

5. Testing, Evaluations, and Criteria for Student Assignment

School districts must use appropriate criteria, evaluation, and testing methods before assigning students to specialized classes or courses of study. Tests must be designed to assess each student's needs, and they should also serve as valid and reliable measures of student achievement. In addition, all tests should be nondiscriminatory.

As it stands now, many are concerned with the education of minority students (e.g., African American learners), and there appears to be a series of recommendations and comments coming from different sources. For example, prior to the reauthorization of IDEA (1997), the U.S. Congress cited the following concerning the education of these students.

1. Greater efforts are needed to prevent the intensification of problems connected with mislabeling and high dropout rates among minority children with disabilities.

2. More minority children continue to be served in special education than would be expected from the percentage of minority students in the general school population.

3. Poor African American children are 2.3 times more likely to be identified by their teacher as having mental retardation than their white counterparts.

4. Although African Americans represent 16 percent of elementary and secondary enrollments, they constitute 21 percent of total enrollments in special education.

5. The dropout rate is 68 percent higher for minorities than for whites.

6. More than 50 percent of minority students in large cities drop out of school. (IDEA, 1997, P.L. 101-476, 20 U.S.C. § 601)

Based on the above recommendations, it is clear that the law requires that general and special educators must avoid misidentification, misassessment, miscategorization, misplacement, and misinstruction of African American learners. There need to be some teeth in the laws; if not, they will be no different from simple reports or suggestions. Teachers and other practitioners must understand that there are consequences for not carrying out these laws. The most notable consequences will be the dangers of not providing equitable educational services that maximize the fullest potential of African American learners.

CONCLUSION

Clearly, the legal foundations of special education for African American learners show that laws have been passed and, in some cases, reauthorized or revised to ensure equal educational opportunities. So, while laws are in place, the implementation of statues may not fulfill the intent of those laws, resulting in bad practice. This may be due in part to a lack of knowledge regarding procedural safeguards set out by IDEA or a lack of cultural understanding because of linguistic and cultural differences. General and special education teachers and administrators should be encouraged to participate in professional development workshops targeting best practices for students with disabilities and culturally diverse learners. In addition, preservice professors must focus on how best to put some teeth in the laws to help African American students to maximize their fullest potential.

REFERENCES

Alexander, K., & Alexander, M. D. (1995). *The law of schools, students and teachers.* St. Paul, MN: West.

Alexander, K., & Alexander, M. D. (2001). *American public school law.* Belmont, CA: Wadsworth Group.

Brown v. Board of Ed. of Topeka, Shawnee County, Kan., 347 U.S. 483, 74 S. Ct. 686, 98 L. Ed. 873, 53 O. O. 326 (1954), Supp. 349 U.S. 294, 75 S. Ct. 753, 99 L. Ed. 1083, 57 O. O. 253 (1955), 197, 199, 200, 201, 206, 208, 214, 411. Title VI. Pub. L. 88-352, Sess. 601 (1964).

Civil Rights Act of 1964, Pub. L. No. 88-352; 42 U.S.C. § 2000 *et seq.*

Dooley, E. A., & Voltz, D. (1999). Educating the African American exceptional learner. In F. E. Obiakor, J. O. Schwenn, & A. F. Rotatori (Eds.), *Advances in special education: Multicultural education for learners with exceptionalities* (pp. 15-31). Stamford, CT: JAI Press.

Education for All Handicapped Children Act (1975), Pub. L. No. 94-142.

Grossman, H. (1995). *Special education in a diverse society.* Boston: Allyn & Bacon.

Individuals With Disabilities Education Act Amendments (1990), Pub. L. No 101-476.

Individuals With Disabilities Education Act Amendments (1997), Pub. L. No 105-17.

Markowitz, J., Garcia, S. B., & Eichelberger, J. (1997, March). *Addressing the disproportionate representation of students from racial and ethnic minority groups in special education: A resource document.* Alexandria, VA: National Association of State Directors of Special Education. (ERIC Document Reproduction Service No. ED 406 810)

Mills v. Board of Education of District of Columbia, 348 F. Supp. 866 (D.C.D.C. 1972).

Osborne, A. (1996). *Legal issues in special education.* Boston: Allyn & Bacon.

Oswald, D., Coutinho, M., Best, A., & Singh, N. (1999). Ethnic representation in special education: The influence of school-related economic and demographic variables. *Journal of Special Education, 32*(4), 194-206.

Pennsylvania Association for Retarded Children v. Commonwealth of Pennsylvania, 343 F. Supp. 279 (D.C. Pa. 1972).

Russo, C., & Talbert-Johnson, C. (1997). The overrepresentation of African American children. *Education & Urban Society, 29*(2), 136-148.

U.S. Department of Education Department of Civil Rights. (1995). *Individuals With Disabilities Education Act: Amendments of 1995.* Washington, DC: Office of Special Programs.

U.S. Department of Education Department of Civil Rights. (1998). *Student assignment and Title VI in elementary and secondary schools.* Washington, DC: Author.

U.S. Department of Education Department of Civil Rights. (1999). *Annual report to congress.* Washington, DC: Author.

U.S. Department of Education Department of Civil Rights. (2000). *Student assignment and Title VI in elementary and secondary schools.* Washington, DC: Author.

Yell, M. (1998). *The law and special education.* Upper Saddle River, NJ: Prentice Hall.

Chapter Three

Functionalizing Assessment for African American Learners in General and Special Education Programs

Cheryl A. Utley

One important underlying principle of the assessment process is that tests should not be racially or culturally discriminatory in the psychological examination of African American learners. From a historical perspective, questions about test bias, issues on psychological testing, factors associated with test construction, and the educational use of tests for African American learners have stimulated debates among psychologists, social scientists, and educators. For example, a major consideration in the evaluation of special education programs for African American learners with exceptionalities is the possibility that the psychological testing process was conceptualized as a means of determining eligibility for placement rather than as a link to the provision of individualized educational programs. A major criticism regarding the use of standardized intelligence tests is that they may be culturally biased against poor, minority children as compared to majority children. Because of differences in cultures, languages, values, and experiential backgrounds, assessment tools are used inappropriately to assess the intelligence of minority children (Utley, Haywood, & Masters, 1992; Valencia & Suzuki, 2001).

If one examines the technical adequacy of the intelligence test for predicting school-related performance, then the assumption that this test is valid for all segments of the population is valid. However, if one examines the quality of educational programming as the conceptual basis for testing, then the psychometric assessment of children is questionable. Given the relatively poor academic achievement and serious behavior problems of some African American learners in different classroom settings, diagnostic information to guide the teaching-learning process is essential. The discriminatory implications of standardized intelligence tests serve as the basis for an examination of functional assessment as a nondiscriminatory procedure for African American learners. This chapter discusses the compelling need for functionalizing assessment for African American learners in general and special education programs.

PSYCHOMETRIC ISSUES IN TESTING AFRICAN AMERICAN LEARNERS

There is a set of assumptions inherent in intelligence quotient (IQ) studies that are still operative in educational research and the assessment of African American learners, some of which are complex and interrelated. Padilla and Lindholm (1995) noted that these

> Identifiable assumptions are: (a) the White middle-class American (typically the male) is the standard against which other groups should be compared; (b) the instruments used for assessing differences are universally applicable across groups, with perhaps only minimal adjustments for culturally diverse populations; and (c) although we need to recognize the sources of potential variance such as social class, educational attainment, gender, cultural orientation, and proficiency in English, these are nuisances that can later be discarded. (p. 97)

The racial differences in intelligence testing have been attributed to the technical and scientific inadequacy of these tests (i.e., test bias and the validation process used in the construction of standardization of intelligence tests).

Conceptually, there are many definitions and empirical methods to detect test bias in intelligence testing. For example, in statistical terminology, bias "refers to the systematic under- or overrepresentation of a population parameter by a statistic based on samples drawn from the population" (Jensen, 1980, p. 375). In psychometrics, test bias is conceived as the systematic (not random) error of some true value of test scores that are connected to group membership (Reynolds, 1980). Therefore test bias or cultural bias is related to variables such as race and ethnicity, sex, age, and social class. In validation theory, test bias is defined as "differential validity of a given interpretation of a test score for any definable, relevant subgroup of test takers" (Cole & Moss, 1989, p. 205). This definition includes features of the validation process such as construct validity, content validity, and criterion validity. Many scholars have conceptualized test bias to include the notion of test unfairness and test fairness, denoting a subjective value judgment regarding how test results are used in selection procedures and decision-making processes. Cole and Moss (1989) explained that:

> There [is] a host of other types of values held by those with an interest in testing situations. These are values about different types of outcomes from testing: instructional

goals, equal opportunity, selection based on qualifications, diverse representation in instructional groups, labels attached to test scores. (p. 204)

In other words, values guide the type of questions asked, the type of information collected, and the conclusions drawn based on empirical evidence. Many scholars have been critical of these definitions of test bias because they exclude any consideration that pertains to the ethical issue of fairness resulting from the use of test scores as criteria for testing and evaluating African American and minority group children in general.

In earlier studies, specific cultural bias has been shown to exist in nonstandardized tests and other forms of clinical assessment (Anderson, 1988; DeHoyos & DeHoyos, 1965; Gross, Herbert, Knatterud, & Donner, 1969; Singer, 1967). In these studies, White psychiatrists diagnosed African American patients with more pathological symptoms. In addition, research has revealed the presence of cultural bias in different forms of psychometric child assessment measures such as personality inventories, ability scales, unstructured clinical interviews, and nonstandardized techniques (Anderson, 1988). Cultural differences in the judgments of appropriate and inappropriate behaviors of African American and White children with emotional disturbance were reported by Kaufman, Swan, and Wood (1980). These researchers found significant differences in the reliability of ratings for African American and White children. Raters reached high levels of agreement in their perceptions of White children, but interrater reliability was very low with regard to the problems of African American children. Also, the interrater reliability was low between teachers and parents of African American children. The arguments against the use of standardized intelligence tests with African American learners have centered on claims of test bias from a variety of sources. Jones (1988) summarized the potential sources of test bias as follows:

1. Standardized tests are biased and unfair to persons from cultural and socioeconomic minorities since most tests reflect largely White, middle-class values and attitudes, and they do not reflect the experience and the linguistic, cognitive, and other cultural styles and values of minority group persons.

2. Standardized measurement procedures have fostered undemocratic attitudes by their use in forming homogeneous classroom groups which severely limit educational, vocational, economic, and other social opportunities.

3. Sometimes, assessments are conducted incompetently by persons who do not understand the culture and language of minority group children and who thus are unable to elicit a level of performance which accurately reflects the child's underlying competence.

4. Testing practices foster expectations that may be damaging by contributing to the self-fulfilling prophecy which ensures low-level achievement for persons who score low on tests.

5. Standardized measurements rigidly shape school curricula and restrict educational change.

6. Norm-referenced measures are not useful for instructional purposes.

7. The limited scope of many standardized tests appraises only part of the changes in children that schools should be interested in producing.

8. Standardized testing practices foster a view of human beings as having only innate and fixed abilities and characteristics.

9. Certain use of tests represents an invasion of privacy. (pp. 16-17)

These psychometric issues in testing compound concerns regarding the appropriate classification of minority children, particularly African American learners, in special education programs. Unfortunately, poorly trained persons with limited experience in urban special education programs, unethical practices in addition to the test unfairness issue, the educational tracking of students, and the classification of minority students as educable mentally retarded or learning disabled culminate in problems associated with testing. The issue of test bias is a hotly debated topic in the psychological literature today as it was in the 1970s, 1980s, 1990s, and 2000s (Grossman, 1995; Karr & Schwenn, 1999; Midgette, 1995; Obiakor, 1994, 1999, 2001; Obiakor et al., 2002; Ogbu, 2002; Samuda, Feuerstein, Kaufman, Lewis, & Sternberg, 1998; Sandoval, Frisby, Gelsinger, Scheuneman, & Grenier, 1998).

EDUCATIONAL ISSUES IN THE ASSESSMENT OF AFRICAN AMERICAN LEARNERS

One very important issue that must be resolved in the psychoeducational assessment of African American children is the utility of standardized assessment in the development of effective educational programs (Utley, Haywood, & Masters, 1990). Although standardized intelligence test scores are used for purposes of classification and diagnosis, they are not prescriptive. Instructional issues raise questions as to the prescriptive contribution of the diagnostic process. Standardized intelligence tests are not used to identify a child's functional needs (e.g., cognitive processing and adaptive motivation); they are used to develop instructional practices designed to minimize discrepancies between learning performance and learning potential. In the case of minority children, Heller, Holtzman, and Messick (1982) eloquently argued that

> the predictive power of IQ does not necessarily make it a good measure of mental processes: different processes may underlie the same IQ scores for different groups of children, and different types of remediation may be necessary in cases of poor performance. For example, it has been frequently argued that levels of motivation and effort of minority students are systematically different from those of White students. Similarly, language factors undoubtedly affect performance more for some groups than others. IQ tests administered entirely in English to students for whom English is a second language are an extreme case in point. Because of these and a host of other factors, there is no way to directly infer the source of a child's difficulty from incorrectly answered test items, nor does a test score or a profile of subscores provide the kinds of information needed to design an individualized curriculum for a child in academic difficulty. (p. 19)

Reflecting a similar perspective, Sewell (1987) stated that "given the relatively poorer academic performance of minority children, assessment dictated by academic problems and geared to provide diagnostic information to guide the teaching-learning process is vitally necessary" (p. 431). He further remarked that "the conceptual model guiding the assessment process should satisfy the fundamental requirement of identifying cognitive processes so that the instructional needs of the individual can be served in a nondiscriminatory context" (p. 433). In this context, psychometric theory is of no particular value if standardized intelligence tests cannot demonstrate a beneficial link to instructional outcomes for African American learners. Therefore it is imperative that teachers and school psychologists demonstrate that the use of standardized intelligence tests leads to effective instructional practices for African American learners with exceptionalities.

FUNCTIONALIZING ASSESSMENT FOR AFRICAN AMERICAN LEARNERS

The underlying principle behind functionalizing assessment is the issue of nondiscriminatory assessment. All laws in special education, for example the Individuals With Disabilities Education Act (IDEA; 1997), have consistently recognized nondiscriminatory assessment as a fundamental ingredient in special education. The idea is to provide an unbiased, multifaceted, multidisciplinary, and professionally sound evaluation. To a large extent, this ensures that an evaluation process adheres to assessment standards and procedures. The evaluation team must follow specific IDEA standards related to cultural bias and the validation of tests. Turnbull and Turnbull (2000) outlined IDEA standards and procedures relating to the student, cultural bias, test validity, and administration, as follows:

1. Tests and other materials are provided and administered in the student's native language or other mode of communication unless it is not feasible to do so [20 U.S.C. § 1414 (b)(3)(A)ii].

2. Tests and other materials that are selected and administered to children with limited English proficiency measure the extent to which the child has a disability and needs special education, rather than measuring the child's English language skills [34 C.F.R. 300.532(a)(2)].

3. The team must ensure that all standardized tests [20 U.S.C. § 1414 (b)(3)(B)] have been validated for the specific purpose for which they are used.

4. Tests and other materials are administered by trained and knowledgeable personnel; and are administered in accordance with any instruction from the test's producers. (p. 140)

Not long ago, Turnbull, Turnbull, Shank, and Leal (1999) noted that nondiscriminatory assessment helps to (a) determine whether or not students have a disability; (b) determine the nature of their disability and the special education and related services that they should receive; and (c) identify specific special education and related services in order to develop an appropriate, individualized educational program (IEP) for a student with a disability. Within nondiscriminatory assessment standards and procedures are (a) breadth of the assessment, (b) administration of the assessment procedures, (c) timing of the assessment, parental notice and consent, and (d) interpretation of the assessment information.

Although the provisions of IDEA (1997) are to guarantee an appropriate education for students with disabilities, problems of misclassification, misidentification, and misassessment continue to exist when African American learners are evaluated using conventional, traditional psychometric testing procedures (Obiakor, 1994, 1999). Recommendations for psychologists when testing minority children, especially African American learners with and without exceptionalities, are presented in Box 3.1. Invariably, these recommended practices will functionalize assessment.

To functionalize assessment, the Council for Children With Behavioral Disorders (1989) suggested an assessment perspective that "clearly recognizes that student learning and/or failure

BOX 3.1   RECOMMENDED ASSESSMENT PRACTICES

AWARENESS AND SENSITIVITY

1.   The assessor must learn as much as possible about the client's culture. This knowledge needs to include the values and beliefs of the culture.

2.   The assessor must learn about the educational process in the client's culture. In particular, one needs to understand the methods of assessment the client has experienced.

3.   One needs to become aware of any stereotypes that are personally held regarding the client and to take steps to minimize the impact of person biases when testing.

4.   The tester must recognize that language issues significantly affect the accuracy of assessment. Using translators or client advocates may improve the fairness of the assessment process when working with limited-English-proficiency clients.

5.   The assessor, either formally or informally, needs to assess the client's level of acculturation. The greater the acculturation, the greater the feasibility of comparing the client's score to the published norms of a test.

6.   The assessor must be aware of professional and ethical considerations when working with diverse clients. These guidelines are discussed in the last chapter of this book.

APPROPRIATE ASSESSMENT SITUATION AND PROCEDURES

1.   Assessors must understand that single-score assessment is inappropriate and select only tests that provide a comprehensive picture of the client's abilities. Information should be sampled from a number of areas in order to demonstrate the client's potential, keeping in mind that comprehensive assessment involves triangulation of testing, observation, and archival analysis in addition to a client's educational, social, and cultural history.

2.   The examiner needs to use tests to power rather than speed, as many culturally diverse clients are not accustomed to high-speed tests. This procedure assures their performance is based on their ability, rather than their inability to finish the test.

3.   An assessor should use both verbal and nonverbal tests. By using both formats, one can promote a more balanced and, therefore, fair assessment process.

4.   Culturally diverse clients exhibit more anxiety during a test situation than mainstream clients, due to the unfamiliarity of the task. To lessen the impact of this anxiety, the assessor must take time, albeit longer than usual, to establish rapport and describe any assessment expectations to the client.

5.   Determination of the client's language dominance must be done prior to testing. If the client's dominant language is not English, the tester must consider supplementing the assessment with nonverbal instruments. For this purpose, the Raven matrices or other culture-reduced tests are recommended.

6.   If the client's dominant language is not English, the assessor needs to use a test translated or adapted into the client's language, in conjunction with a nonverbal instrument. It is incumbent upon the assessor to evaluate translated and adapted instruments.

7.   The assessor needs to ensure that the examinee understands the test directions. This allows the tester to evaluate the viability of using a particular test.

8.   An assessor should view nonverbal tests as culture-reduced, rather than culture-free, instruments. The structure of the items and strategies to obtain correct responses have a cultural component and, therefore, remain culturally loaded.

9.   The System of Multicultural Pluralistic Assessment (SOMPA) provides useful adaptive behavior indicators and sociocultural information, but it is not to be used to make clinical or psychoeducational decisions on culturally diverse children because the validity of the Estimated Learning Potential (ELP) score is questionable.

10.   Testing-of-limits procedures must be implemented whenever feasible. These procedures need to be used with individual tests of ability, as well as with group measures of aptitude. The client's ability to improve test performance when procedures are modified will help an assessor gain a clearer picture of a client's functioning.

11.   The assessor must become skilled at test-train-test via mediation methods. Using a formal dynamic assessment procedure, such as the Learning Potential Assessment Device (LPAD), helps the tester identify a client's learning style and ability to profit from tutorial guidance. This shift from product-oriented to process-oriented assessment allows the clients to demonstrate learning potential within the context of their social and cultural background.

CULTURALLY APPROPRIATE INTERPRETATIONS

1.   The assessor cannot assume that the rules of test interpretation are applicable to the test results of a minority client in the same way they are applied to the test results of a middle-class, mainstream client. Testers need to be flexible when judging cultural factors that are clearly affecting a client's test performance.

2.   Acknowledgment of the client's level of acculturation and the effect this level might have on the test result is required. If a lack of acculturation is suspected to have had a role in determining the client's performance, it is necessary to reassess the client when the level of acculturation has increased.

3.   The assessor needs to use comprehensive assessment data, testing-of-limits results, and other dynamic assessment intervention methods. A qualitative description is needed to outline the strengths and possible deficits of the client.

4.   When interpreting scores, the tester must take into account that many traditional tests have not been normed adequately with various cultural groups. They need to be wary of the fact that some examinees are not well represented by national test norms and make interpretations accordingly.

5.   When making recommendations, the examiner must focus on describing strengths rather than weaknesses, potential rather than deficiencies.

6.   Recommendations must link assessment to culturally appropriate interventions. These interventions need to focus on helping clients develop their potential.

7.   One must never use a single test score to categorize and place a client into a program. A comprehensive approach must always be used.

8.   Test results need to eliminate prejudice, racism, and inequities, rather than promote inadequate treatment of culturally diverse clients, by providing accurate, meaningful scores linked to appropriate intervention strategies.

SOURCE: J. E. Lewis (1998).

occurs in an instructional context, and as such it is affected by both student characteristics and environmental influences (e.g., the quantity and quality of instruction received)" (p. 269). Maheady, Algozzine, and Ysseldyke (1984) identified three guiding principles for the assessment process: (a) the collection of data that are directly relevant to instructional decision making, (b) the assessment of alterable instructional variables, and (c) the gathering of assessment information that reflects students' responsiveness to existing pedagogy. Specifically, a functional assessment perspective is based on three underlying assumptions.

First, learning is an interactive process that is influenced by both characteristics of the learner and instructional variables in the classroom. As Bijou (1993) pointed out:

The interaction between the child and the environment is continuous, reciprocal, interdependent. We cannot analyze a child without reference to an environment, nor is it possible to analyze an environment without reference to a child. The two form an inseparable unit consisting of an interrelated set of variables, or an interactional field. (p. 29)

There is no doubt that the academic and behavioral performance of African American learners must be observed under existing teaching and learning conditions. Tucci and Hursh (1994) agreed:

A learning environment is composed of (1) teachers and the repertoires they bring to the environment, (2) learners and the repertoires they bring to the environment, (3) curricular materials and instructional formats available to the environment, and (4) the physical structures and furnishings in the environment. Instructional conditions created by various arrangements of the parts of the learning environment either establish, strengthen, maintain, or weaken the learners' repertoires. These instructional conditions have different effects with respect to the learners' repertoires because the relative strength of the repertoires determines the manner in which a given instructional condition will function. (p. 261)

BOX 3.2   ALTERABLE INSTRUCTIONAL PROCESSES

- Low amounts of time devoted to academic instruction
- High amounts of time lost to instruction, transitions, and pullout labs
- Low academic responding or infrequent opportunities to respond
- Infrequent opportunities to learn academic subjects or to gain exposure to lessons, materials, and independent practice
- Instructional materials, media, and practices that play a role in accelerating or decelerating students' engagement in academic responding and the rate of students' academic growth
- Low fidelity of the curriculum
- Little use of instructional-effectiveness criteria
- High use of teacher behaviors that decelerate academic achievement outcomes

SOURCE: Adapted from C. R. Greenwood (1996).

The second assumption is that African American learners are responsive to good teaching and altered instructional practices that facilitate the opportunity to respond, or academic responding to improve student performance. In earlier research, Greenwood, Delquadri, & Hall (1984) defined opportunity to respond as "the interaction between (a) teacher formulated instruction . . . (the materials presented, prompts, questions asked, signals to respond), and (b) its success in establishing the academic responding desired or implied by materials, the subject matter goals of instruction" (p. 64). Evaluation of how the behaviors of low-achieving, at-risk, and high-achieving students interact with the instructional environment has revealed that certain classroom factors, as illustrated in Box 3.2, promote lower levels of academic performance and reinforce negative classroom behavior.

Third, the academic and behavioral performance of African American learners can be substantially improved without labels and classification systems that diagnose these students as deviant. Empirical research has demonstrated that classification systems and labels do not provide assessment information linked to student variables (e.g., cognitive styles, motivational influences, language proficiency, and experiential background) and alterable school-related and instructional variables. In fact, a functional assessment approach requires the use of procedures that include the direct observation of the teaching-learning environment, referred to as *instructional ecology*. This term refers to the relationships between schools and their instructional environments. The environment in which they are taught influences the behavior and academic performance of African American learners. More specifically, student outcomes are a function of (a) content goals of the school and (b) the instructional and pedagogical approaches employed by teachers, as expressed in terms of their success in managing students' responses to academic tasks (Greenwood, Carta, Kamps, & Arreaga-Mayer, 1990). In citing research by Chun, Hilliard (1990) noted that there is a protocol of interactive behaviors of teachers who, for whatever reasons, have low expectations for students which affect the delivery of instruction. This body of research shows that teachers tend to

- Give low-achieving students the answer or call on someone else rather than try to improve the response of these students through repeating the question, providing clues, or asking a new question

- Provide low-achieving students with inappropriate reinforcement by rewarding inappropriate behaviors or incorrect responses
- Criticize low-achieving students more often than high-achieving students
- Fail to give informative feedback to low-achieving students' questions and public responses
- Pay less attention to low-achieving students and interact with them less frequently
- Use more rapid pacing and less extended explanations or repetition of definitions and examples with high-achieving students compared to low-achieving students
- Use more effective instruction with high-achieving students compared to low-achieving students.

The range of teacher behavior and classroom teaching strategies observed in classrooms is a critical aspect of the systematic assessment of African American learners and whether or not they are successful learners. According to Salvia and Ysseldyke (1998), research on

> instructional environments is focused on classroom structures, the amount of time allocated to instruction, the amount of time students are actively engaged in responding to instruction, the ways in which instructions are given for school tasks, the pacing of instruction, and the ways in which teachers use information on student performance to change or adapt instruction. (p. 222)

The results of this research have shown that (a) academic engaged time was related positively to achievement gains, and (b) students who are failing spend very little time actively engaged in academic subject matter. For example, research on classroom instruction has substantiated the hypothesis that growth in academic achievement is a function of the time spent learning a content area and the level of active student engagement in tasks with a direct relationship to those skills which will be assessed as evidence of academic achievement. In other words, instructional programs that accelerate and maintain the time spent learning a subject matter and student engagement will accelerate students' growth on measures of achievement. Conversely, those instructional programs that reduce the time spent and time engaged decelerate this growth and contribute to student failure (Greenwood et al., 1990).

CONCLUSION

In this chapter, I have proposed a functional assessment approach to examine the instructional ecology of classroom settings as a viable alternative or supplement to current psychometric approaches in testing African American learners. It is my belief that in conducting assessments with African American learners, psychologists must be knowledgeable about the weaknesses of traditional standardized testing procedures. In prior research, Carroll (1985) presented a model of school learning where quality instruction is a function of the nature, objectives, content, and hierarchical structure of teacher-provided instruction and instructional materials. In addition, quality of instruction varies as a "function of the clarity of task requirements, adequacy of task presentation and of sequencing and pacing, and the degree to which the learner's unique needs have been considered during the instructional presentation" (p. 63). It is imperative that psychologists and practitioners focus their efforts on classroom and school learning environments and move away from perspectives that divert their attention from quality instruction issues. These professionals must also examine the relationship between observable student behaviors, teacher behaviors, and classroom contexts to establish instructionally based standards for academic performance.

For all assessments to be fair, nondiscriminatory, and functional for African American learners, regular and special educators and other service providers (e.g., psychologists) must increase their "understanding of behavior and communication within a social/cultural context, and expand their acceptance of individual differences so that it reflects a cross-cultural perspective" (Salend, 1994, p. 423). Professionals must have knowledge, skills, and experiences in order to differentiate between minor learning problems and major forms of exceptionalities. Moreover, psychologists and practitioners must (a) be sensitive to the cultural and linguistic backgrounds of African American learners, (b) provide assessment situations with suitable testing procedures for African American learners, and (c) provide culturally appropriate descriptions and interpretations of skills of African American learners. As Obiakor and his associates (2002) concluded, to functionalize assessment, we must consider

1. Needs of the students across all components of the ecological system in which he or she lives

2. Instruction as the primary purpose of assessment

3. The importance of emphasizing functional levels rather than qualified statements of performance based on extrapolations from limited samples of behavior

4. The functioning of a child at home, on the bus, on the playground, and with peers as more relevant than his or her performance in a specialist's office (e.g., offices of counselors, diagnosticians, and school psychologists)

5. Where children are, what they can do, and what they are doing, not want they cannot do

6. The importance of using assessment to determine what the child needs to become the most competent human being possible

7. Intelligence as a phenomenon that can be defined in multiple ways (p. 143)

Obiakor and associates (2002) maintain that

Good schools are defined by how they address student diversity. If this vision is embraced, misidentification, discrimination, and mistreatment will be reduced and the benefits of having a "good school". . . . will be realized by all learners, all teachers, all parents, and all communities. It is toward this lofty goal that we must direct our efforts with regard to both research and practice. (p. 57)

REFERENCES

Anderson, W. A. (1988). The behavioral assessment of conduct disorder in a Black child. In R. L. Jones (Ed.), *Psychoeducational assessment of minority group children: A casebook* (pp. 193-224). Berkeley, CA: Cobb & Henry.

Bijou, S. W. (1993). *Behavior analysis of child development* (2nd ed.). Reno, NV: Context Press.

Carroll, J. B. (1985). The model of school learning: Progress of an idea. In L. W. Anderson (Ed.), *Perspectives on school learning: Selected writings of John B. Carroll* (pp. 82-102). Hillsdale, NJ: Lawrence Erlbaum.

Cole, N. S., & Moss, P. A. (1989). Bias in test use. In R. L. Linn (Ed.), *Educational measurement* (3rd ed., pp. 201-219). New York: Macmillan.

Council for Children With Behavioral Disorders. (1989). Best assessment practices for students with behavioral disorders: Accommodation to cultural diversity and individual differences. *Behavioral Disorders, 14*(4), 263-278.

DeHoyos, A., & DeHoyos, G. (1965). Symptomatology differentials between Negro and White schizophrenics. *International Journal of Social Psychiatry, 11*, 245-255.

Delquadri, J., & Hall, R. V. (1984). Opportunity to respond and student academic performance. In W. L. Heward, T. E. Heron, J. Trapp-Porter, & D. S. Hill (Eds.), *Focus on Behavior Analyais and Education* (pp. 58-88). Columbus, OH: Charles Merrill.

Greenwood, C. R. (1996). The case for performance-based instructional models. *School Psychology Quarterly, 11*(4), 283-296.

Greenwood, C. R., Carta, J. J., Kamps, D., & Arreaga-Mayer, C. (1990). Ecobehavioral analysis of classroom instruction. In S. Schroeder (Ed.), *Ecobehavioral analysis and developmental disabilities: The twenty-first century* (pp. 33-63). New York: Praeger.

Gross, H. S., Herbert, M. R., Knatterud, G. L., & Donner, L. (1969). The effect of race and sex on the variation of diagnosis and disposition in a psychiatric emergency room. *Journal of Nervous and Mental Disease, 148*, 628-642.

Grossman, H. (1995). *Teaching in a diverse society*. Needham Heights, MA: Allyn & Bacon.

Heller, K. A., Holtzman, W. H., & Messick, S. (1982). *Placing children in special education: A strategy for equity*. Washington, DC: National Academy Press.

Hilliard, A. G. (1990). *ABCD Teachers Project training manual* (Vol. 2). Ann Arbor: Michigan Department of Education.

Individuals With Disabilities Education Act Amendments of 1997, Pub. L. No. 101-476, 20 U.S.C. § 1400.

Jensen, A. (1980). How much can we boost IQ and scholastic achievement. *Harvard Educational Review, 38*, 1-123.

Jones, R. L. (1988). *Psychoeducational assessment of minority group children: A casebook*. Berkeley, CA: Cobb & Henry.

Karr, S., & Schwenn, J. O. (1999). Multimethods of assessment of multicultural learners. In F. E. Obiakor, J. O. Schwenn, & A. F. Rotatori (Eds.), *Multicultural education for learners with exceptionalities* (Vol. 12, pp. 105-120). Stamford, CT: JAI Press.

Kaufman, A. S., Swan, W. W., & Wood, M. M. (1980). Do parents, teachers and psychoeducational evaluators agree in their perceptions of the problems of Black and White emotionally disturbed children? *Psychology in the Schools, 17*(2), 185-191.

Lewis, J. E. (1998). Nontraditional uses of traditional aptitude tests. In R. J. Samuda, R. Feuerstein, A. S. Kaufman, J. E. Lewis, & R. J. Sternberg and Associates (Eds.), *Advances in cross-cultural assessment* (pp. 218-241). Thousand Oaks, CA: Sage.

Maheady, L., Algozzine, B., & Ysseldyke, J. (1984). Minority overrepresentation in special education: A functional assessment perspective. *Special Services in the Schools, 1*, 5-19.

Midgette, T. E. (1995). Assessment of African American exceptional learners: New strategies and perspectives. In B. A. Ford, F. E. Obiakor, & J. M. Patton (Eds.), *Effective education of African American exceptional learners: New perspectives* (pp. 3-26). Austin, TX: Pro-Ed.

Obiakor, F. E. (1994). *The eight-step multicultural approach: Learning and teaching with a smile*. Dubuque, IA: Kendall/Hunt.

Obiakor, F. E. (1999). Teacher expectations of minority exceptional learners: Impact on "accuracy" of self-concepts. *Exceptional Children, 66*, 39-53.

Obiakor, F. E. (2001). *It even happens in "good" schools: Responding to cultural diversity in today's classrooms*. Thousand Oaks, CA: Corwin.

Obiakor, F. E., Algozzine, B., Thurlow, M., Gwalla-Ogisi, N., Enwefa, S., Enwefa, R., & McIntosh, A. (2002). *Addressing the issue of disproportionate representation: Identification and assessment of culturally diverse students with emotional or behavioral disorders.* Arlington, VA: Council for Children With Behavioral Disorders, Council for Exceptional Children.

Ogbu, J. U. (2002). Cultural amplifiers of intelligence: IQ and minority status in cross-cultural perspective. In J. M. Fish (Ed.), *Race and intelligence: Separating science from myth* (pp. 241-278). Mahwah, NJ: Lawrence Erlbaum.

Padilla, A. M., & Lindholm, K. J. (1995). Quantitative educational research with ethnic minorities. In J. A. Banks & C. A. McGee-Banks (Eds.), *Handbook of research on multicultural Education* (pp. 201-225). New York: Macmillan.

Reynolds, C. R. (1982). The problem of bias in psychological measurement. In C. R. Reynolds & T. B. Gutkin (Eds.), *The handbook of school psychology*. New York: Wiley.

Salend, S. J. (1994). *Effective mainstreaming: Creating inclusive classrooms*. New York: Macmillan.

Salvia, J., & Ysseldyke, J. E. (1998). *Assessment* (7th ed.). Boston: Houghton Mifflin.

Samuda, R., Feuerstein, R., Kaufman, A. S., Lewis, J. E., & Sternberg, R. J. (1998). *Advances in cross-cultural assessment*. Thousand Oaks, CA: Sage.

Sandoval, J., Frisby, C. L., Gelsinger, K. F., Scheuneman, J. D., & Grenier, J. R. (1998). *Test interpretation and diversity: Achieving equity in assessment*. Washington, DC: American Psychological Association.

Sewell, T. E. (1987). Dynamic assessment as a non-discriminatory procedure. In C. S. Lidz (Ed.), *Dynamic assessment: An interactional approach to evaluating learning potential* (pp. 426-445). New York: Guilford Press.

Singer, B. D. (1967). Some implications of differential psychiatric treatment of Negro and White patients. *Social Science and Medicine, 1*, 77-83.

Tucci, V., & Hursh, D. E. (1994). Developing competent learners by arranging effective learning environments. In R. Gardner, D. M. Sainato, J. O. Cooper, T. E. Heron, W. L. Heward, J. Eshleman, & T. A. Grossi (Eds.), *Behavior analysis in education: Focus on measurably superior instruction* (pp. 258-264). Pacific Grove, CA: Brooks/Cole.

Turnbull, H. R., & Turnbull, A. P. (2000). *Free appropriate public education: The law and children with disabilities* (6th ed.). Denver, CO: Love.

Turnbull, H. R., Turnbull, A. P., Shank, M., & Leal, D. (1999). *Exceptional lives: Special education in today's schools* (2nd ed.). Upper Saddle River, NJ: Merrill.

Utley, C. A., Haywood, H. C., & Masters, J. C. (1992). Policy implications of psychological assessment of minority children. In H. C. Haywood & D. Tzuriel (Eds.), *Interactive assessment* (pp. 445-469). New York: Springer-Verlag.

Valencia, R. R., & Suzuki, L. A. (2001). *Intelligence testing and minority students: Foundations, performance factors, and assessment issues*. Thousand Oaks, CA: Sage.

Chapter Four

Categorization: Impact on African American Learners With Exceptionalities

Angela Stephens McIntosh

To the real question, "How does it feel to be a problem?" I answer seldom a word.

—W. E. B. DuBois (1903/1961, p. 15)

When DuBois made this statement in his seminal work, *The Souls of Black Folk*, his point of reference was the issue of racism in the southern United States. He contended that, regardless of the so-called rights and liberties afforded to Blacks at that time, being different was innately problematic. DuBois described how it felt to be a powerless outsider, to be in an environment that judged and assessed African Americans as different, and to be, therefore, a problem for "the majority."

Categorization and labeling have always been a part of special education. These actions determine, at least in some measure, which students will be served, where they will be served, who will provide the services, and how much funding will be allocated for the provision of services. But they also identify individuals as "different" and as "outsiders" (Hobbs, 1975; Obiakor, 1999, 2001). Because labels and categorization are so inherently a part of special education, educational practitioners seldom give judicious regard to the impact of these actions on their clients (i.e., students). When they assign a categorical special education label to a student, they directly or indirectly say to that student, "You are a problem." This chapter addresses issues of labeling and categorization in special education and their impacts on African American learners with and without exceptionalities.

THE POWER OF WORDS

Words matter! They can help or harm, assuage or enrage, obscure or elucidate, obviate or exacerbate, exalt or denigrate, elevate or subjugate (Obiakor, 1996). Like other semantic elements, words, names, and labels are efficient and effective as communication tools when, and only when, they are understood in the same way by both the sender and the receiver of the language. For example, when special education professionals use labels like *learning disabled* or *seriously emotionally disturbed*, these terms are effective only to the extent that the receiver of those words understands the characteristics of, and concepts related to, *learning disabled* or *seriously emotionally disturbed* in the same way that the sender (special education professional) understands them. This perfect congruency seldom exists. More often than not, these and other special education categorical labels take on specific levels of meaning or ambiguity that depend on when, where, and by whom they are used. This creates a communicative fissure—an irreparable abyss wherein the power of words is gained or lost, generalizations are made, and stigmas develop as words are defined and redefined through informal applications and associations (Obiakor, 2001).

Kovel (1984) coined the term *thingification* to explain how members of the dominant society use language to establish distance between themselves and others. The dominant group then has the power to differentiate outsiders: to classify, label, and categorize others. Well-intentioned as it may be, the special education categorization and labeling system creates thingification and the power to dichotomize between those who assign labels and those who receive them. Delpit (1995) explained that "traditional bastions of academe distance people from one another as they create power relationships whereby one group maintains the power to 'name' the other" (p. 91). This long-established power of labeling and categorization in special education is well-known. Also far from new are the pros and cons of labeling and categorization that continue to be topics of contention and debate. Few would deny the indispensable utility of labels and classification systems in the special education process, yet there are valid concerns regarding the potential for abuse and misuse. About 3 decades ago, Hobbs (1975) warned of the potential for the well-intended classification system established by the Education for All Handicapped Children Act (1975) to have negative consequences for some students in special education programs. As he noted,

> Categories and labels are powerful instruments for social regulation and control, and they are often employed of obscure, covert, or hurtful purposes; to degrade people, to deny them access to opportunity, to exclude "undesirables" whose presence in some ways offends, disturbs familiar custom, or demands extraordinary effort. (p. 11)

Under the law, labeling and categorization create the opportunity for students to receive special educational services that would otherwise be unavailable; in reality, labels sometimes create lifelong barriers. These concerns make it necessary to pay particular attention to the ways in which the education of African American students with exceptionalities is affected by the use and misuse of categorization and labeling.

THE EVOLUTION OF SPECIAL EDUCATION LABELS

The history of special education is aligned with changes in the words used to identify or describe the recipients of special education services. The terms *idiot* and *feebleminded* have long since been replaced by designations of the degree of mental retardation as mild, moderate, severe, or profound—considered to be less demeaning and more socially acceptable. The American Association on Mental Retardation (AAMR; 1992) now recommends a classification system based on levels of support required by individuals with mental retardation. AAMR posits that such terms deemphasize interpersonal deficits. The term *handicapped* has been replaced in current special education literature by people-first terminology: for example, *individuals with disabilities* instead of disabled or handicapped people. "What a student is called, where he or she is placed, and how he or she is taught speak volumes about how much we value that student" (Obiakor et al., 2002, p. 57). Practicing the delicate art of describing difference, the authors of the Individuals With Disabilities Education Act (IDEA; U.S. Department of Education, 1997) sought to use language that expressed affirmation and equity consistent with the intent of the law. Yet of the 13 categorical labels prescribed by IDEA, most contain language that, in a literal sense, is negative, devaluing, and disempowering. Consider the synonyms shown in Table 4.1.

People in educational quarters and the society at large are now concerned about political correctness of terms and words. It is true that every word is prone to positive or negative interpretations. However, words must ensure equity and promote empowerment, especially if they are used in laws and regulations. No doubt, words are consistently used to describe particular and varied conditions of students who, if they are to realize their full human potential, require specially designed instruction that meets their unusual needs. Some critical questions deserve attention. What words would an individual with a disability choose? What words describe the educational needs of exceptional students and also connote power, equality, and positive characteristics? If there are such affirming words, will the affirming qualities of those words endure? How can one know what measure of resistance these words hold against the development of stigma through generalizations and associations? How can one be sure that the newfangled terms will not sooner or later become imbued with expectations and predictions that do not represent the positive characteristics of exceptional students?

The important thing to gain from the above inquiry is the understanding that words, and the images and ideas conjured up by those words, are merely social constructs (Obiakor, 1996). Social constructs are in themselves unstable. They are the collective perspectives of a particular group of people, and they are subject to change in response to changes in the composition of the group, with the gathering of new information, or simply with the passage of time. Categorical labels are ideas resting, for the present time, in the language of the special education profession. This understanding is not particularly difficult to come by. What *is* difficult to come by within this dilemma is the commitment to protect the philosophical principles of special education— that exceptional children deserve and have the right to specialized educational services that meet their individual needs. This requires that, despite the negative connotations in the particular

Table 4.1   Terms Commonly Used in Special Education Categorization and
Their Synonyms

Special Education Terminology	*Synonyms*
Disability	Impotence
	Imbecility
	Caducity
	Ineptitude
	Indocility
	Helplessness
	Incompetence
	Disqualification
	Invalidity
Disordered	Deranged
	Discomposed
	Embroiled
	Unsettled
	Confused
	Troubled
	Disrupted
Disabled	Weakened
	Rendered powerless
	Reduced in strength
	Invalidated
	Enfeebled
	Debilitated
Disturbed	In a state of pain
	Hapless
	Discontented
	Stricken
	Crushed
	Miserable
	Horrified
	Broken
	In a state of despair
Impaired	Unimproved
	Deteriorated
	Altered
	Injured
	On the decline
	Degenerate
	Imperfect
	Second-rate

SOURCE: P. M. Roget (1972).

language of the categorical labels, the intent of categorical definitions must be the focus. To that end, the label must be, at best, a tertiary consideration, following complete investigation of individual student characteristics and thorough, appropriate evaluation of educational needs.

SYSTEMIC WEAKNESSES IN THE USE OF CATEGORICAL LABELS IN SPECIAL EDUCATION

The categorization system in special education was designed to facilitate decision making about which students will receive services. The implicit assumptions of the system are that all exceptional students who require special education can be assigned to at least one of the 13 categories, based on the definitions and the eligibility criteria of each category, and that students within each category share some commonalities with regard to educational needs. The latter assumption is supported by the differentiation of funding allocations across the categories. More money is allocated to the education of students in some categories than in others. Several fundamental problems regarding the use of categories and labels in special education reside in these assumptions.

The specific definitions and eligibility criteria for each of the 13 categories suggest that the categories are distinct and mutually exclusive. There is an implied level of objectivity that is inaccurate and impractical given the manner in which eligibility and placement decisions are made. The special education labeling and categorization system rests on the presumptive notion of pathology within the individual (Adelman, 1996). The impact of environmental factors is, therefore, deemphasized. Additionally, the structure of this system suggests within-category similarities among students that may or may not exist (Brenner, 1998). This faulty perspective supports the practice of differentiating instruction based on categorical labels, and leads to a lack of individualization of instruction, the major thrust of special education.

The definitions and eligibility criteria are not well understood by African American parents and others outside of the special education profession. Furthermore, the definitions and criteria are loosely constructed and permit a broad range of interpretations and applications. According to Oswald, Coutinho, Best, and Singh (1999), African American students with exceptionalities, particularly those who live in urban environments and those who experience poverty, are at a high risk for poor educational outcomes as a result of inappropriate identification, placement, and services. These poor educational outcomes are, in part, a result of attitudes and actions influenced by the negative connotations of special education categorical labels. In the following sections, I discuss the impact of these labels on teacher behaviors, student behaviors, and institutional behaviors.

THE IMPACT OF CATEGORICAL LABELING ON TEACHER BEHAVIORS

For African American students with exceptionalities, the behaviors and attitudes of general and special education classroom teachers can either mediate or exacerbate the negative impact of categorization and labeling. These teachers have responsibilities that extend far beyond the walls of the classroom. They are tasked with preparing students to fit into and achieve within the existing institutions of school and society. Mutual and congruent interpretations and values of the institutions of school and society make fertile ground for education. When goals and values between teachers and students are well aligned, teachers hold high expectations for student performance and for positive educational outcomes. Likewise, when this mutuality does not exist, teacher expectations are low, and the opportunity for positive educational outcomes is diminished (Obiakor, 1999, 2001).

The influence of teacher attitudes and behaviors on student outcomes and on the self-esteem of students is well documented in the literature (Brophy, 1983). In both general and special education settings, teachers' expectations become self-fulfilling (Persell, 1997; Obiakor, 1999). Yet, according to Dunn (1968), "We must expect that labeling a child 'handicapped' reduces the teacher's expectancy for him to succeed" (p. 9). When teachers have low expectations for students, they direct precious time and resources toward other students. Teachers who are not able to see beyond the stigma and stereotype of special education labels cannot recognize individual capability and potential in exceptional students. Because of this, such teachers will be ineffective in facilitating positive educational outcomes, even if they use prescribed interventions and comply with individualized education plan requirements. "When teachers do not understand the potential of the students they teach, they will underteach them, no matter what the methodology" (Delpit, 1995, p. 176). In fact, for African American students with exceptionalities, the categorical label presents yet another variable that sometimes widens the gap of student-teacher discordance and decreases the potential for positive educational outcomes.

THE IMPACT OF CATEGORICAL LABELING ON STUDENT BEHAVIORS

At the dawn of the current era in special education history, Dunn (1968) realized the potential adverse effects of labeling and categorization. In his words:

> We must examine the effects of these disability labels on the pupils themselves. Certainly none of these labels are badges of distinction. Separating a child from other children in his neighborhood—or removing him from the regular classroom for therapy or special class placement—probably has a serious debilitating effect upon his self-image. (p. 9)

In many cases, African American students respond to these self-image problems in ways that are contrary to positive educational outcomes. Students often decide to act the part and adjust their behavior and academic performance to what they perceive as the level of expectation from teachers and peers (Anderson, 1994). Peer influence is powerful among African American students, and they often opt for the esteem that is gained from peers by acting out.

Even students who are labeled gifted experience pressures with regard to being categorized. Fordham and Ogbu (1986) described the pressure placed on high-achieving African American students by their peers. Accepting the identity of a good student is complicated for African American students with gifts and talents if they have not been exposed to high expectations for academic achievement in the home and community, and if the value of academic achievement is not demonstrated in the community through role models. When a direct relationship between school performance and adult success is not evident, school engagement diminishes (Obiakor, 2001).

THE IMPACT OF CATEGORICAL
LABELING ON INSTITUTIONAL BEHAVIORS

The Eurocentric cultural perspective that drives public education in America posits assumptions about African American students that perpetuate the negative impact of special education labeling (Obiakor, 1992). In addition to specific classes of behaviors by teachers and students, categorical labeling can be viewed as the upholding of institutionalized attitudes, policies, and actions. In a reciprocal fashion, special education labeling and categorization perpetuate institutionalized behaviors that have deleterious effects on the educational outcomes of African American students with exceptionalities. The systematic and widespread occurrences of the institutionalized behaviors of misidentification, misassessment, and misplacement of African American students with exceptionalities result in an overrepresentation of African American students in special education programs. These institutional behaviors are so widespread that they are given particular attention in the text of IDEA (U.S. Department of Education, 1997). The relevant sections read as follows:

(8) (A) Greater efforts are needed to prevent the intensification of problems connected with mislabeling and high dropout rates among minority children with disabilities.

(B) More minority children continue to be served in special education than would be expected from the percentage of minority students in the general school population.

(C) Poor African American children are 2.3 times more likely to be identified by their teacher as having mental retardation than their white counterpart.

(D) Although African Americans represent 16 percent of elementary and secondary enrollments, they constitute 21 percent of total enrollments in special education.

(E) The dropout rate is 68 percent higher for minorities than for whites.

(F) More than 50 percent of minority students in large cities drop out of school.
(P.L. 105-17, § 601(8))

The aforementioned issues have been the focus of attention among special education professionals for more than 20 years (Artiles & Zamora-Duran, 1997), yet, as data from a recent report to Congress (U.S. Department of Education, 2000) on the implementation of IDEA reveal, the disproportionate representation of African American students in special education programs still exists. The resilience of this issue supports the notion that the institution of American public education may be intolerant of some characteristics of African American learners in general and of African American males in particular. Anderson (1994) suggested that "the primary view of the world that evidences itself in the overrepresentation of African American males in behavior-disorder (BD) class placements was constructed contrary to a commonality of experience with the Afro-centric perspective" (p. 93). See Table 4.2.

Table 4.2   Percentage of Students Ages 6 Through 21 Served by Disability and Race/Ethnicity, in the 1998-1999 School Year

Disability	American Indian	Asian/Pacific Islander	Hispanic	Black/ Non-Hispanic	White/ Non-Hispanic
Specific Learning Disabilities	1.4	1.4	18.3	15.8	63.0
Speech/Language Impairments	1.2	2.4	16.5	11.6	68.3
Mental Retardation	1.1	1.7	34.3	8.9	54.1
Emotional Disturbance	1.1	1.0	26.4	9.8	61.6
Multiple Disabilities	1.4	2.3	19.3	10.9	66.1
Hearing Impairments	1.4	4.6	16.8	16.3	66.0
Orthopedic Impairments	.8	3.0	14.6	14.4	67.2
Other Health Impairments	1.0	1.3	14.1	7.8	75.8
Visual Impairments	1.3	3.0	14.8	11.4	69.5
Autism	.7	4.7	20.9	9.4	64.4
Deaf-Blindness	1.8	11.3	11.5	12.1	63.3
Traumatic Brain Injury	1.6	2.3	15.9	10.0	70.2
Developmental Delay	.5	1.1	33.7	4.0	60.8
All Disabilities	1.3	1.7	20.2	13.2	63.6
Resident Population	1.0	3.8	14.8	14.2	66.2

SOURCE: U.S. Department of Education (2000).

BEST PRACTICES TO AMELIORATE THE IMPACT OF LABELING AND CATEGORIZATION ON AFRICAN AMERICAN EXCEPTIONAL LEARNERS

The use of categorical labels in the context of providing specialized educational services creates a false dilemma. In a true dilemma, there are only two real choices. In a false dilemma, there are only two apparent choices, but there are other less-evident options. The false dilemma created by the pros and cons of categorical labels is the notion that either we must use labels to identify students who receive special education services, or else we must abandon the use of labels, yet serve all students equitably. Less apparent, but far more reasonable, are the options to take particular caution regarding the use of labels and to nurture an increased awareness of the long-term implications and impact of assigning labels. If we are staunchly prudent in the exercise of best practices related to the use of labels and categorization, we will increase the probability of positive educational outcomes for all learners, especially African American students with exceptionalities (Obiakor, 2001). As a consequence, general and special educators must

1.   Practice effective cross-cultural communication. According to Lynch (1998), "effective cross-cultural communication includes the willingness to engage in discussions that explore differences openly and respectfully, interactions that dispel myths and open doors to understanding" (p. 76). Cross-cultural communication will reduce the stigmatizing effects of categorical labels by generating the exchange of useful and specific information.

2.   Have realistic expectations of all students. Teachers in particular should not be influenced by negative stereotypes. Responding to labels "blocks the essential agenda of good teaching, namely inquiry through dialogue and interaction, teacher with student" (Kliewer & Bilkin, 1996, p. 93).

3.   Use comprehensive assessment methodologies. Assessment methodologies that provide an evaluation of students' strengths and weaknesses in an ecological context are useful in planning instruction and interventions. Educators should adapt a functional behavioral assessment perspective to ensure that you know the whole child (Obiakor et al., 2002).

4.   Affirm individualism in positive ways. Educational programming must respond to individual differences in more specific terms (Obiakor, 1994).

5.   Pay particular attention to the contextual meanings of labels. Categories and labels are subject to use according to local interpretations (Obiakor, 2001).

6.   Ensure that language is not a barrier to communication. The use of special education terminology can obscure and complicate communication with those who are not in the field of special education, and can alienate and disempower parents and students (Kalyanpur & Harry, 1999).

7.   Look beyond the label to see the needs of the individual (Obiakor, 1992, 1994, 1999, 2001). There is always more to know about students and how best to serve their educational needs than what is revealed in the paperwork.

8.   Evaluate labels and categories critically for information about the student. Educators must remember that labels identify, they do not inform. They must also never make assumptions about the characteristics or educational needs of students based on the categorical labels they have been assigned (Obiakor, 2001; Obiakor et al., 2002).

9.   Remember the dimensional nature of categories. Special education categories must be viewed as dimensional, with the understanding that the educational needs they identify exist on a continuum (Obiakor, 2001). Categorical labels do not neatly overlay the problem behaviors or specific academic needs of a student and cannot be applied like Post-it notes.

10.   Understand that categorical special education labels are neither precise nor stable. Additions to the categorical system and modifications to eligibility criteria demonstrate that change is probable (Obiakor, 2001).

11.   Avoid programming instruction or planning interventions based on a categorical label. Interventions and instructions should be individualized based on the specific needs of each student as recorded in the individualized education plan, not on generalized presumptions about the needs of students in a particular special education category (Obiakor et al., 2002).

12.   Beware of one-size-fits-all interventions and instructional techniques promoted for a particular disability category (Obiakor, 2001). While current research supports the notion that some interventions work better than others (Lloyd, Forness, and Kavale, 1998), the notion of category-specific intervention and instructional methods is not supported.

13.   Develop a vigilant awareness of the possibility for negative consequences as a result of the misuse of categorization and labeling. These consequences can have long-term implications (Obiakor et al., 2002).

Obiakor (2001) articulated the following principles for truly good teachers regarding labeling and categorization:

1. Because words have power, they must be used to empower students.

2. Race matters in labels and categories.

3. Parents must be empowered as equal partners to reduce the effects of labels and categories.

4. It is better to document behaviors than to use gut feelings.

5. Children and youths are best served when programs emphasize services needed and not types of or labels for children.

6. If a categorical label is absolutely needed, it should be used to identify the specific problem and not the child.

7. No child or youth is a disordered child or youth.

8. Behaviors are good or bad depending on the culture, age, gender, time, and circumstance.

9. Negative behaviors of teachers have far-reaching consequences.

10. Individual differences in students must be valued to reduce labels and categories.

11. When students' differences are loaded with deficit perspectives, good students and good teachers fail.

12. "Good" labels can open educational doors for children, and "bad" labels can close those same doors.

13. Education should build trust and not destroy it.

14. Inappropriate identifications lead to inappropriate assessments which, in turn, lead to inappropriate labels.

15. All students are exceptional—they can learn when we provide nondiscriminatory labels, remediating services, and conducive learning environments. (pp. 74-75)

CONCLUSION

If we are to identify and serve the needs of African American children with exceptionalities, we must have language that allows us to exchange information and knowledge about exceptionalities and about exceptional students. No matter what words we use or how we identify individuals for special education services, any act of differentiation that allows us to provide specialized educational services to some, but not all, students is prone to the development of negative connotation and stigma. The problem resides in the tendency to be casual with the use of labels, to assume too much about the meanings vested in labels, and to take overgeneralized views about the individuals to whom we assign labels. We have given labels and categories descriptive and prescriptive powers that they do not deserve. What is needed is not so much the annihilation of special education language as it is an awareness of the power of words to condition attitudes and to trigger behaviors. If we at least recognize and acknowledge that underpinnings of discrimination and prejudice reside in the practice of special education labeling and categorization, then we may be in a position to deal with the impact they have on African American learners.

REFERENCES

Adelman, H. S. (1996). Appreciating the classification dilemma. In W. Stainback & S. Stainback (Eds.), *Controversial issues confronting special education: Divergent perspectives* (2nd ed., pp. 96-111). Needham Heights, MA: Allyn & Bacon.

American Association on Mental Retardation, Ad Hoc Committee on Terminology and Classification. (1992). *Mental retardation: Definition, classification, and systems of support* (9th ed.). Washington, DC: American Association on Mental Retardation.

Anderson, M. G. (1994). Perceptions about behavioral disorders in African American cultures and communities. In R. L. Peterson & S. Ishii-Jordan (Eds.), *Multicultural issues in the education of students with behavioral disorders* (pp. 93-104). Cambridge, MA: Brookline.

Artiles, A. J., & Zamora-Duran, G. (1997). *Reducing disproportionate representation of culturally diverse students in special and gifted education.* Reston, VA: Council for Exceptional Children.

Brenner, S. M. (1998). *Special education issues within the context of American society.* Belmont, CA: Wadsworth.

Brophy, J. (1983). Research on self-fulfilling prophecy and teacher expectations. *Journal of Educational Psychology, 75,* 631-661.

Delpit, L. (1995). *Other people's children.* New York: New Press.

DuBois, W. E. B. (1961). *The souls of black folk.* Greenwich, CT: Fawcett. (Original work published 1903)

Dunn, L. M. (1968). Special education for the mildly retarded—is much of it justifiable? *Exceptional Children, 35,* 5-22.

Education for All Handicapped Children Act (1975), P.L. 94-142, 20 U.S.C. § 1401 *et seq.*

Fordham, S., & Ogbu, J. (1986). Black student's school success: Coping with the burden of "acting white." *Urban Review, 18,* 176-206.

Hobbs, N. (1975). *The future of children: Categories, labels, and their consequences.* San Francisco: Jossey-Bass.

Kalyanpur, M., & Harry, B. (1999). *Culture in special education: Building reciprocal family-professional relationships.* Baltimore: Paul H. Brookes.

Kliewer, C., & Biklin, D. (1996). Labeling: Who wants to be called retarded? In W. Stainback & S. Stainback (Eds.), *Controversial issues confronting special education: Divergent perspectives* (2nd ed., pp. 83-95). Needham Heights, MA: Allyn & Bacon.

Kovel, J. (1984). *White racism: A psychohistory.* New York: Columbia University Press.

Lloyd, J. W., Forness, S. R., & Kavale, K. A. (1998). Some methods are more effective than others. *Intervention in School and Clinic, 33,* 195-200.

Lynch, E. W. (1998). Developing cross-cultural competence. In E. W. Lynch & M. J. Hanson (Eds.), *Developing cross-cultural competence: A guide for working with children and their families* (2nd ed., pp. 47-86). Baltimore: Paul H. Brookes.

Obiakor, F. E. (1992). Self-concept of African American students: An operational model for special education. *Exceptional Children, 59,* 160-167.

Obiakor, F. E. (1994). *The eight-step multicultural approach: Learning and teaching with a smile.* Dubuque, IA: Kendall/Hunt.

Obiakor, F. E. (1996, January 24). The power of the word. *Emporia Gazette,* p. 7.

Obiakor, F. E. (1999). Teacher expectations of minority exceptional learners: Impact on "accuracy" of self-concepts. *Exceptional Children, 66,* 39-53.

Obiakor, F. E. (2001). *It even happens in good schools: Responding to cultural diversity in today's classrooms.* Thousand Oaks, CA: Corwin.

Obiakor, F., Algozzine, B., Thurlow, M., Gwalla-Ogisi, N., Enwefa, S., Enwefa, R., & McIntosh, A. (2002). *Addressing the issue of disproportionate representation: Identification and assessment of culturally diverse students with emotional or behavioral disorders.* Arlington, VA: Council for Exceptional Children.

Oswald, D. P., Coutinho, M. J., Best, A. M., & Singh, N. N. (1999). Ethnic representation in special education: The influence of school-related economic and demographic variables. *Journal of Special Education, 32,* 194-206.

Persell, C. (1997). Social class and educational equity. In J. A. Banks & C. A. M. Banks (Eds.), *Multicultural education: Issues and perspectives* (3rd ed., pp. 87-107). Needham Heights, MA: Allyn & Bacon.

Roget, P. M. (1972). *Roget's thesaurus of synonyms & antonyms.* Framingham, MA: Dennison Manufacturing.

U.S. Department of Education. (1997). *Individuals With Disabilities Education Act Amendments of 1997.* Washington, DC: Author.

U.S. Department of Education. (2000). To assure the free appropriate education of all children with disabilities. *Twenty-second annual report to Congress on the implementation of the Individuals With Disabilities Education Act.* Washington, DC: Author.

Part II

Managing Learning Environments

Chapter Five

Instructional Strategies for African American Learners With Cognitive Disabilities

Helen Bessant Byrd

Successful education programs result from a good fit between the child, with careful attention to the frame of reference from which the child comes, and the education program in which the child is engaged. While this assertion is consistent with education philosophy articulated for some time, it is not yet a reality for many African American students in today's schools.

The continuing shrinkage of the supply of African American schoolteachers and administrators and the increasing demand for these personnel necessitate action by state and local education agencies. Two paths represent the options: (a) opening the pipeline for the preparation and licensure of more African American teachers or (b) designing and implementing teacher preparation programs which are infused with content that inculcates cultural competence in all candidates for teaching careers. Indeed, both paths should be taken. Such paths would facilitate appropriate identification, assessment, placement, and instruction of all learners who actually have cognitive and adaptive problems.

This chapter focuses on instructional strategies that are appropriate for African Americans learners with cognitive disabilities. After the population of learners is delineated, the traits of a competent teacher will be enumerated. The multicognitive, multicultural model is described, followed by a collection of exemplary, cognitively focused—as well as culturally focused—strategies for instruction.

LEARNERS WITH COGNITIVE DISABILITIES

In an effort to conveniently categorize and label learners in the school setting, numerous appellations have been used to identify those learners whose intellectual ability falls significantly below the norm. That is, limitations in cognition or intellectual ability are evident. This status has been variously labeled a mental defect, mental deficiency, and mental retardation. Designations of levels of tested intelligence have been idiot, imbecile, moron, custodial, as well as educable, mild, trainable, moderate, and severe profound. For the purposes of this chapter, cognitive disabilities refer to all levels of mental retardation as defined by Luckasson and associates (1992). They pointed out that

> mental retardation refers to substantial limitations in present functioning. It is charac-
> terized by significantly subaverage intellectual functioning, existing concurrently with
> related limitations in two or more of the following applicable adaptive skill areas: com-
> munication, self-care, home living, social skills, community use, self-direction, health
> and safety, functional academics, leisure, and work. Mental retardation manifests
> before age 18. (p. 1)

There is considerable disaffection in the field with this definition of mental retardation. Smith (2001) cites some of the concerns and reports that a new definition will likely be drafted soon with a possible name change for the category to cognitive disabilities or developmental disabilities. Suffice it to note that, for discussion in this chapter, cognitive disability refers to significant functional limitations due to low intellectual performance and adaptive ability occurring before the 18th birthday.

AFRICAN AMERICAN LEARNERS
WITH COGNITIVE DISABILITIES

African American learners with cognitive disabilities have been observed to display some common cultural behaviors. Because of the role that race plays in educational programming, it is those culturally manifested behaviors that result in misidentification, misassessment, miscate-gorization, misplacement, and misinstruction of African American learners. Although there is also much variability, characteristic proclivities have continued in ethnic and cultural groups over generations. Hale-Benson and Byrd have documented behavioral patterns and practices based on literature review and classroom observations (Hale-Benson, 1986; Byrd, 1995). Pertinent charac-teristics of African American learners include preferences for kinesthetic and tactile learning, reliance on visual rather than auditory input, musical rhythm and movement in learning, and coop-erative learning.

The presence of cognitive disability among African American learners increases the challenges that face teachers who seek to provide for them an effective education. Provision of a culturally centrist curriculum necessitates a response to the aforementioned characteristics of disabilities and, at the same time, a focus on the African Americanism of the learner. Bessant (1975) addressed such special education more than 3 decades ago. A teacher who can respond to cognitive variance should be able to respond to cultural variance and vice versa.

Prevalence statistics suggest that there is disproportionate representation of culturally diverse special education students receiving services (Artiles & Zamora-Duran, 1997). Particularly, African American learners constitute a disproportionately high number of students identified as having cognitive disabilities. Many African American learners have been misidentified, misassessed, misplaced, and misinstructed. Indeed, many of these learners may have educational needs that would not necessitate the label cognitive disabilities. Therefore it is most critical that, in addition to steps toward prevention, intervention strategies must be undertaken through general and special education programs to effectively meet the needs of African American learners identified as having cognitive disabilities.

The teacher who is effective in creating environments for African American learners with cognitive disabilities is generally a competent educator. In other words, the teacher can effectively serve all learners. Some traits that are inherent in the competent teacher include

- Facile use of basic skills
- Skill in curriculum development
- Genuine positive regard for children in general and for those with cognitive disabilities specifically
- Large repertoire of tactics for differentiated instruction
- Pleasant, outgoing disposition
- Creative and analytical thinking
- Excellent skills in classroom management
- Effective and positive interpersonal relations with peers and learners
- Effective use of humor in the classroom
- Recognition of the worth of each individual

In addition to the generic competencies of an effective teacher cited above, to be effective in providing for the education of African American learners, the teacher must be culturally competent. There are competencies that should be mastered by the teachers that more directly address the needs of African American students in the schools. Several scholars have addressed the teacher and the education of African American learners. Hale-Benson (1986) agrees that the teacher should believe in the ideology of the school; live in the school community; ideally, share, understand, and participate in Black culture; assimilate into mainstream culture; be trained in child development; respect Black culture; and work well with parents.

When teachers teach African American students in positive ways, the results are positive. Ladson-Billings (1994) made the following five statements about teaching and learning:

(1) When students are treated as competent they are likely to demonstrate competence; (2) when teachers provide instructional scaffolding, students can move from what they know to what they need to know; (3) the focus of the classroom must be instructional; (4) real education is about extending students' thinking and abilities; and (5) effective teaching involves in-depth knowledge of both the students and the subject matter. (pp. 123-125)

For students with cognitive disabilities, it is even more urgent that the teacher is generally competent and culturally competent. Inasmuch as the learners often have met with failure, it is all the more necessary that they have positive experiences. Marshall (2002) identified five characteristics of successful teachers of African American students, namely: (a) the belief that all students can succeed; (b) promotion of student development across several dimensions; (c) a focus on the collective; (d) recognition that no knowledge is sacrosanct; and (e) respect for teaching as a profession and an art. The combination and integration of the proven characteristics of teaching students with cognitive disabilities along with techniques that work with African American learners can yield an excellent compendium of desired traits of teachers. The professional who evinces these traits will orchestrate the teaching-learning environment that helps the students to maximize their fullest potential.

A CULTURALLY CENTRIC CURRICULUM FOR AFRICAN AMERICAN LEARNERS WITH COGNITIVE DISABILITIES

Just like other students with exceptionalities, African American learners with exceptionalities need a culturally centrist curriculum. The overall purpose of such a curriculum is to design and implement a plan to successfully manage the learning environment for the student to achieve. Wiggins and McTighe (1998) stated that "a curriculum is a specific blueprint for learning that is derived from content and performance standards. Curriculum takes content and shapes it into a plan for effective teaching and learning" (p. 4). Any curriculum should be designed or modified with the specific learner as the focus.

This is especially important for the learner with cognitive disabilities, inasmuch as this learner is less able to make inferences and transfer knowledge. Learning experiences should be directly related to the learner. Byrd's (1995) learner-centered curriculum model reflects the centrism advocated. (See Figure 5.1.) The learner is at the core of the curriculum. All content and pedagogy focus on that specific culture. A larger circle, which includes the common culture, encircles the learner's culture. The latter comprises some aspects of other specific cultures and some traits specific to the common culture.

The curriculum based on the learner-centered cultural centrism model serves five functions critical to the success of the African American learner with cognitive disabilities. Such a curriculum (a) affirms the child's identity, (b) ensures understanding of the child's own culture, (c) promotes understanding of other individual cultures, (d) serves as a foundation for valuing a common culture, and (e) provides cohesion that sustains a nation. The merit of this curriculum has recently escalated. The self-understanding, understanding of others, awareness for and appreciation of commonalities, with recognition of connection with others, are direly needed to cement a patriotic bond of all citizens—black, white, red, yellow, and brown—of the United States. By the same token, the learner-centered cultural centrism model is consonant with and extends Byrd's (1994) multicognitive multicultural curriculum. This paradigm provides a schema for understanding strategies that aid the management of successful learning environments for African American learners. (See the multicultural multicognitive model in Figure 5.2.) Application of the model to learners with cognitive disabilities facilitates understanding for the overlay of the four components on the learner: (a) cognition, (b) curriculum, (c) culture, and (d) pedagogy.

Figure 5.1   Learner-Centered Cultural Centrism Model

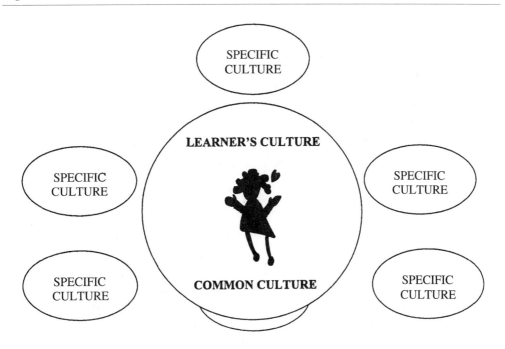

These components provide the controls, the content, the context, and the conduit respectively for the teaching-learning process.

Cognition is the component that serves as the *control* or framework for the teaching-learning experience. Cognition is the authority that guides the teacher's decisions and planning. The extent of the perceived potential and style of the learner are identified to provide the structure that supports the teaching-learning process. The level of cognitive disability, whether it is mild, moderate, or severe, influences the teacher's decisions about the curriculum and pedagogy.

An additional critical aspect of the cognition component is determination of the cognitive style of the learner. Individuals exhibit preferences for interaction with stimuli that have been catalogued in varied models by theorists. Exemplary among the models are (a) Guilford's (1980) structure of intellect that organizes intelligence in content, process, and product categories; (b) Gardner's (1989) and Silver, Strong and Perini's (2000) multiple intelligences, including logical-mathematical, linguistic, musical, spatial, bodily-kinesthetic, interpersonal, intrapersonal, and naturalist; (c) Sternberg's (1988) triarchic theory of intelligence that specifies practical, creative, and analytical abilities; and (d) Woods's (2002) learning styles based on sensory input and output preferences, which may be visual, auditory, or kinesthetic. Although the literature equivocates on documentation of the import of cognitive or learning styles, it is herein averred that knowledge of the learner's preferences does indeed facilitate the teaching-learning process.

Curriculum is key to the teaching-learning environment that engenders successful experiences for African American learners with cognitive disabilities; curriculum is the *content* that is imparted. For the students with mild disabilities, little difference is made in the content except for a focus on functionality. As the capacity for mastery lessens, the breadth of the curriculum narrows, with emphases on survival and independence.

Figure 5.2   Multicognitive Multicultural Curriculum

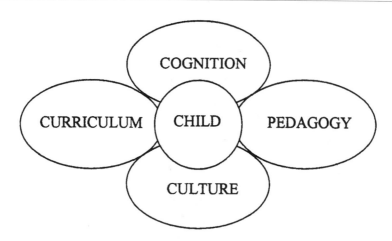

Culture is the third component of the multicultural multicognitive model. The focus in this component is on the *context* of the educational environment. The progression of the learner from the familiar to the novel and mastery thereof is eased when the learner's own image is seen in the learning material and when the environment is imbued with nurturance and empowerment. The culturally centrist curriculum recognizes and values the language, traditions, and values of the learner. It infuses the curriculum with content about the traditions and contributions of people like the learner. The curricular content adheres to the guidelines of the state and local education agencies' standards of learning.

Pedagogy is the final of the four components of the multicultural multicognitive model. Herein is specified the *conduit* for the teaching-learning process. Specific tactics serve as the channel through which the cognitive control, the curriculum content, and the cultural context come together to consummate the teaching-learning process.

VISIONARY PEDAGOGY FOR AFRICAN AMERICAN LEARNERS WITH DISABILITIES

A conceptual framework grounded in cultural centrism has been posited. This multicultural-multicognitive model provides for a successful learning environment for African American students with cognitive disabilities. The approaches to instruction may be demarcated into those that are cognitively focused and those that are culturally focused.

Determination of appropriate, cognitively focused instructional strategies for teaching learners with cognitive disabilities emanates from understanding the characteristics of this population of students. The literature of the discipline is replete with discussions on this topic. Points of consensus on characteristics include slow or limited intellectual performance and academic functioning due to low tested intelligence, delayed or deficient communication skills, delayed or maladaptive ability, poor social skills, limited economic efficiency, and, sometimes, poor motor skills. Since the advent of special education programs which gave significant focus to learners with cognitive disabilities in the early 1960s, educators have sought to determine what strategies work effectively. Numerous efforts have been made to chronicle and categorize these strategies for preservice and inservice education purposes. Mastropieri and Scruggs (2000) specified classroom adaptations for students with disabilities. Many scholars and educators have provided extensive enumeration and discussion of strategies for teaching students with disabilities (e.g., Henley, Ramsey, & Algozzine, 1999; Ysseldyke & Algozzine, 1995; Ysseldyke, Algozzine, & Thurlow, 2000).

Recognition of the need to individualize or personalize instruction for learners in general education has led to publications of specific instructional strategies that have applicability to learners with cognitive disabilities. Orlich, Harder, Callahan, and Gibson (2001) provided a thorough exploration of teaching strategies. Some of the many strategies cited in these sources will be enumerated and discussed later in this chapter for use with African American learners with cognitive disabilities.

Culturally focused strategies comprise techniques and approaches that seek to accentuate the culture as the entrée to motivating the learner and are an excellent way to reach the student. While such strategies for reaching the learner are not always unique to a cultural or ethnic group, the universe of strategies for teaching all children includes a subset of strategies for teaching culturally and linguistically diverse learners. This subset includes a subset of strategies for instruction of African American students. The critical factor is that the learning activity for any student taps into the experiential background or frame of reference of the particular learner. Since this chapter addresses the African American learner, the strategies proposed must be congruent with the characteristics or traits common among African American learners. Strategies have been chronicled that are commensurate with characteristics common among African American learners enumerated earlier in the chapter (Byrd, 1995; Hale-Benson, 1986), recognizing that they have much in common with other culturally diverse groups. Given the nature of pedagogical tactics, some of the strategies appropriate to African American learners are also appropriate for learners with cognitive disabilities and vice versa.

SUGGESTED PEDAGOGICAL STRATEGIES

There are specific teaching tactics that have proven worth for African American learners with cognitive disabilities. The strategies and activities described in this section have come from a variety of sources (e.g., Henley et al., 1999). The strategies that follow are grouped for discussion in seven broad categories: work and leisure habits, study skills, prompting, thinking skills, literacy skills, academic skills, and social skills.

Work and Leisure Habits. Attention to attendance and promptness is important to aid the student in preparation for a vocation. The student with cognitive disabilities requires intentional instruction instead of leaving mastery of these abilities to incidental learning. African American students may be predisposed to completing activities "in time" rather than "on time." Therefore they need a focus on punctuality. Having students sign in and record the time when they arrive in class and keep a record of productivity during certain class periods are excellent prevocational skill development activities. Students with cognitive disabilities also often require formal instruction in daily living and in leisure time activities. This is especially so for those who function below the mild disability level.

Study Skills. African American students and those with cognitive disabilities should be taught how to study and how to take tests. The Powerful Preparation for Successful Testing (PPST) model (Morris & Byrd, 2001) provides a scheme to facilitate instruction on varied aspects of study including psychological and physical readiness for test taking, the ecology of study, and time orientation and management.

Prompting. Activities in this category serve to give extra encouragement to the learner to respond correctly. There are three types cited. The first is *advance organizers*. The structure and guidance imposed by the teacher in the teaching-learning process is critical for the African American learner with cognitive disabilities. It aids in focusing the learner on the desired content. Following are some preliminary steps:

- Alert students to the transition to a new activity.
- Identify topics and activities that students will do.
- State the concepts to be learned and give examples.
- Introduce new vocabulary.
- State the expected outcomes of an activity.

Likewise, in preparation for a story, teachers pose questions that prompt answers to issues of who, what, when, and why? The second type of prompting is *guiding directions*. The teacher who uses this strategy gives guidelines before an activity that will aid in directing the learner's attention to the task. Often students fail to complete an assignment correctly because they have not attended to the critical dimensions. Early on, students need to learn terms such as copy, underline, draw, circle, line, alike, and different. *Physical assist* is the third type of prompting which is useful, especially for learners who have moderate to severe cognitive disabilities. In this case, the teacher actually moves the learner's body through an act, for example, buttoning a shirt. The teacher grasps the learner's hands that are holding the button and shirt; then the teacher takes the learner through the motions. This act gives the student the kinesthetic experience. This type of prompting is withdrawn as the learner acquires the skills.

Thinking Skills. Higher-order thinking skills activities strengthen the cognitive facility of the learner. The Byrd and Morris model (1998) provides a schema for acquisition of convergent and divergent thinking as well as imaging and transcending. Exemplary activities are included. Additional higher-order thinking skills include mindmapping, ladders (progression of changing one letter to make a new word), mnemony (memory cues), and other metacognitive skills.

Literacy Skills. Vital to the academic progress of African American learners with cognitive disabilities is the mastery of literacy skills. These academic skills provide the foundation for subsequent learning and represent minimum standards in each area. Most often the term *literacy skills* refers to concepts in reading and language arts. However, it is proposed that literacy skills are equally important in other areas as well. In the area of reading and language arts literacy, basic skills are decoding and encoding symbol systems of a language. Strategies used in the language arts should accentuate the African American's preference for the oral traditions. This includes story reading, storytelling, play production, and so forth. Quantitative literacy entails mastery of the basic content in mathematics. Learning activities for mastery of number operations include counting money, telling time, shopping, and budgeting. An understanding of everyday concepts in science leads to science literacy. These skills include biological concepts such as human growth, diet and health, pets and their care, and gardening. Chemical concepts include understanding of cleaning agents, personal toiletries, and medications. Citizenship literacy includes the skills and actions exhibited by Americans who enjoy the privileges and exercise the responsibilities of the status. These skills and actions include being a registered voter and having a grasp of certain basic information (e.g., the pledge of allegiance, the national anthem, senatorial and congressional district of residence, and one's voting precinct and polling place).

Academic Skills. This category of instructional strategies includes a wide variety of activities that lead to mastery of academics. Some specific activities that are of great aid to African American learners with cognitive disabilities include tiered activities, scaffolding, staggered starts, limited choice, peer tutoring, cooperative learning, and problem-based instruction.

Social Skills. The final category of pedagogical strategies is social skills acquisition. Because the African American learner comes from a different cultural milieu, the child may not be predisposed to sit quietly in class. Thus the student often may be at odds with expectations in the classroom. On the other hand, the learner with cognitive disabilities acquires less via incidental learning and more through intentional learning. The African American learner with cognitive disabilities may require much more instruction for social-skills acquisition. Some specific areas of instruction include social decorum, continual verification, and conflict resolution.

CONCLUSION

Key Points to Remember

Enumerated below are 10 crucial points from the chapter:

1. Learners with cognitive disabilities are those who have intellectual deficits generally referred to as mental retardation.

2. A disproportionately high number of African American students are identified as having cognitive disabilities.

3. A culturally centric curriculum shapes all content and activities with a focus on the specific learner, bridging from the learner's own culture to the common culture to other specific cultures.

4. There are necessary traits that teachers must have to be effective in teaching African American students in the areas of self-understanding, child focus, content mastery, and strategic proficiency.

5. The curriculum affirms the child's identity, ensures understanding of the child's own culture, promotes understanding of other individual cultures, serves as a foundation for valuing a common culture, and provides cohesion that sustains a nation.

6. Byrd's (1995) multicultural multicognitive model comprises curriculum content, cognitive controls, cultural context, and pedagogical conduits for the teaching-learning process.

7. The culturally centrist curriculum recognizes and values the language, traditions, and values of the learner, infusing the curriculum with content about the traditions and contributions of people like the learner.

8. Cognitively focused strategies are teaching techniques that are responsive to the intellectual parameters of the learner. Culturally focused strategies seek to accentuate the culture of the learner as the learner's entry point to acquisition of new information or skills.

9. Specific pedagogical strategies are grouped in the following categories: work and leisure habits, study skills, prompting, thinking skills, literacy skills, academic skills, and social skills.

10. Literacy skills are fundamental concepts in several categories including reading and language arts, quantitative literacy, science literacy, and citizenship literacy.

Final Comments

This chapter has addressed specific avenues of instruction for African American learners with cognitive disabilities. After defining the population, an enumeration and discussion followed of characteristics that evince competence in the teacher. The concept of cultural centrism in the curriculum was elucidated. Finally, a collection of specific strategies for instruction was listed and described. Application of these strategies will lead to the establishment and maintenance of an environment conducive to learning for African American learners with cognitive disabilities.

Discussion Issues

1.   Cite and discuss at least three driving forces for increasing the cultural competence of all teachers.

2.   From the context of this chapter, explain and discuss the proverb, "They who learn, teach."

3.   Rahman is a 12-year-old African American boy with a mild cognitive disability. He pays little attention during classes. Most of the day, he is drawing pictures of rap singing artists or beating on the desktop and rapping. Outline some steps that his teacher may take to connect him to the curricular content and engage him in the learning process.

4.   Name and explain four specific pedagogical strategies. What features commend them for use with African American learners with cognitive disabilities?

5.   Explain the idea that all education must be founded on the nature of the child.

REFERENCES

Artiles, A. J., & Zamora-Duran, G. (Eds.). (1997). *Reducing disproportionate representation of culturally diverse students in special and gifted education.* Reston, VA: Council for Exceptional Children.

Bessant, H. P. (1975). Interfacing special education with multicultural education in a performance-based teacher education model. In C. Grant (Ed.), *Sifting and winnowing: An exploration of the relationship between multicultural education and CBTE* (pp. 55-68). Madison, WI: Teacher Corps Associates.

Byrd, H. B. (1994, April). *Inclusive curricula for African American exceptional students*. Paper presented at the 72nd annual convention of the Council for Exceptional Children, Denver, CO.

Byrd, H. B. (1995). Cultural and pedagogical procedures for African American learners with academic and cognitive disabilities. In B. A. Ford, F. E. Obiakor, & J. M. Patton (Eds.), *Effective education of African American exceptional learners: New perspectives* (pp. 123-150). Austin, TX: Pro-Ed.

Byrd, H. B., & Morris, C. (1998). Improving academic performance through higher order thinking skills acquisition model. In A. W. Freeman, H. B. Byrd, & C. Morris (Eds.)*, Enfranchising urban learners for the twenty-first century* (pp. 55-65). Kearney, NE: Morris.

Byrd, H. B., Morris, C., & Lang, S. (1998). Contemporary theoretical applications to urban learners. In A. W. Freeman, H. B. Byrd, & C. Morris (Eds.), *Enfranchising urban learners for the twenty-first century* (pp. 6-20). Kearney, NE: Morris.

Finegan, C., & Helms, R. G. (2002). *On the net 2002: Multicultural education*. Boston: Allyn & Bacon.

Garcia, E. (2000). *Student cultural diversity: Understanding and meet the challenge* (3rd ed). Boston: Houghton Mifflin.

Gardner, H. (1989). Multiple intelligences to go to school. *Educational Researcher, 18*(8), 410.

Guilford, J. P. (1980). Cognitive styles: What are they? *Educational and Psychological Measurements, 40,* 715-735.

Hale-Benson, J. E. (1986). *Black children, their roots, culture and learning styles* (Rev. ed.). Baltimore: Johns Hopkins Press.

Henley, M., Ramsey, R. S., & Algozzine, B. (1999). *Characteristics of and strategies for teaching students with mild disabilities* (3rd ed.). Boston: Allyn & Bacon.

Ladson-Billings, G. (1994). *The dreamkeepers: Successful teachers of African American children*. San Francisco: Jossey-Bass.

Luckasson, R., Coulter, D. L., Polloway, E. A., Reis, S., Shalock, R. L., Snell, M. E., Spitalnik, D. M., & Stark, J. A. (1992). *Mental retardation: Definition, classification, and systems of supports*. Washington, DC: American Association on Mental Retardation.

Marshall, P. L. (2002). *Cultural diversity in our schools*. Belmont, CA: Wordsworth/Thompson.

Mastropieri, M. A., & Scruggs, T. E. (2000). *The inclusive classroom: Strategies for effective instruction*. Upper Saddle River, NJ: Prentice-Hall.

Morris, C., & Byrd, H. B. (2001, May). *Powerful preparation for successful testing*. Paper presented at the 47th annual convention of the International Reading Association, New Orleans, LA.

Orlich, D. C., Harder, R. J., Callahan, R. C., & Gibson, H. W. (2001). *Teaching strategies: A guide to better instruction* (6th ed.). Boston: Houghton Mifflin.

Silver, H. F., Strong, R. W., & Perini, M. J. (2000). *So each may learn: Integrating learning styles and multiple intelligences*. Alexandria, VA: Association for Supervision and Curriculum Development.

Smith, D. D. (2001). *Introduction to special education: Teaching in an age of opportunity* (4th ed.). Boston: Allyn & Bacon.

Sternberg, R. J. (1988). *The triarchic mind: A new theory of human intelligence*. New York: Viking.

Wiggins, G., & McTighe, J. (1998). *Understanding by design*. Alexandria, VA: Association for Supervision and Curriculum Development.

Woods, J. W. (2002). *Adapting instruction to accommodate students in inclusive settings* (4th ed.). Upper Saddle River, NJ: Pearson Education.

Ysseldyke, J. E., & Algozzine, B. (1995). *Special education: A practical approach for teachers* (3rd ed.). Boston: Houghton Mifflin.

Ysseldyke, J. E., Algozzine, B., & Thurlow, M. (2000). *Critical issues in special education* (3rd ed.). Boston: Houghton Mifflin.

Chapter Six

Working With African American Students With Specific Learning Disabilities

Patrick A. Grant and Pauline B. Grant

If we look at learning disabilities as differences in learning style, or the way a student approaches learning, we may see the interaction between the student and the environment as a cause of the learning disability.

—Nancy Hunt and Kathleen Marshall (2002, p. 118)

Learning disability has been viewed as a perplexing category of exceptionality. Hunt and Marshall (2002) reported that children with learning disabilities have always existed, but for many years, educators failed to recognize their unique problems and characteristics.

Based on the Individuals With Disabilities Education Act (IDEA) and amendments (1990, 1997), students have a learning disability if they (A) do not achieve at the proper age level and ability level in one or more of several specific areas when provided with appropriate learning experiences; and (B) have a severe discrepancy between achievement and intellectual ability in one or more of the following areas: (a) oral expression, (b) listening comprehension, (c) written expression, (d) basic reading skills, (e) reading comprehension, (f) mathematics calculation, and (g) mathematics reasoning. The key element of the federal definition is the emphasis on the performance of students with learning disabilities, which is often tied to their ability to receive or express information (Hunt & Marshall, 2002). This chapter explores ways to work with African American students with specific learning disabilities.

HISTORICAL AND CONCEPTUAL FRAMEWORKS OF LEARNING DISABILITIES

The learning disabilities story actually began long before Kirk (1975) introduced the term at a meeting of parents advocating special educational services for their children who were having difficulty in school. In earlier decades, these children's difficulties had been variously categorized as mild exogenous mental retardation (mild mental retardation caused by brain injury), minimal brain dysfunction (behavior associated with brain injury, although brain damage cannot be verified), perceptual impairment (persistent difficulty in making sense of sensory stimulation), hyperactivity (excessive and socially inappropriate behavior accompanied by problems in learning), and slow learning (a child whose achievement is not far enough below average to indicate mental retardation) (Hallahan & Cruickshank, 1973; Hallahan & Kauffman, 1977; Mann, 1979; Wiedherhold, 1974). The difficulties mentioned above and other terms were eventually assimilated into the concept of learning disabilities.

Today, people from nearly every walk of life and every ethnicity recognize the term learning disability—the general public often uses it generically to indicate that someone's behavior is highly unusual or inadequate for the circumstances. Learning disability is a separate category in the special education literature, a disability defined by federal and state laws, and a specialization for which teachers in many states must obtain special certification. The term has gained almost universal acceptance among regular educators, special educators, and the general public in the United States and in many foreign countries (Mazurek & Winzer, 1994; Winzer, 1993). Hallahan, Kauffman, and Lloyd (1996) reported that the history of learning disabilities could be summarized in relation to themes that have emerged as the field has developed. These themes are critical to understanding that learning disabilities (a) represent an interdisciplinary field that is international and multicultural in scope; (b) have a variety of possible causes; (c) are, in part, a social construct; (d) are heterogeneous in nature; (e) vary in severity and pervasiveness; (f) are characterized by individual differences; (g) affect a diverse group of people; (h) may coexist with other disabilities or giftedness; (i) require training in systematic approaches to tasks; (j) require educators to minimize the contribution of poor teaching; (k) are developmental disorders persisting over the lifespan. Additionally, it must be acknowledged that advances in the field of learning disabilities can occur only through careful, persistent research.

The field of learning disabilities is complicated by controversy in the areas of definition, prevalence, and demographics. One explanation for why people have attempted to define learning disabilities is that it is necessary to describe for whom funds and legislation are being advocated.

Kirk's Definition

Kirk (1962) defined learning disability as follows:

A learning disability refers to a retardation, disorder, or delayed development in one or more of the processes of speech, language, reading, writing, arithmetic, or other school subject resulting from a psychological handicap caused by a possible cerebral dysfunction and/or emotional or behavioral deprivation, or cultural and instructional factors. (p. 263)

There are five components of Kirk's definition that have appeared in many of the later definitions of learning disability: (a) subaverage achievement (reading, writing, arithmetic) or achievement-related (speech or language) behavior; (b) intraindividual differences—the possibility that the subaverage achievement or achievement-related behaviors occur in only some areas or one area, with average or above-average achievement occurring in the other areas; (c) reference to psychological handicaps (often referred to as psychological processes by Kirk and others) as causal factors; (d) reference to cerebral dysfunction as a possible causal factor; (e) exclusion of other disabling conditions (e.g., mental retardation) and environmental conditions as causal factors.

Bateman's Definition

Bateman (1965), a student of Kirk, offered the following definition:

Children who have learning disorders are those who manifest an educationally significant discrepancy between their estimated intellectual potential and actual level of performance related to basic disorders in the learning process, which may or may not be accompanied by demonstrable central nervous system dysfunction, and which are not secondary to generalized mental retardation, educational or cultural deprivation, severe emotional disturbance, or sensory loss. (p. 220)

Bateman's definition differed from Kirk's in at least two important respects. First, it did not include reference to emotional factors as a cause of learning disabilities. In fact, it mentioned severe emotional disturbance as one of the disabilities that does not cause learning disabilities. No major definitions since Bateman's have mentioned emotional disturbance as a possible causal factor. Second, and even more important, it included reference to a discrepancy between intellectual potential and actual performance.

The Federal Government's Definition

The federal government defined learning disabilities in the Education for All Handicapped Children Act (1975) and subsequent amendments. In the 1975 law, disability is defined:

Specific learning disability means a disorder in one or more of the basic psychological processes involved in understanding or in using language, spoken or written, which may manifest itself in an imperfect ability to listen, think, speak, read, write, spell, or to do mathematical calculations. The term includes such conditions as perceptual handicaps, brain injury, minimal brain dysfunction, dyslexia, and developmental aphasia. The term does not include children who have problems that are primarily the result of visual, hearing, or motor disabilities, or mental retardation, emotional disturbance, or of environmental, cultural, or economic disadvantage. (Hunt & Marshall, 1994)

Lokerson (1992) noted that although the federal definition governs the identification of, and services to, children with learning disabilities (LD), there are variations between states and among school systems. In an attempt to clarify the identification, some states specify an intelligence range. Others add a concept of a discrepancy between potential and achievements, sometimes quantifying the discrepancy using test scores. These slightly different yardsticks are indicative of a lack of clear consensus about exactly what learning disabilities are.

Despite the apparent logic of explaining learning disabilities as a discrepancy between intellectual potential and academic achievement, many people have criticized the concept. Researchers have pointed to at least four problems inherent in the discrepancy between concepts of ability, achievement, and discrepancy:

A. Disputes continue regarding the definition and measurement of intelligence.

B. The intelligence of students with learning disabilities may be underestimated by IQ tests, because the tests are affected by the disabilities to some extent.

C. It is difficult to distinguish between groups of poor readers whose achievement is discrepant from IQ.

D. Using discrepancy makes it difficult to identify young children, because they are not yet old enough to have demonstrated a discrepancy.

As one researcher (Stanovich, 1989) put it, "The decision to base the definition of a reading disability on a discrepancy with measured IQ is . . . nothing short of astounding. Certainly one would be hard pressed to find a concept more controversial than intelligence in all of psychology" (p. 487).

According to the figures kept by the federal government, the public schools have identified approximately 2.3 million students 6 to 21 yeas of age as learning disabled, which represents 4.09% of those in this age range (U.S. Department of Education, 1994). However, this is a slight underestimation because students in private schools identified with learning disabilities have tripled. Critics have suggested that this rapid growth is evident because learning disabilities is an ill-defined category, and even defenders of the field are concerned that much of the growth is indicative of the confusion over definition and diagnostic criteria. Others have noted that the increase in the numbers of students identified with learning disabilities is inversely related to the numbers identified for several reasons:

1. Hallahan (1992) speculated that there may be many reasons for some of the growth. The field of learning disabilities was quite new in 1976 when the government started keeping prevalence data, and it may have taken professionals several years to decide how to identify children.

2. Hallahan identified a number of social and cultural changes that have occurred in the last 30 years that have heightened children's vulnerability to developing learning disabilities. Earlier, Baumeister, Kupstas, and Klindworth (1990) suggested that an increase in poverty has placed more children at risk for biomedical problems, including central nervous system dysfunctions.

3. Hallahan further speculated that stress on parents may result in their being less able to provide the social support necessary to help their children, who themselves are experiencing an increasing amount of stress. The result may be that children who, in a previous time of less stressful lifestyles and more support, would have gotten by in their schoolwork are now experiencing failure.

AFRICAN AMERICANS IN THE WORLD
OF LEARNING DISABILITIES: CRITICAL ISSUES

Brown v. Board of Education of Topeka (1954) called for the desegregation of schools in America and set the stage for equal education for African Americans. Banks (1997) contended that perhaps more than any other single event, this decision by the high court helped pave the way for the civil rights movement of the 1960s and 1970s. Today, segregation still exists in schools in the form of disproportionate placement of African American children in special education programs. To truly understand the African American learner with learning disabilities, it is imperative to understand DuBois (1996),who suggested that the world of African Americans does not lead them to true self-consciousness but only lets them see themselves through the revelation of the other world. The ramification of this double consciousness is tremendous. This sense of always looking at one's self through the eyes of others, of measuring one's soul by the tape of a world that looks on in amused contempt and pity, creates self-hatred and an inaccurate sense of self-worth.

Slavery in its disguised form still exists today, and general and special educators seem to be the greatest slave masters in this century. What is not taught in schools and may not be either known or understood by educators today is that the Africans came to America long before Columbus. Banks (1997) suggested Africans established a colony in Mexico before Columbus in 1492. They were the first Europeans to explore America, and they had been living in Europe for many years when European exploration of America began. What seems to have occurred over the years is the branding of African Americans in America. More than 2 decades ago, Graves (1978) observed that institutional racism brands African American children as inferior from birth. These students are branded through IQ testing, classroom ability grouping, and negative teacher attitudes. Some educators (e.g., Howard, 1985; Kuykendall, 1992) have discovered that rumors, myths, and innuendoes have strong effects on the aspirations and academic achievement of many African American and Hispanic youth. It is ironic that the longer African American youths stay in school, the further they fall behind the academic achievement of their White counterparts. Nadell (1995) determined that this condition could be counteracted when progressive Whites recognize that African American people historically and currently make the greatest contribution to a universal humanity. Interestingly, African American students are often excluded from classes for students with learning disabilities and placed in classes for people with mental retardation and emotional disturbance. A persistent and pervasive problem in the education of African American students is their disproportionate representation in special education settings (Heller, Holtzman, & Messick 1982; Serwatka, Deering, & Stoddard, 1989). This problem is most pronounced in the rate of underrepresentation of African American students in gifted programs. Conversely, there exist a disproportionately high representation of African American students in classes for students with educable mental retardation (EMR) (Serwatka, Deering, & Grant, 1995). It appears that African American students are more frequently placed in more restrictive, self-contained special education classes than in less restrictive, inclusive settings. This occurs in disability categories such as educable mental retardation (EMR) and specific learning disabilities (SLD).

Gay (1997) reported that despite legal mandates prohibiting discrimination, educational inequalities continue to prevail at crisis levels today. A report on the education status of African Americans by the College Entrance Examination Board (1985) concluded that "although many of the legal barriers to educational opportunity have been removed, education—to a large extent—remains separate and unequal in the United States" (p. vii). This inequality becomes clear when the current educational status of students of color—especially African Americans, Mexican Americans, Puerto Ricans, and American Indians—and the pervasiveness of the problems these groups encounter in schools are analyzed. The situation is not quite as serious for Asian Americans, at least on some standardized test measures of school achievement, school attendance, and graduation rates. We live in a society that is enriched by the traditional values of people from different national origins, different language backgrounds, different areas of the country, and different genders. Yet, with this diversity comes the dilemma of having been steeped in customs, knowledge, language, modes of thought, and styles of behavior that may not be well matched to the expectations of our schools. Our school curriculum is built on middle income, White expectations for what is the appropriate language to learn, the best knowledge to learn, and the behaviors that are most acceptable. Rather than celebrate the differences among different people, our curricula give the message that the White middle-class ways of behavior and thinking are more important than any other. Smith (1994) explained that the problem is exacerbated when we weigh the importance of teachers in the equation. Teachers are the referring agents, and Whites represent between 80% and 90% of all teachers in the educational system, who base their referrals of African American students on their personal stereotypes. Moreover, Smith concluded that poor teaching involves far more than an inappropriate match of tasks to learning characteristics. It also involves (a) the kinds of expectations teachers communicate to students, (b) the teacher's ability to deal with special needs in the classroom, (c) the teacher's knowledge of normal child development, and (d) the teacher's sensitivity to the different learning strategies and behavioral styles youngsters bring to the school environment. About 3 decades ago, Adelman (1971) noted that when teachers do not personalize instructions to accommodate individual differences, the number of children with learning problems increases. Later, Larsen (1978) contended that some students might be erroneously identified as learning disabled because they fall behind as a result of inappropriate learning opportunities. This misidentification leads us to understand why many African American children end up being misdiagnosed, misreferred, and, most often, misplaced. General and special educators must understand that many other factors may contribute to the misclassification of learners from diverse cultures as behaviorally disordered instead of learning disabled. The Executive Committee of the Council for Children With Behavior Disorders (1989) listed many factors that may contribute to the misclassification of learners from diverse cultures, for example:

1. Language, which affects how the educational community interacts and perceives the learner's behavior

2. Faculty perceptions and lower expectations

3. The higher rates at which learners from cultural minorities enter the referral-to-placement process, which increases their likelihood of identification or misidentification

WORKING WITH AFRICAN AMERICAN STUDENTS WITH LEARNING DISABILITIES

To work with African Americans with learning disabilities, general and special educators must focus on appropriate identification and assessment. About 2 decades ago, Ysseldyke and associates (1983) summarized several issues related to learners identified as learning disabled. In

5 years of research, they found no reliable psychometric differences between students labeled learning disabled and those who were perceived to be low achievers. In addition, identification as learning disabled depended on the criteria used, with different children being identified dependent on the definition applied: If individual children move to a different school district, they may no longer be identified as being learning disabled (Shea & Bauer, 1994). Algozzine (1991) argued that the new move toward "excellence" in education might increase the likelihood that low-performing students will be referred as having learning disabilities. For the African American learner, it will most often be based on behavior; therefore they will be referred for the emotionally disturbed or the mentally retarded classification. In addition, the shortage of well-prepared and certified individuals to conduct the necessary evaluation makes the situation even worse.

In order to diagnose a child with a suspected learning disability, the following procedures must be considered: clinical interview, ecological assessment, parent interview, teacher interview, review of cumulative reports and records, intelligence testing, and achievement testing.

Clinical Interview

The clinical interview involves a series of interviews with the child to assess where the ultimate problem may lie. When interviewing the African American child with suspected learning disabilities, it is important to look and listen for confusion over questions, poor use of vocabulary, problems expressing ideas and thoughts, awkward gait, poor memory, short attention span, lack of focus, poor fine-motor skills, and a history of academic difficulties.

Ecological Assessment

Ecological assessment involves observing the African American child in a variety of settings, such as the classroom, playground, and other structured and nonstructured settings to determine where the student manifests the greatest difficulties. In the case of an African American child, general and special educators may observe social withdrawal, alienation from peers, inability to focus in unstructured setting, and class clown type of behavior as a means of being removed from an academically stressful setting.

Parent Interview

A parent interview requires a personal meeting with the parents to determine background history that may be essential for appropriate diagnosis. In the case of an African American child with a suspected learning disability, general and special educators must try listening during an interview for statements such as (a) has difficulty dressing self; (b) avoids housework; (c) is disorganized; (d) has a short attention span; (e) forgets easily; (f) forgets to bring books home; (g) gets stomachaches in the morning before school; (h) gets frequent headaches; (i) has few friends; (j) is unwilling to try new things; and (k) gives up easily.

Teacher Interview

Teacher interviews may require several meetings with the classroom teacher to ascertain the child's basic intellectual, social, and academic performance. In the case of an African American child with potential learning disability, the interviewer should be aware of certain LD symptom clusters that may appear in the classroom. Examples include poor memory; gross-motor coordination difficulties; lack of focus; short attention span; procrastination; failure to hand in written work or homework; lack of confidence; self-derogatory statements such as, "I'm so stupid"; consistently low academic performance in certain subjects over time; social difficulties; lack of motivation for schoolwork; poor handwriting; and poor fine-motor skills.

Review of Cumulative Reports and Records

In the case of an African American child with potential learning disability, a review of cumulative records by general and special educators may reveal consistently low achievement scores in certain subjects over a period of years, past teacher comments showing a pattern similar to what the child's present teacher reports, a historical pattern of academic difficulties, frequent absences (which may occur when the child feels frustrated and overwhelmed by the work), and a discrepancy between ability and class performance as indicated by report card pattern.

Intelligence Testing

In the case of an African American child with a suspected learning disability, the psychologist ought to administer an individual intelligence test to look for an average to above-average potential intellectual level. This does not mean that the child's IQ need be in the average range, but analysis of the profile indicates that greater potential may be shown through a significantly uneven pattern of scores within the same test. Many children are commonly misdiagnosed as having a learning disability when, in actuality, they may be slow learners, children with emotional issues, or underachievers not performing for reasons other than a learning disability.

Achievement Testing

Children with learning disabilities usually exhibit a severe discrepancy between potential ability (as measured on an individual IQ test) and academic achievement. This is a debatable criterion because it is possible that an African American child functioning on grade level, according to standardized achievement tests, may actually have a severe discrepancy if one takes into account ability levels (Pierangelo & Giuliani, 2002).

Overview

Turnbull, Turnbull, Shank, Smith, and Leal (2002) reported that in diagnosing learning disabilities, it is necessary to use a nondiscriminatory approach to ensure compliance with the mandates of IDEA. An important aspect of nondiscriminatory evaluation for African American students with learning disabilities is establishing a discrepancy between ability as measured by an IQ test, and achievement, as measured by a standardized test. While many professionals understand the biases inherent in standardized tests as they relate to the African American student, it is sometimes satisfying to put a label on a disability or at least to identify a condition that can be treated. This was the case of Ennis William Cosby (the son of actor Bill Cosby) when he found out he had dyslexia—a form of learning disability: "The happiest day of my life occurred when I found out I was dyslexic. I believe that life is finding solutions, and the worst feeling in the world to me is confusion" (Turnbull et al., 2002, p. 131).

With proper assessment comes proper instruction and intervention for African American learners. One of the best ways for teachers to address the needs of African American students with learning disabilities is to adapt instruction and materials. Many textbooks include teachers' manuals to assist in the presentation of instruction. Too often, however, the lessons in the manuals are brief and potentially confusing. General and special education teachers need to modify these lessons before presenting them to the class (Hunt & Marshall, 2002). African American students with learning disabilities have different learning styles and cultural values. As a result, parents and extended family members must be involved in the educational process.

CONCLUSION

Key Points to Remember

Following are 10 key points that general and special educators should note to help African American students with learning disabilities:

1. Family support is a must.

2. Caring and good teachers are essential.

3. Nondiscriminatory assessments are crucial.

4. In-school support systems are a necessity.

5. Understanding how children learn is a major component.

6. It is important to adapt the classroom environment to meet the needs of the student.

7. Materials can be adapted to meet a student's needs.

8. Peer tutors can be used to increase opportunities for learning.

9. Patience is a must to avoid unnecessary categories.

10. Students must always be allowed to be creative in their presentation of information.

Final Comments

Students with learning disabilities face an enormous amount of problems daily. They are faced with the problem of failure in the academic arena, problems making friends, and problems being accepted by adults. For African American students, the problems go even deeper. They are evaluated with instruments that have historically left them out of the equation and are excluded from quality education. These students face the daily battle of racism from teachers with a Eurocentric frame of reference, and their referrals often come from teachers who would rather not have them in their class. In addition, they are faced with trying to fit in with students who define *Blackness* for them. In order to get along in predominantly White schools, they have to play the stereotypical Negro to be accepted, and find themselves being accused of acting White when they are in predominantly Black settings. For the African American student with a learning disability, the pressure to do well, to fit in, and to satisfy others, may lead to dropping out, suicide, continuous fighting, or constant outbursts that are totally unacceptable to teachers and administrators.

Discussion Issues

1. Briefly explain traditional problems facing African American students with learning disabilities.

2. Describe visible signs of learning disabilities.

3. Identify and explain learning characteristics of students with learning disabilities.

4. Evaluate strategies to empower African American families whose children have learning disabilities.

5. Summarize how the potential of African American students with learning disabilities can be maximized in an inclusive setting.

REFERENCES

Adelman, H. S. (1971). The not so specific learning disability population. *Exceptional Children, 37*, 528-533.

Algozzine, B. (1991). Decision-making and curriculum-based assessment. In B. Y. L. Wong (Ed.), *Learning about learning disabilities* (pp. 40-55). San Diego, CA: Academic Press.

Banks, J. A. (1997). *Teaching strategies for ethnic studies* (6th ed.). Boston: Allyn & Bacon.

Bateman, B. (1965). An educational view of a diagnostic approach to learning disorders. In J. Hellmuth (Ed.), *Learning disorders* (Vol. 1, pp. 219-239). Seattle, WA: Special Child Publications.

Baumeister, A. A., Kupstas, F., & Klindworth, L. M. (1990). New morbidity: Implications for prevention of children's disabilities. *Exceptionality, 1*(1), 1-6.

Brown v. Board of Education of Topeka, 347 U.S. 483 (1954).

College Entrance Examination Board. (1985). *Equality and excellence: The educational status of black Americans*. New York: Author.

DuBois, W. E. B. (1996). *The souls of black folk*. New York: Modern Library. (Original work published 1903)

Executive Committee of the Council for Children With Behavioral Disorders. (1989). White paper on best assessment practices for students with behavioral disorders: Accommodation to cultural and individual differences. *Behavioral Disorder, 14*, 263-278.

Gay, G. (1997). Educational equality for students of color. In J. A. Banks & C. A. McGee-Banks (Eds.), *Multicultural education: Issues and perspectives* (3rd ed., pp. 195-228). Boston: Allyn & Bacon.

Graves, T. L. (1978, September). Broken promise for many. *Black Enterprise*, p. 7.

Hallahan, D. P. (1992). Some thoughts on why the prevalence of learning disabilities has increased. *Journal of Learning Disabilities, 25*(8), 523-528.

Hallahan, D. P., & Cruickshank, W. M. (1973). *Psycho-educational foundations of learning disabilities*. Englewood Cliffs, NJ: Prentice Hall.

Hallahan, D. P., & Kauffman, J. M. (1977). Labels, categories, behaviors: ED, LD, and EMR reconsidered. *Journal of Special Education, 11*, 139-149.

Hallahan, D. P., Kauffman, J. M., & Lloyd, J. W. (1996). *Introduction to learning disabilities*. Needham Heights, MA: Allyn & Bacon.

Heller, K., Holtzman, W., & Messick, S. (1982). *Placing children in special education: A strategy for equity*. Washington, DC: National Academy Press.

Howard, J. (1985, December). Race and how it affects our every day life. *Detroit Free Press*, p. 8.

Hunt, N., & Marshall, K. (1994). *Exceptional children and youth: An introduction to special education*. Boston: Houghton Mifflin.

Hunt, N., & Marshall, K. (2002). *Exceptional children and youth: An introduction to special education* (3rd ed.). Boston: Houghton Mifflin.

Individuals With Disabilities Education Act Amendments of 1997, Pub. L. No. 101-476, 20 U.S.C. § 1400 *et seq.*

Kirk, S. A. (1962). *Educating exceptional children*. Boston: Houghton Mifflin.

Kirk, S. A. (1975). Behavioral diagnosis and remediation of learning disabilities. In S. A. Kirk & J. J. McCarthy (Eds.), *Learning disabilities: Selected papers* (pp. 7-10). Boston: Houghton Mifflin.

Kuykendal, C. (1992*). From rage to hope: Strategies for reclaiming black and Hispanic students*. Bloomington, IN: National Educational Service.

Larsen, S. C. (1978). Learning disabilities and the professional educator. *Learning Disability Quarterly, 1*, 5-12.

Lokerson, J. (1992). *Learning disabilities* (EC Digest No. E516). Arlington, VA: ERIC Clearinghouse on Disabilities and Gifted Education. (ERIC Document Reproduction Service No. 352 779).

Mann, L. (1979). *On the trail of progress*. New York: Grune & Stratton.

Mazurek, K., & Winzer, M. A. (1994). *Comparative studies in special education*. Washington, DC: Gallaudet University Press.

Nadell, J. (1995). Boyz n the hood: A colonial analysis. *Journal of Black Studies, 25*(4), 447-464.

Pierangelo, R., & Giuliani, G. A. (2002). *Assessment in special education: A practical approach*. Boston: Allyn & Bacon.

Serwatka, T. S., Deering, S., & Grant P. A. (1995). Disproportionate representation of African Americans in emotionally handicapped classes. *Journal of Black Studies, 25*(4), 492-506.

Serwatka, T. S., Deering, S., & Stoddard, A. (1989). Correlates of underrepresentation of Black students in classes for gifted students. *Negro Education Review, 58*, 520-530.

Shea, T. M., & Bauer, A. M. (1994). *Learners with disabilities: A social systems perspective of special education*. Dubuque, IA: Brown & Benchmark Communications.

Smith, C. R. (1994). *Learning disabilities: The interaction of learner, task, and setting* (3rd ed.). Boston: Allyn & Bacon.

Stanovich, K. E. (1989). Has the learning disabled field lost its intelligence? *Journal of Learning Disabilities, 22*(8), 487-492.

Turnbull, R., Turnbull, A., Shank, M., Smith, S., & Leal, D. (2002). *Exceptional lives: Special education in today's schools* (3rd ed.). Upper River Saddle, NJ: Merrill-Prentice Hall.

U.S. Department of Education. (1994). *Sixteenth annual report to Congress on the implementation of the Individuals With Disabilities Education Act*. Washington, DC: Author.

Wiedherhold, J. L. (1974). Historical perspectives on the education of the learning disabled. In L. Mann & D. Sabatino (Eds.), *The second review of special education* (pp. 103-152). Philadelphia: Journal of Special Education Press.

Winzer, M. A. (1993). *The history of special education: From isolation to integration*. Washington, DC: Gallaudet University Press.

Ysseldyke, J. E., Thurlow, M. L., Graden, J. L., Wesson, C., Algozzine, B., & Deno, S. L. (1983). Generalizations from five years of research on assessment and decision-making: University of Minnesota Institute. *Exceptional Education Quarterly, 4*(1), 75-93.

Chapter Seven

Interventions for African American Learners With Behavioral Problems

Cathy D. Kea, Gwendolyn Cartledge,
and Lisa J. Bowman

African American children and youth may be the most misunderstood of all the cultural groups within U.S. society. Dorn (1997) stated that "much of America is convinced that young people—particularly African American youth and children of color—are a menace; that these children, violent and without remorse, must be contained and feared" (p. 45). Aggression among African American youth in urban centers is readily evident (Prothrow-Stith, 1991). However, rather than signs of individual, family, or community pathology, these levels of aggression may be more accurately attributed to environmental and social conditions such as poverty, stress, and hopelessness (Mitchell & Logan, 1996; Prothrow-Stith, 1991). These effects all too often spill over into schools to undermine the successful development of African American children.

Schools are a principal institution for nurturing intellectual, social, and emotional development. However, for many African American children, schools do not hold this promise. Cartledge and Talbert-Johnson (1997) reiterated that U.S. schools are failing their students and disproportionately fail poor students who come from culturally diverse backgrounds. Accordingly, they argued that schools disenfranchise these students through practices such as educational tracking, monocultural curricula, monocultural school staff, competitive classroom environments, inhospitable school climates, and instructional methods that fail to capitalize on learners' abilities and backgrounds. Similarly, other educators have exposed unwholesome school environments for many African American students because of academic difficulties or unrecognized talents (Ford, 1998), harsh discipline policies (Townsend, 2000), and immersion year after year in culturally irrelevant and incongruent curricula (Day-Vines, 2000).

Although the school dropout rate between African Americans and Anglo Americans continues to narrow, African American youth are still more likely to drop out of school than their Anglo American peers (U.S. Department of Education, 1999). Furthermore, the dropout rate is higher among students with disabilities—namely, those with emotional disturbances (ED) and learning disabilities (LD)—than for their peers without disabilities. Research has indicated that African American males in particular are disproportionately placed in programs for students with behavioral disorders and mental retardation (Oswald, Coutinho, Best, & Singh, 1999; Toppo, 2001), receive more restricted placements (Harry & Anderson, 1995), and are plagued with lower-paying employment once they leave public school (U.S. Department of Education Department of Civil Rights, 1993).

A few years ago, Snyder (1996) observed that African American youth are overrepresented at each stage of the juvenile court process relative to their representation in the general population. According to a study funded by the U.S. Department of Education, 19% of adolescents with disabilities were arrested after being out of school 2 years (Wagner et al., 1991). Of students in special education, 37% of students with emotional disturbances and 20% of students with learning disabilities had been arrested. In addition, students with emotional disturbances were more likely to be African American and male, and males were arrested more frequently than females (U.S. Department of Education Department of Civil Rights, 1993). The purpose of this chapter is to examine more closely some of the factors that contribute to school misbehavior and to suggest proactive strategies that might ameliorate poor outcomes for African American students. To buttress our examination, we focus our discussions on teacher beliefs and expectations, discipline, and ineffective instruction.

WAYS SCHOOLS FAIL AFRICAN AMERICAN LEARNERS

Teachers' beliefs are extremely important; their beliefs influence their expectations and judgments about students' abilities, effort, and progress in school (Obiakor, 1999). Biased beliefs can color the way children's behaviors are perceived, causing some actions to be misperceived and inappropriately handled (Obiakor, 2001; Obiakor et al., 2002). Both the verbal and nonverbal communication styles of African American students, for example, are noted to baffle school personnel, especially White teachers, who have little or no understanding of their students' expressive styles (Irvine, 1990). When such misinterpretations occur, school staff may unfairly or too harshly administer punishing consequences, causing students to respond with anger and, potentially, leading to vicious conflict cycles between students and school authority figures. It becomes imperative, then, for school personnel to be more culturally competent.

Over the past decade, several authors have questioned the cultural competence of both general and special educators (e.g., Dandy, 1990; Ford, 1992; Pang & Sablan, 1998). Irvine (1990), for example, noted that White teachers had more negative attitudes and beliefs about African American children than did African American teachers. Similarly, Pang and Sablan (1998) reported that "teachers believe African American students have little potential and expect less performance from them. They also may be less willing to use a variety of instructional methods that will motivate and support students who are trying to learn" (p. 509). In Pang and Sablan's investigation of how confident a predominantly White sample of general education preservice and inservice teachers felt about their skills to teach African American students, they found that (a) racial attitudes affected teacher self-efficacy, (b) teachers had limited knowledge of African American students and their culture, and (c) preservice teachers reported more confidence about their ability to teach this population than did inservice teachers. One speculation by the researchers was that the confidence expressed by novice teachers is eroded by the socialization provided by their more negative, experienced colleagues once they enter the system. In another study that investigated preservice students' reflections on multicultural experiences, Kea and Bacon (1999) found that preservice teachers had little cultural knowledge of students outside their own cultural group. One interesting finding of this study, however, was that African American preservice teachers also reported limited cross-cultural experiences. Cultural competence is critical to the accurate interpretation of behaviors of children from culturally diverse backgrounds. Cultural misunderstandings and a lack of sensitivity on the part of teachers, administrators, ancillary personnel, and even other students can result in undesired disciplinary practices.

DISCIPLINE

Students from culturally diverse backgrounds are disciplined more often and receive far more severe consequences than White students for similar infractions (Cartledge, Tillman, & Talbert-Johnson, 2001; Townsend, 2000). Earlier, Sheets and Gay (1996) studied discipline within the context of race and ethnicity and found that males, across ethnic groups, were disciplined more frequently, publicly, and severely than females. A second finding was that African American males and females were disciplined more than other groups, followed sequentially by Latinos, Filipinos, and Caucasians. Interviews on disciplinary conflict with these culturally diverse students within an urban high school revealed that, overwhelmingly, students wanted teachers to be fair and respectful to them, listen to what they had to say about the event, build teacher-student relationships, be sensitive to their feelings, help them solve their problems, assign relevant classwork, and learn different ways to teach them.

The data on suspensions and expulsions are particularly disconcerting. African American students, especially males, are reportedly suspended or expelled two to five times more often than their majority counterparts for the same infractions (Cartledge et al., 2001). Not only do these exclusionary practices rob students of valuable learning time, but there is also no evidence that suspension results in more adaptive student behaviors. Lo and Cartledge (2001), for example, studied the office disciplinary referral data for two elementary urban schools and found that the most common disciplinary action in the school with mostly African American students was out-of-school suspensions (57%), compared to only 8.1% in the predominately White school. A closer look at the data also revealed that for students with the most office referrals (five or more), the number of out-of-school suspensions increased, and that by spring, at least three of the students were on homebound instruction. At the very least, these data fail to support that out-of-school suspensions contributed to school success or served as a deterrent for at least 30% of the school population, who also had disciplinary referrals and out-of-school suspensions.

The culture of the school often differs markedly from that in which many African American students have been socialized. According to Shade, Kelly, and Oberg (1998), institutionalized ways of behaving in a classroom developed by European Americans may contribute to cultural misunderstandings. For example, these classrooms promote the idea and expect that (a) assigned tasks need not be connected to personal interest, experience, or children's needs; (b) individual competition is prized over collective collaboration; and (c) there must be low levels of physical movement and stimulation. In contrast, many low-socioeconomic African American students come from backgrounds that are directly opposite to many of these expectations. These young-sters, for example, are encouraged to be active, spontaneous, and passionate, and to explore things according to their interests and to personal relevance (Neal, McCray, & Webb-Johnson, 2001). Apparently, teacher prejudice, racial bias, expectations, beliefs, and differential treatment influence referral decisions and the instructional process of African American students (Bondy & Ross, 1998). These perspectives act as barriers for teacher reflection about issues of culture and equality. For African American students to achieve their fullest potential, teachers must iden-tify the cognitive and learning styles of each and be sensitive to the sociocultural processes of their ethnic communities (Bos & Fletcher, 1997). This is particularly true for males, who are at risk for dropping out of school or for being labeled as having emotional and behavioral dis-orders (EBD). Many African American males do not succeed in school because their cultural, social, and linguistic characteristics are unrecognized; hence they are often misdiagnosed and miseducated (Cartledge, Kea, & Ida, 2000; Kea & Utley, 1998). Furthermore, African American students are often socialized to respect authority figures according to competence rather than simply according to title (Irvine, 1990). Therefore teachers who fail to demonstrate their author-ity are less likely to command respect and compliance from these students than are teachers who are skilled at managing the classroom academic and social environment.

INEFFECTIVE INSTRUCTION

Effective instruction is the first line of defense for behavior problems (Kauffman, 2001). Structured, direct environments are important for all students and are especially critical for students who often come to school unprepared (e.g., African American students) for the ambigu-ous rules and communication styles typical of middle-class schools (Delpit, 1988, 1995). Teachers who fail to structure their classroom and academic day not only run the risk of losing valuable instructional time but also invariably encounter increases in disruptive pupil behavior. It appears that poor and culturally diverse children present the greatest educational need; how-ever, they are least likely to be recipients of effective instruction (Haycock, 2001). Inadequate services for children in poor, urban settings are evident after examining students' performance in basic skills and the high rate of school failure experienced by them (Hart & Risley, 1995). For a large percentage of these students, failing experiences start in the early elementary grades (Greenwood, Delquadri, & Bulgren, 1993). Urban, poor children not only start out behind, coming to school with fewer skills than their middle-class peers, but also the quality and quantity of instruc-tion that they receive is most often inferior to instruction at schools in the suburbs (Greenwood, Delquadri, & Hall, 1989; Hart & Risley, 1995, 1999).

Several scholars and educators (e.g., Delpit, 1995; Hirsch, 1999; Irvine, 1990; Kozol, 1991) offer explanations for the poor academic performance of urban poor students, including African American learners. For instance, Irvine observed that new and inexperienced teachers often teach these children. Kozol provided extensive documentation of the poor and substandard conditions within which many of these students are schooled. Hirsch, who believed naturalistic or progressive models (e.g., whole language) are almost exclusively responsible for these poor outcomes, gives additional rationales. Similarly, Delpit (1995) contends that progressive models are too foreign for many African American students who have been raised with different cultural influences in the home. In a review of the relevant literature, Arreaga-Mayer and Greenwood (1986) observed that when given structured learning conditions, culturally diverse children learned in the same manner as children in the majority culture with respect to response fluency, slope of learning curves, learning trials, use of discriminative stimuli, and reinforcement procedures. They added, however, that compared to their suburban counterparts, inner city, culturally diverse students were given significantly fewer opportunities to respond. In order to receive comparable opportunities, these students would have to remain in school for the entire summer. Interestingly, a reciprocal relationship appears to exist between academic instruction and social behavior: Good instruction minimizes behavior problems (Armendariz & Umbreit, 1999), and socially appropriate students experience higher academic achievement (Cartledge & Milburn, 1995). Thus it may be safe to assume that poor instructional environments contribute to disruptive behaviors.

EFFECTIVE INTERVENTIONS

Conceptual Framework

With regard to the efficacy of instruction, the issue of culturally relevant pedagogy comes into play in the works of Ladson-Billings (1994, 2000, 2001). Her research with experienced and novice teachers who were successful with African American students presents an important theoretical frame of reference on this issue. This theory of culturally relevant pedagogy is based on three propositions about what contributes to success for all students, especially African American learners. These propositions are that successful teachers focus on students' academic achievement, develop students' cultural competence, and foster students' sense of sociopolitical consciousness. A logical extension is that teachers play a role in creating culturally responsive school environments where African American children feel safe and where learning takes place. These schools have strong principals, small student-teacher ratios, fair discipline policies that are clearly stated and consistently implemented, teachers with high expectations for every student, and an ongoing effort to consistently include parents in the educational process. The goal of such schools is to affirm and remotivate students who have been demoralized by failure. Schools can help prevent behavior problems by ensuring that culturally responsive instruction, curricula, and instructional materials are implemented along with teaching students how to manage conflict and anger. Logically, in culturally responsive schools, behavioral management techniques respond to students' cultural backgrounds.

Behavior Management

A major factor in improving the schooling and overall success of African American students is to empower school personnel to be proactive rather than reactive. This means that school personnel must become skilled in behavior management strategies that enable them to create school environments that motivate students to act according to school and classroom rules, as well as foster positive interpersonal interactions with peers and authority figures. A promising model that has emerged in recent years is positive behavior supports (e.g., Lewis & Sugai, 1999). In contrast to the zero tolerance policies that emphasize punishing instead of positive consequences, positive behavior supports is a model designed to stress positive incentives to motivate students to behave. Within this model, schools are encouraged to create schoolwide interventions, classwide interventions, individual interventions, social-skills instruction, effective instruction, and home-school relationships. In culturally responsive schools, school personnel first take time to assess the school culture and conditions to determine the incentives that motivate student behavior and areas where intensive interventions are needed. Being proactive means that administrators and teachers devise strategies to reward appropriate behaviors before problems occur rather than try to put in place corrective measures following misbehavior. For example, students might randomly receive hand stamps and praise for following school and class rules rather than waiting for students to act out to get punished for not following them.

Culturally responsive school personnel need to study closely their particular population and to design interventions accordingly. To illustrate, in the predominantly African American school Lo and Cartledge (2001) studied, they observed that the most common infraction that resulted in expulsion involved some form of aggression such as fighting or assaulting peers. Social-skills instruction that centered on alternatives to aggression would be culturally responsive and sensitive for this group. Poor students, particularly African American students in urban environments, are sometimes reared under conditions where aggressive behavior is socialized. General and special educators can teach these students to learn to make an assertive comment, walk away, change the subject, use humor, or report some provocation to an authority figure, when the preceding alternatives do not work. If this type of instruction is intensified schoolwide, if students receive powerful reinforcers for displaying the desired social behaviors and are reinforced socially by all school personnel and peers, there is no doubt that their most disturbing behaviors could be greatly curbed. Current practices of suspending students are ineffective since, in some cases, they find suspensions rewarding and, in other cases, they produce more anger, thereby increasing the likelihood that the student will engage in more maladaptive behavior. To motivate students to be more adaptive in their behavior, they need to be taught using culturally responsive strategies (e.g., Cartledge & Milburn, 1996).

Teachers are important to the success of all students. African American children often view teachers as significant others in their lives (e.g., mentors and role models). Through their actions, subtle or overt, teachers send messages to children about whether they are accepted and competent and can accomplish tasks given, and about whether they are true members of the learning community. Shade, Kelly, and Oberg (1998) asserted that teachers must set the stage and climate for learning that facilitates cognitive engagement. As they pointed out, teachers send verbal and nonverbal messages to students indicating their capabilities for success, establish intellectually stimulating classroom climates by setting time limits, select appropriate tasks, and deliver presentation styles that meet the information processing and learning preferences of all students. They further asserted that teachers can establish a culturally responsive learning community if they practice and implement the following seven principles:

1. Teachers are personally inviting.

2. Classroom is physically inviting.

3. Students are reinforced for academic development.

4. Changes made to accommodate culture are essential to learning.

5. Classroom is managed with firm, consistent, loving control.

6. Interactions stress cooperation rather than individuality.

7. Children are affirmed in their cultural connections. (p. 57)

A culturally responsive learning community can be sustained through the acknowledgment, acceptance, and infusion of African American history and culture in the curriculum emphasizing a strengths-based approach. King (1994) noted that culturally relevant and inviting classrooms can enhance the teaching and learning process for African American learners if they (a) recognize and affirm students' collective identification with persons of African heritage; (b) heighten a sense of mutual responsibility among students for their own and their peers' learning, and use it to benefit their community, society, and humanity; (c) include a meaningful curriculum in all areas from the African American cultural ethos (e.g., proverbial wisdom, metaphoric language, African orality, public performance, artistic expression); (d) retain the cultural values and style of the African American community; (e) use the strengths of African American cultural patterns in the teaching-learning process; and (f) focus critical thinking and inquiry around the strengths, weaknesses, and challenges faced by the African American community. Similarly, in a literature review on juvenile delinquency among African American males, Bowman (2000) found that some African American youths' negative attitudes toward, and experiences in, school were tied to the lack of a culturally relevant curriculum. It follows that the culture of African American students, as well as the culture of other students, must be embraced and infused throughout the curriculum and classroom to help create a disruption-free environment.

Effective Instruction

One of the most significant things that teachers can do to make a difference in the educational progress of African American learners with instructional and behavioral challenges is to make a firm personal commitment to use effective instructional procedures. Students with behavior problems typically have significant learning problems (Kauffman, 1997). Regardless of where students are taught (i.e., general or special education support classroom), teachers must ensure that students are taught in accordance with what is known about effective instructional principles. Most curricula for EBD students focus on controlling behavior rather than the total picture (e.g., student needs, a meaningful and challenging curriculum, and academic achievement) (Johns, 1998). Preservice and inservice programs often focus on behavior management rather than on effective teaching methods or meaningful curriculum. In fact, behavior management is usually the primary concern, and meaningful instruction is secondary. Meaningful instruction is a critical component of successful programs for students with EBD. Students with behavioral problems typically have significant learning problems (e.g., difficulties with short and long-term memory skills, selective attention skills, metagcognitive skills, storing and accessing verbal information, and organizational skills). Appropriate instruction and appropriate student behaviors are intertwined. Unchallenging or boring instruction and a poorly defined and culturally irrelevant curriculum contribute to misbehaviors of African American learners. Poor instruction may be an antecedent for inappropriate behavior and, at the very least, may be a factor in causing behavior problems to worsen. Addressing instructional variables can reduce inappropriate behaviors (Lloyd, Forness, & Kavale, 1998). Unfortunately, classes and programs for EBD students are not typically characterized by high-quality instruction. Teacher-directed presentations or carefully planned curricular sequences are the exception, not the rule (Walker et al., 1998). It is still unclear why so many teachers of EBD students fail to implement rigorous programs of academic instruction (Scheuermann, 1998).

Based on their review, Lloyd et al. (1998) offered that curricula and instruction for EBD students must be inclusive of learning strategies, social skills, transition skills, technology, and direct-instruction principles. Culturally responsive instruction must be added for African American learners. Teachers can make a difference if they spend most of their time teaching the subject content matter, using empirically validated interventions, and are able to demonstrate that African American students are learning. They must know how to teach and what to teach, as shown in Figure 7.1. Kea (1998) provided a comprehensive summary of teaching behaviors that can promote learning for African American students. Effective teachers of culturally diverse students acknowledge both individual and cultural differences enthusiastically and build relationships with the learner. They also focus on ways students learn—they identify their task orientations to develop a variety of instructional strategies. More important, structure is provided during the teaching and learning process. Teachers who manage behaviors engage in critical teaching behaviors that include (a) using advance and post organizers, (b) giving rationales, (c) communicating expectations, (d) reviewing and checking for understanding, (e) facilitating independence, (f) intensifying instruction, (g) monitoring instruction, (h) providing feedback, and (i) requiring mastery of learning (Kea, 1987, 1995).

Lesson presentations involve structure, clarity, redundancy, enthusiasm, appropriate rate, maximum engagement through questioning, positive specific feedback, and use of cultural affirmations for success. Although it may be questioned whether African American children require special instructional approaches (Ferguson, 1998), other authorities argue persuasively that many African American children profit from more explicit, direct instructional and disciplinary practices (Delpit, 1995; Hirsch, 1999).

African American children learn when the teachers makes themselves the clear authority figure in the classroom; make clear, unambiguous requests; and present the material in a precise way so that the students know exactly what they are learning (Cartledge & Milburn, 1996; Delpit, 1995). Direct instruction, as opposed to indirect-process approaches, are most beneficial for increasing academic and socially appropriate behaviors. A critical component of direct instruction is giving students the opportunity to respond to the academic material. Techniques such as classwide peer tutoring, response cards, guided notes, and choral responding repeatedly have been shown to have a robust, positive effect on student learning in the classroom (Greenwood, Arreaga-Mayer, Utley, Gavin, & Terry, 2001; Heward, 2000).

African American students want to be active participants in class. Like most students, they learn best when they provide an active response to instructional material rather than passively attending. Ironically, less active instructional time is observed in schools today, and students from urban environments receive even fewer opportunities to respond actively to instruction than their suburban peers (Arreaga-Mayer & Greenwood, 1986). A study by Armendariz and Umbreit (1999) showed that students had fewer intervals of disruptive behavior when they were taught under conditions of active student responding. Specifically, during active student responding, all students simultaneously answered the teacher's questions by writing the answers on response cards. This is in contrast to traditional methods where the teacher solicits a response from one student while the others sit passively, often off-task or being disruptive. Lambert (2001) obtained similar findings in his study of active student responding within a math class with fourth-grade urban students. These studies provide solid evidence that African American students need to be taught under conditions where they respond at high rates and with accuracy to academic materials. High response rates will not only lead to improved academic performance but also will help to counter disruptive behavior.

Figure 7.1   Effective Instruction for EBD Students Incorporates Student, Parent, and Community Involvement

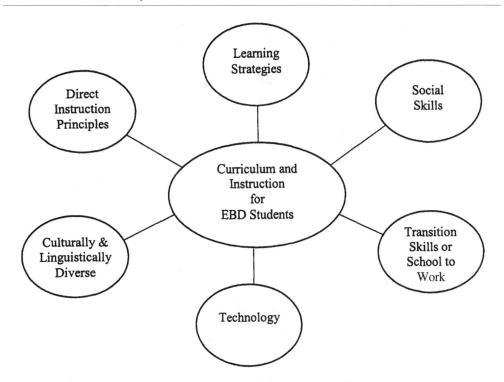

Peer Tutoring

Additional interventions have been found successful for African American learners. Classwide Peer Tutoring (CWPT) is an effective instructional intervention that is used to teach a variety of content areas (e.g., spelling, math, and reading) to a wide range of students in a variety of settings (Arreaga-Mayer, 1998; Greenwood, Delquadri, & Carta, 1997). In CWPT, teachers randomly divide students into two groups, and students are assigned to tutoring dyads or triads within both groups. Members of each group take turns in the role of tutor and tutee. High levels of student mastery have been consistently reported because of the systematic nature of CWPT that allows students increased opportunities to respond. Furthermore, its game-like format makes CWPT motivating and interesting to students. Individual and classwide progress are monitored daily and are evaluated on a weekly basis.

The implementation of effective instructional practices is essential to the educational progress of African American learners with academic and behavioral difficulties. Generalization, mnemonic strategies, and social-skills instruction are among those that research indicates help students to make academic gains. Integrated strategies such as mediated scaffolding and judicious review, as well as CWPT, are also proven strategies.

CULTURAL PRINCIPLES

A strong attachment to the African American community, the development of caring relationships, and the respect of extended family members and their role in the educational process is a must to bring about a sense of connectedness for the well-being of the African American learner. It is important that teachers encourage African American students to bring their community experiences into the classroom, and that they listen to their voices as students relate their sociopolitical consciousness to mainstream society. As teachers link classroom content to these students' experiences, they will infuse the hidden curriculum (e.g., inequalities in society) and foster self-determination that will help students cope with society and both institutional and educational racism (Foster, 1995, 1997). To this end, teachers will be able to focus on the development of the whole child and nurture students and explicitly teach and model personal values, persistence, and responsibility to self and others. This will serve as a foundation for current and future learning. It is critical that teachers do the following:

1. Create a family-type learning community

2. Use cultural rituals and routines to reinforce a sense of collectivity

3. Promote familiar participation patterns (e.g., call and response, analogies, and rhythm)

4. Organize learning as a social event rather than a competitive or individual endeavor

5. Implore the use of expressive language and code switching to teach situational adjustable behavior

6. Increase motivation, engagement, and collaborative support of peers

7. Create a sense and system of familial responsibilities in the classroom that approximate home communities

8. Use cooperative learning and peer and cross-age tutoring strategies as means to encourage and reinforce skill development and positive, communal peer interactions

9. Create socially just and caring learning communities in the classroom, in which both students' and teachers' voices, experiences, and perspectives are recognized and respected

10. Know how different cultural groups sanction behavior, celebrate accomplishments, and use rules of decorum and deference

11. Analyze the curriculum for cultural and linguistic family and student relevance

Positive support interventions can be fostered for African American learners with behavior problems when general and special educators:

1. Identify and affirm students' individual and cultural strengths

2. Respect, relate, and like their students and communicate acceptance of students even when it's necessary to reject specific behaviors

3. Listen and communicate openly

4. Understand and honor their family, culture, language, and race

5. Develop knowledge and skills from cross-cultural, interpersonal interactions

6. Build relationships with all students

7. Employ culturally responsive discipline (culturally contextualized competence, caring, connectedness, and community)

8. Know the value orientation, standards for achievements, social taboos, relational patterns, communication styles, motivational systems, and learning styles of different African American learners

9. Learn the communication styles of African American youth, and differentiate between animated, cultural conversation and verbal aggression.

10. Teach positive and validated behaviors in the classroom

In addition, general and special educators can empower African American parents when they:

1. Create a welcoming environment for parents and students

2. Provide information and resources to parents on an ongoing basis

3. Locate support groups for parents and students

4. Use natural networks (e.g., churches, sororities, fraternities, community social groups) that can provide parent training and leadership skills for the student

5. Identify family management techniques for discipline and problem solving

6. Adapt interventions to the learning and lifestyle of the family

7. Include extended family members in the development of interventions if they are highly involved with the student or are primary caregivers

8. Make sure at least two family members understand the interventions to be carried out

9. Create a home and school contract or behavior-management plan collaboratively with family members, and stress the need for adult consistency in the use of the plans developed

10. Incorporate cultural values in the behavior intervention plan

African American learners with behavioral problems will achieve both academically and socially if their teachers use a strengths-based approach and infuse cultural relevancy throughout the classroom, curriculum, and instructional process. Educational practitioners should have pride in their profession and students, be strict but positive disciplinarians, encourage African American students to succeed, use effective, empirically validated instructional strategies, and be willing to challenge the status quo for social justice measures.

CONCLUSION

Key Points to Remember

Below are 10 key points to remember:

1. Teacher beliefs and expectations influence their interactions with their students.

2. Cultural competence is critical to the accurate interpretation of behaviors for children from culturally diverse backgrounds.

3. Effective instruction is the best defense for behavior problems.

4. Culturally responsive instruction and curricula can help prevent behavior problems.

5. School personnel must become skilled in behavior management strategies that enable them to create school environments that motivate students to act according to school rules, and foster positive interactions with peers and authority figures.

6. Being proactive means that administrators and teachers devise strategies to reward appropriate behaviors before problems occur.

7. Culturally responsive school personnel need to study their population and design interventions accordingly.

8. One of the most significant things that teachers can do to make a difference in students' educational progress is to use effective instructional practices.

9. Appropriate instruction and appropriate student behaviors are intertwined.

10. Students learn best when they are actively engaged in their learning.

Final Comments

African American learners often encounter and present special challenges that most of our schools fail to overcome. Impoverished and ill prepared, many of these young people enter schools demanding more, not the less-than-adequate education they often receive. The culture of the school is likely to be foreign to them, expecting behaviors and understandings that are at odds with their previous socialization. These conditions, combined with misguided instructional practices, make up a formula for school failure, particularly for African American youth with, or at risk for, behavior problems.

Educators and other policymakers need to become aware of the ways in which we are failing these students in our schools: Policies of containment and punishment are not only ineffective but counterproductive, and curriculum and instructional practices tend not to reflect the students' specific learning needs. The behavior change research literature clearly shows that positive interventions are highly effective in bringing about more adaptive school behavior. Such procedures can motivate children to want to comply with school rules and classroom expectations, yet these strategies are applied too sparsely or ineffectively, if at all.

Good instruction is one of the best means for addressing behavior as well as learning problems. Current curriculum and instructional practices often fail to take into consideration the learning and skill deficits these youngsters bring to school. Many language-based programs are predicated on unrealistic assumptions about the child's language and concept development. Instead of employing process approaches, designed to build upon skills not yet in the repertoire of many African American children with special needs, educators would be well advised to use more direct approaches to teach for these deficits and help children to build the foundation of skills needed for higher-level learning. Empirical support exists for this position.

Educators also need to become cognizant of the cultural discontinuities that may occur between the culture of the school and the background of some African American students. Not all behavior differences are indicative of behavior disorders. School personnel need to view many nonfunctional student behaviors as opportunities for instruction, not just punishment. Knowledge about the child's culture can be instructive for ways to structure the classroom and learning activities to make school a more inviting and productive environment for African American students with and without learning and behavior problems.

Discussion Issues

1. Analyze how a student's behavior can have cultural implications.

2. Briefly explain why teacher preparation is an asset in behavior management.

3. Describe how what the teacher does in class affects students' behavior.

4. Evaluate how teacher expectations affect academic and social behaviors of African American learners.

5. Identify the basic components of an effective instructional program to address academic and behavioral needs of African American learners.

REFERENCES

Armendariz, F., & Umbreit, J. (1999). Using active responding to reduce disruptive behavior in a general education classroom. *Journal of Positive Behavior Interventions, 1*(3), 152-158.

Arreaga-Mayer, C. (1998). Increasing active student responding and improving academic performance through classwide peer tutoring. *Intervention in School and Clinic, 34*(2), 89-94, 117.

Arreaga-Mayer, C., & Greenwood, C. R. (1986). Environmental variables affecting the school achievement of culturally and linguistically different learners: An instructional perspective. *NABE: The Journal for the National Association for Bilingual Education, 10*(2), 113-135.

Bondy, E., & Ross, D. D. (1998). Confronting myths about teaching African American children: A challenge for teacher educators. *Teacher Education and Special Education, 21*(4), 241-254.

Bos, C. S., & Fletcher, T. V. (1997). Sociocultural considerations in learning disabilities inclusion research: Knowledge gaps and future directions. *Learning Disabilities Research & Practice, 12,* 92-99.

Bowman, L. (2000). Juvenile delinquency among African American males: Implications for special education. *Multiple Voices, 4*(1), 62-72.

Cartledge, G., Kea, C. D., & Ida, D. J. (2000). Anticipating differences—celebrating strengths: Providing culturally competent services for students with serious emotional disturbance. *Teaching Exceptional Children, 32*(3), 30-37.

Cartledge, G., & Milburn, J. F. (1995). *Teaching social skills to children and youth: Innovative approaches.* Boston: Allyn & Bacon.

Cartledge, G., & Milburn, J. F. (1996). *Cultural diversity and social skills instruction: Understanding ethnic and gender differences.* Champaign, IL: Research Press.

Cartledge, G., & Talbert-Johnson, C. (1997). School violence and cultural sensitivity. In A. P. Goldstein & J. C. Conoley (Eds.), *School violence intervention handbook* (pp. 391-425). New York: Guildford.

Cartledge, G., Tillman, L. C., & Talbert-Johnson, C. (2001). Professional ethics within the context of student discipline and diversity. *Teacher Education and Special Education, 24*(1), 25-37.

Dandy, E. B. (1990). *Sensitizing teachers to cultural differences: An African American perspective.* Paper presented at the National Dropout Prevention Conference, Nashville, TN. (ERIC Document Reproduction Service No. ED 323 479)

Day-Vines, N. L. (2000). Ethics, power, and privilege: Salient issues in the development of multicultural competencies for teachers serving African American children with disabilities. *Teacher Education and Special Education, 23*(1), 3-18.

Delpit, L. (1988). The silenced dialogue: Power and pedagogy in educating other people's children. *Harvard Educational Review, 58*(3), 280-298.

Delpit, L. (1995). *Other people's children*. New York: New Press.

Dorn, B. (1997). Youth violence: False fears and hard truths. *Educational Leadership, 55*(2), 45-47.

Ferguson, R. (1998). Teachers' perceptions and expectations and the Black-White test score gap. In Christopher Jencks and Meredith Phillips (Eds.), *The Black-White test score gap*. Washington, DC: Brookings Institute.

Ford, B. A. (1992). Multicultural education training for special educators working with African American youth. *Exceptional Children, 59*(2), 107-114.

Ford, Y. D. (1998). The underrepresentation of minority students in gifted education: Problems and promises in recruitment and retention. *The Journal of Special Education, 32*(1), 4-14.

Foster, M. (1995). African American teachers and culturally relevant pedagogy. In J. A. Banks & C. A. McGee (Eds.), *Handbook of research on multicultural education* (pp. 570-581). New York: Macmillan.

Foster, M. (1997). *African American teachers on teaching*. New York: New Press.

Greenwood, C., Arreaga-Mayer, C., Utley, C., Gavin, K., & Terry, B. (2001). Classwide peer tutoring learning management system: Applications with elementary-level English language learners. *Remedial and Special Education, 22*(1), 34-47.

Greenwood, C. R., Delquadri, J., & Bulgren, J. (1993). Current challenges to behavioral technology in the reform of schooling: Large-scale, high-quality implementation and sustained use of effective educational practices. *Education and Treatment of Children, 16*(4), 401-440.

Greenwood, C., Delquadri, J., & Carta, J. (1997). *Together we can! Classwide peer tutoring to improve basic academic skills*. Longmont, CO: Sopris West.

Greenwood, C. R., Delquadri, J. C., & Hall, R. V. (1989). Longitudinal effects of classwide peer tutoring. *Journal of Educational Psychology, 81*(3), 371-383.

Harry, B., & Anderson, M. G. (1995). The disproportionate placement of African American males in special education programs: A critique of the process. *Journal of Negro Education, 63*(4), 602-619.

Hart, B., & Risley, T. R. (1995). *Meaningful differences in the everyday experience of young American children*. Baltimore: Brookes.

Hart, B., & Risley, T. R. (1999). *The social world of children learning to talk*. Baltimore: Brookes.

Haycock, K. (2001). Closing the achievement gap. *Educational Leadership, 58*(6), 6-11.

Heward, W. L. (2000). *Exceptional children: An introduction to special education* (6th ed.). Upper Saddle River, NJ: Prentice-Hall.

Hirsch, E. D. (1999). *The schools we need and why we don't have them*. New York: Anchor.

Irvine, J. J. (1990). *African American students and school failure: Policies, practices, and prescriptions*. Westport, CT: Greenwood.

Johns, B. (1998). Reaching them through teaching them: Curriculum and instruction for students with E/BD. *Beyond Behavior, 10*(1), 3-6.

Kauffman, J. M. (1997). *Characteristics of emotional and behavioral disorders of children and youth* (6th ed.). Columbus, OH: Merrill.

Kauffman, J. M. (2001). *Characteristics of emotional and behavioral disorders of children and youth* (7th ed.). Upper Saddle River, NJ: Merrill.

Kea, C. D. (1987). *An analysis of critical teaching behaviors employed by teachers of students with mild handicaps*. Unpublished doctoral dissertation, University of Kansas, Lawrence.

Kea, C. D. (1995, July). Critical teaching behaviors. *Strategram, 7*(6), 1-8. Lawrence, KS: Center for Research on Learning.

Kea, C. D. (1998). Focus on ethnic and minority concerns: Critical teaching behaviors and instructional strategies for working with culturally diverse students. *Council for Children With Behavioral Disorders Newsletter, 11*(4), 4-6.

Kea, C. D., & Bacon, E. H. (1999, Summer). Journal reflections of preservice education students on multicultural experiences. *Action in Teacher Education, 21*(3), 34-50.

Kea, C. D., & Utley, C. A. (1998). To teach me is to know me. *Journal of Special Education, 32*(1), 44-47.

King, J. (1994). The purpose of schooling for African American children: Including cultural knowledge. In E. R. Hollins, J. E. King, & W. C. Hayman (Eds.), *Teaching diverse populations: Formulating a knowledge base* (pp. 25-56). Albany: State University of New York Press.

Kozol, J. (1991). *Savage inequalities*. New York: Crown.

Ladson-Billings, G. (1994). *Dreamkeepers: Successful teachers of African American children*. San Francisco: Jossey-Bass.

Ladson-Billings, G. (2000, May/June). Fighting for our lives. *Journal of Teacher Education, 51*(3), 206-214.

Ladson-Billings, G. (2001). *Crossing over to Canaan*. San Francisco: Jossey-Bass.

Lambert, M. C. (2001). *The effects of increasing active student responding in the classroom with response cards on disruptive behavior and academic performance for urban learners*. Unpublished doctoral dissertation, Ohio State University, Columbus.

Lewis, T. J., & Sugai, G. (1999). Effective behavior support: A systems approach to proactive school-wide management. *Focus on Exceptional Children, 31*, 1-24.

Lloyd, J. W., Forness, S. R., & Kavale, K. A. (1998). Some methods are more effective than others. *Intervention in School and Clinic, 33*, 195-200.

Lo, Y.Y., & Cartledge, G. (2001). They are more than just reports: Using office discipline referrals to increase school disciplinary effectiveness. *Principal Magazine, 20*(2), 1-3.

Mitchell, S. G., & Logan, S. L. (1996). Reconceptualizing youth violence: Implications for positive change. In S. L. Logan (Ed.), *The African American family: Strengths, self-help, and positive change* (pp. 83-107). Boulder, CO: Westview.

Neal, L. I., McCray, A. D., & Webb-Johnson, G. (2001). Teacher's reactions to African American students' movement styles. *Intervention in School and Clinic, 36*(3), 168-174.

Obiakor, F. E. (1999). Teacher expectations of minority exceptional learners: Impact on "accuracy" of self-concepts. *Exceptional Children, 66*, 39-53.

Obiakor, F. E. (2001). *It even happens in "good" schools: Responding to cultural diversity in today's classrooms*. Thousand Oaks, CA: Corwin.

Obiakor, F. E., Algozzine, B., Thurlow, M., Gwalla-Ogisi, N., Enwefa, S., Enwefa, R., & McIntosh, A. (2002). *Addressing the issue of disproportionate representation: Identification and assessment of culturally diverse students with emotional or behavioral disorders*. Arlington, VA: Council on Children With Behavioral Disorders, Council for Exceptional Children.

Oswald, D. P., Coutinho, M. J., Best, A. M., & Singh, N. N. (1999). Ethnic representation in special education: The influence of school-related economic and demographic variables. *Journal of Special Education, 32*, 194-206.

Pang, V. O., & Sablan, V. A. (1998). Teacher efficacy: How do teachers feel about their abilities to teach African American students? In M. E. Dilworth (Ed.), *In being responsive to cultural differences: How teachers learn* (pp. 39-58). Thousand Oaks, CA: Corwin.

Prothrow-Stith, D. (1991). *Deadly consequences*. New York: Harper Collins.

Scheuermann, B. (1998). Curricular and instructional recommendations for students with emotional/behavioral disorders. *Beyond Behavior, 9*(3), 3-4.

Shade, B. J., Kelly, C., & Oberg, M. (1998). *Creating culturally responsive classrooms*. Washington, DC: American Psychological Association.

Sheets, R. H., & Gay, G. (1996). Students' perceptions of disciplinary conflict in ethnically diverse classrooms. *NASSP Bulletin, 80*(580), 84-94.

Snyder, H. (1996). The juvenile court and delinquency cases. *Future of Children, 6*(3), 53-63.

Toppo, G. (2001, March 3). African Americans tracked into special education at higher rates. *News & Record*, pp. A1 & A5.

Townsend, B. L. (2000). The disproportionate discipline of African American learners: Reducing school suspensions and expulsions. *Exceptional Children, 66*(33), 381-391.

U.S. Department of Education. (1999). *Dropout rates in the United States: 1997*. Washington, DC: National Center for Education Statistics.

U.S. Department of Education Department of Civil Rights. (1993). *1990 elementary and secondary school civil rights survey: National summaries*. Washington, DC: DBS Corp.

Wagner, M., Newman, L., D'Amico, R., Jay, E., Butler-Nalin, P., Marder, C., & Cox, R. (1991). *Youth with disabilities: How are they doing? The first comprehensive report from the National longitudinal transition study of special education students*. (ERIC Document Reproduction Service No. ED 341 228).

Walker, H. M, Forness, S. R., Kauffman, J. M., Epstein, M. H., Gresham, F. M., Nelson, C. M., & Strain, P. S. (1998). Macro-social validation: Referencing outcomes in behavioral disorders to societal issues and problems. *Behavioral Disorders, 24*(1), 7-18.

Chapter Eight

Maximizing the Learning Potential of African American Learners With Gifts and Talents

Vera I. Daniels

Although children with gifts and talents exist in all racial, ethnic, cultural, and socio-economic groups, the availability of assessment tools that effectively evaluate their cognitive potentials is still lacking. In the United States, children from culturally different and economically disadvantaged backgrounds constitute a large percentage of the school-age population. Yet these youngsters make up only an inconsequential percentage of the population of children in gifted education programs. National figures published by the U.S. Department of Education Department of Civil Rights (Richert, 1985) indicate that minority groups—for example, African Americans, Hispanics, and Native Americans—are underrepresented in gifted education programs by 30% to 70%. A number of theories have been advanced to explain the reason for the disproportionately low representation of minority students in gifted education programs. These theories have emphasized the role of heredity (e.g., genetic makeup) and the environment (e.g., family, culture, school) in determining intelligence or intellectual ability. Although evidence suggests that both play an important role in the development of giftedness, it is generally believed the environment has the greatest influence on its development.

For most children from culturally different and low-income backgrounds, equal educational opportunity and justice for all is not yet a reality. For decades, educators have addressed equity issues in the use of traditional assessment measures that prejudice educational outcomes of minority children. In spite of their limited usefulness and the realization that "the traits that are valued and measured, as well as the choice of vocabulary and content in some of the test items, tend to exclude abilities and experiences of many African American children" (Byrd, 1995, p. 129), these measures are still being widely used today to identify African Americans and other minority children for gifted education programs. The overreliance on such tests to assess the developing abilities of minority and low-income, disadvantaged children has contributed substantively to the disproportion of minority student representation in gifted education programs (Shaklee, 1992). What is ironic is that even with the use of nontraditional assessments, multicultural students, especially African Americans, still remain disproportionately underrepresented in programs for the gifted. Moreover, despite the extraordinary efforts of researchers such as Frasier (1979), Hilliard (1976), and Torrance (1969) to address the unique needs of young, gifted African American learners, the causes of the differential representation of African American students in gifted education programs still are not fully understood. However, what is obvious in a racially biased society such as ours is that programs for gifted students tend to serve two primary purposes— as a haven for upper- and middle-class White students and as a more subtle form of continual and perpetual racial and ethnic discrimination (Gallagher, 1995). Thus our inability to effectively identify giftedness among African American students and other racially and culturally diverse students may be attributed to a number of factors. For example, our concept and definition of giftedness; the procedures and assessment measures used for identification and program placement; and teachers' lack of knowledge and skills in the ability to recognize giftedness, the indicators of giftedness, or the potential for giftedness within multicultural populations. Other plausible explanations include test bias, misuse of standardized tests, racial biases among teachers and administrators (Bracey, 1992), lack of multiple criteria, lack of multiple data sources, selective referrals (Frasier, Garcia, & Passow, 1995), limited role models, and conflicts between teaching and learning styles.

The question that arises is, how, then, can we become more effective in our identification procedures? Clark (1997) suggested that we can be more effective in our identification of culturally diverse learners if we "seek the basic intellectual abilities that are common to all gifted students, regardless of their cultural background and the manner in which they express their abilities" (p. 296). Characteristics evidenced as common to gifted learners include

- A strong desire to learn
- An intense, sometimes unusual interest
- Unusual ability to communicate with words, numbers, or symbols
- Use of effective, often inventive strategies for recognizing and solving problems
- Exceptional ability to retain and retrieve information, resulting in a large storehouse of information
- Extensive and unusual questions, experiments, and explorations
- Quick grasp of new concepts, connections; sense of deeper meanings
- Logical approaches to figuring out solutions
- Ability to produce many highly original ideas
- Keen, often unusual sense of humor (Frasier & Passow, cited in Clark, 1997, p. 296)

These characteristics tend to be downplayed by general and special educators who are tied to the apron strings of tradition. In this chapter, I address ways to maximize the learning potential of

African American students with gifts and talents. In addition, I present conceptual frameworks and pedagogical implications for helping these students in educational achievement.

CONCEPTUAL FRAMEWORK: AFRICAN AMERICANS WITH GIFTS AND TALENTS

The unmasking of giftedness or hidden potential among African American students is a persistent concern in the field of gifted education. Even though most states formally subscribe to the federal definition of giftedness, in practice, many local school districts tend to seek White, middle-class, academic achievers (Richert, 1985). A number of theories have been postulated to account for the relatively small percentage of giftedness among African Americans. These theories, as noted in the writings of Patton and Baytops (1995), range from the inability of minority students to demonstrate behaviors associated with giftedness, to the lack of their ability to demonstrate capacity, abilities, or aptitudes characteristic of persons with gifts and talents. Efforts to maximize the learning potential of African American youngsters with gifts and talents require that teachers infuse cultural constructs of African American culture in the instructional paradigm. It also requires that instruction be undergirded by learning and cognitive styles that match the cognitive and learning styles of African American learners. Programmatic efforts that fall short of this undertaking seem to be less effective in empowering African American gifted learners to develop and transform their potential.

Culturally focused research on the cognitive and learning styles of African American students reveals that they often have cognitive orientations and preferences that are markedly different from European American children (Patton & Townsend, 1997). Most African American children are field-dependent and field-sensitive (Franklin, 1992; Shade, 1997), holistic, relational, and visual learners (Ford, 1996). As a group, they tend to "relate best to teachers who are flexible, supportive, accepting, creative, tolerant of individual differences, and determined to ensure that learning occurs" (Banks, 1977, p. 24). In addition, they are characterized as having a preference for group, rather than individual, learning experiences; cooperative, rather than competitive, learning situations (Byrd, 1995; Ford & Webb, 1994; Grossman, 1990; Hale-Benson, 1986); and instructional settings with subdued rather than bright light (Byrd, 1995). Most important, these learners are described as being able to (a) learn better when information is presented in a visual manner; (b) rely more heavily on external clues and information when formulating opinions, viewpoints, perspectives, and the like (Grossman, 1990); (c) seek feedback, guidance, and approval from others; and (d) prefer tactile and kinesthetic learning and teaching experiences (Ford, 1996). Also, it has been noted that African American students are more people oriented. They are often depicted as being more sociable, more sensitive to the feelings of others, and of being more sensitive to praise and criticism (Grossman, 1990). In addition, they are recognized as having a remarkable interest in helping others and in maintaining close physical proximity between themselves and others when engaged in verbal dialogue. Moreover, these students are characterized as (a) relying on external cues and information when forming judgments and opinions; and (b) responding best to personal forms of rewards and reinforcements such as praise, smiles, pats on the back, and the like. Although research on the strengths and learning preferences of African American learners with gifts is limited, that which is available has led to the development of identification modules and instructional methodologies supported by theoretical frameworks that accentuate the cognitive, affective, and creative strengths of African American students with gifts and talents (Baytops & Reed, 1997).

PEDAGOGICAL IMPLICATIONS

African American students with gifts and talents have always demonstrated the need for specifically designed instructional programs to meet their unique and varied cognitive, affective, and creative needs (Baytops & Reed, 1997). Despite this well-known fact, many problems still persist in terms of how to best provide appropriate educational opportunities for these youths within our educational systems. This may be due, in part, to the composition of our nation's teaching force. Supply and demand research reveals that our teaching force largely comprises females of European American decent, which is a sharp contrast to the backgrounds of many of the students they teach. Students from ethnic, racial, and culturally diverse groups make up an increasingly large proportion of our nation's school population, and this trend is expected to continue. The question is, what impact will the demographic gap between the ethnic backgrounds of students and their teachers have on learning?

Based on what is revealed in the literature on cognitive-styles research, one can surmise that such a discontinuity could have some potentially harmful effects on student learning. For one reason, many African American students engage in field-dependent and field-sensitive approaches to learning. For another reason, our public school teachers, who are mostly European American females, employ a field-independent teaching style (Grossman, 1990). When the cognitive styles of African American learners (field-dependent and field-sensitive) are incompatible with the styles of teaching (field-independent) and learning (field-independent) required to succeed in school, it can result in educational neglect and inappropriate programming. As Ford (1996) pointed out, "African American [Black] students do not fail in school because of learning style differences but because schools fail to accommodate these differences" (p. 63). In essence, general and special education teachers who employ predominately field-independent teaching methods when instructing African American students place many of these youngsters at risk for having learning and behavioral problems in school (Grossman, 1990). Some may become underachievers, while others may become dropouts, drug addicts, and the like.

If highly intelligent African American learners are to experience success in school and in life, general and special educators must promote a knowledge base that is culturally sensitive, and a teaching style that is congruent with the learning and behavioral styles that dominate African American culture. They must also have curricula and instruction adapted to their abilities and knowledge. Although the use of field-independent teaching styles permeates most instructional settings in our public schools, the use of such styles does not mean that instructional standards or learning expectations must be lowered or compromised. Neither does it mean that African Americans are inferior learners. It does mean that by using a field-dependent approach to accommodate the learning and behavioral styles of African American students, teachers equalize their students' opportunities, when compared to their European American counterparts, and maximize their learning and potential for learning. Success for gifted African American learners requires that they be taught through their preferred modes of learning. It also requires the implementation of a culturally responsive curriculum, one which provides culturally sensitive, challenging, informative, and intriguing instruction within a learning environment designed to develop their abilities, skills, and interests without their losing a sense of membership as part of the class (Baytops & Reed, 1997).

It should be noted, however, that irrespective of their intellectual abilities, teachers, especially those from the cultural majority, often have faulty perceptions and understanding about the learning and social behaviors of African American students. This may be attributed to such variables as a lack of knowledge about ethnic, cultural, socioeconomic, learning, and behavioral style differences of this population as well as conflicting value systems, goals, and beliefs (Obiakor, 1999, 2001). When teachers misperceive, misunderstand, or misinterpret behaviors of African American students and other multicultural and multiethnic youngsters, it can cause them to "perceive behavior problems that don't exist, misunderstand the causes of students' behaviors, and use culturally inappropriate responses to deal with students' behavior problems" (Grossman, 1990, p. 339).

Using instructional methodologies that are sensitive to the manner in which students receive, process, comprehend, synthesize, and respond to instruction is critical to maximizing not only their achievement but also their potential for achievement. As noted by Baytops and Reed (1997),

> As long as traditional instructional methodologies continue to be held as the standard by which all students are measured, without specific attention to the strengths and needs of individual students and the cultural bases from which they originate, what we do in the name of schooling may continue to miss the mark. (p. 42)

If we are to maximize the learning potential of African American gifted learners, it will necessitate major changes not only in how we assess and identify this population for giftedness (or the potential for giftedness), but also in how we view teaching and learning. While the impact of our failure to identify these children can be difficult to measure, we can surmise that our failure to do so will lead to academic underachievement, social-behavior problems, and other school-related concerns.

A number of factors can affect the ability and performance of highly able, gifted, and talented multicultural children and prevent them from fully demonstrating their potential. These factors may include

- Experiential deprivation, especially in childhood, which would include lack of cognitive stimulation
- Limited language development
- Differences in learning styles
- Lack of role models
- Low expectations on the part of parents and teachers
- Peer pressure
- Lack of parental involvement
- Strained relationships with one or both parents and siblings
- Cultural differences
- Racial bias
- Lack of opportunity (Cline & Schwartz, 1999, pp. 103-104).

Other factors may include the curriculum, teachers' attitudes toward minority children in gifted programs, and the school's atmosphere. Without question, teachers of gifted learners play a central role in the instructional process. Not only are they key to the development of methodologies, strategies, techniques, and effective practices that enable gifted learners to maximize their potential, but they are also responsible for organizing enrichment activities, and coordinating and integrating general education curricula activities so that students can work at a pace and level commensurate with their ability.

What are the characteristics of effective teachers of African American learners with gifts? Effective teachers of African American learners with gifts recognize and establish programs for diverse levels of ability, differences in learning styles (modes of learning), student interest, and the like. They possess a broad repertoire of teaching skills and techniques and an extensive knowledge of cultural differences. In addition, they (a) are empathetic and caring, (b) acknowledge and respect cultural differences, (c) find ways to increase the relevance of lessons to make them more meaningful, and (d) infuse cultural constructs of their students within the curriculum. It appears that there are many African American students with high abilities who have legitimate educational needs. Unfortunately, these students remain diamonds in the rough because of a lack of opportunity to demonstrate their extraordinary potential. To increase the probability of equal opportunity and justice for all, barriers that stand in the way of appropriate instruction for gifted African American learners must be eradicated.

Given the premise that each student concentrates, processes, absorbs, and remembers new and difficult information in a different way (Dunn, 1995), it can be conceived that African American students with gifts also learn differently from each other. It may also be conceived that these students, by virtue of their cognitive styles (field-dependent and field-sensitive) will need teachers who teach globally rather than analytically. As Dixon, Mains, and Reeves (1996) pointed out,

> Educating gifted students demands stepping out of the traditional mode, rethinking the classroom, restructuring tests, being flexible, providing independent learning time and assistance, using many more manipulatives, creating hands-on classrooms that allow much more movement, and sometimes simply allowing the gifted students to take charge of his or her own learning. Such a classroom also requires a teacher who is tolerant and encourages active, hands-on learning. (p. 23)

There are many possible combinations and variations of programs and service delivery models (e.g., acceleration programs, enrichment programs, resource programs, and self-contained programs) for educating African American students with gifts and talents. Since there is no cookbook recipe or a one-size-fits-all instructional strategy that has proven to be effective for all or most African American gifted learners, it is hoped that the strategies below provide renewed insight into practices that can be employed to cultivate and crystallize the abilities and potential abilities of these youngsters. While the strategies presented represent some of the most effective principles and techniques for students referred to as at-risk learners, they also have considerable applicability to African American gifted learners because of the problems (e.g., underachievement and low self-esteem and self-concept) generally associated with this unique population. General and special educators must

1. Provide instruction in a manner that corresponds with (matches) the student's cognitive (learning) style and build on the student's strengths (Carbo & Hodges, 1988). Traditional instructional modes (field-independent) are generally oppositional to the learning styles (field-dependent) of many African American learners, thereby creating a classroom climate that may not be conducive to helping them maximize their potential.

2. Decrease cultural discontinuity between home and school; infuse cultural variables in instruction and interact more with students by using personal, conversational techniques (Franklin, 1992; Gollnick & Chinn, 1991); and provide multiple opportunities to learn and practice new skills.

3. Deemphasize skill work that requires a strong analytic learning style with high-interest materials in which students can become actively engaged in lessons (Carbo & Hodges, 1988). It is widely known that active learners learn better and faster (Johnson, 1998).

4. Start lessons globally, rather than analytically, to reduce confusion and frustration (Carbo & Hodges, 1988); use visual aids, emphasize and develop relevant concepts, provide concrete examples and experiences to deepen student's understanding (Carbo & Hodges, 1988), and establish an experiential base for learning (Johnson, 1998).

5. Allow students to work with peers in small groups on a frequent basis. Cooperative learning arrangements (a) provide opportunities for interactions with others, (b) enhance student learning, (c) improve intergroup relations (Franklin, 1992; Johnson, 1998), and (d) reduce some of the stress associated with placement in a gifted classroom environment.

6. Maintain high expectations (Johnson, 1998). The learning potential of African American, field-dependent, gifted learners is equivalent to that of their European American, field-independent counterparts. It is important to organize the learning environments so that students with field-dependent and field-independent cognitive styles can benefit equally from instruction (Gollnick & Chinn, 1991).

7. Provide frequent feedback at multiple levels (e.g., acknowledging a correct response, prompting with clues, repeating or paraphrasing a question) (Burnett, 1999). It is important to use affective types of behavioral responses (e.g., praise, encouragement) to build and motivate student interest and enthusiasm for learning (Franklin, 1992; Johnson, 1998).

8. Teach learning strategies (e.g., organizing information, study strategies, higher-order thinking skills) to facilitate the acquisition, manipulation, integration, storage, and retrieval of information (Johnson, 1998).

9. Use a variety of instructional strategies and activities to offer students opportunities to learn in ways that are responsive to their communication styles, cognitive styles, and aptitudes (Burnette, 1999). Such variety also helps them develop, acquire, and strengthen other approaches to learning new and different information.

10. Address students' social, emotional, and psychological needs (Ford, 1996; Patton & Townsend, 1997).

It is not uncommon for African American gifted learners to express feelings of isolation and alienation. Once placed in gifted programs, these youngsters make numerous social sacrifices and take many risks. For example, they risk rejection from their African American peers who may perceive them as being untrue to their cultural and racial group; they risk isolation and alienation from their European American peers who do not understand, and they risk being under the guidance of teachers who also do not understand them (Ford, 1996). Such an emotional tug-of-war can cause many of these youngsters to develop behaviors that mask their gifts and talents to avoid identification and placement in gifted programs.

CONCLUSION

Key Points to Remember

Following are 10 key points to remember, to maximize the fullest potential of African American learners with gifts and talents.

1. The underrepresentation of African American students in programs for the gifted may be attributed to a number of factors, such as our concept of giftedness, the procedures and assessment measures used for identification and program placement, test bias, misuse of standardized tests, racial biases among teachers and administrators, lack of multiple criteria for giftedness, overreliance on traditional standardized tests, the lack of multiple data sources, the inability of African American youngsters to demonstrate behaviors associated with giftedness, and teachers' lack of knowledge and skills in the ability to recognize giftedness or the potential for giftedness among African American students.

2. We can be more effective in our identification of African American learners with gifts if we seek the basic intellectual abilities that are common to all students with gifts.

3. Efforts to improve the educational outcomes of African American learners with gifts and talents cannot be fully realized without the infusion of cultural constructs within the instructional paradigm.

4. Most African Americans are field-dependent (field-sensitive) learners who perform best when instruction and teaching methodologies and strategies are introduced in their preferred modes of learning. Consequently, when they are introduced to new and difficult information, they will remember significantly more.

5. Teachers' use of field-dependent teaching styles to instruct African American learners with gifts does not mean that instructional standards or learning expectations must be lowered. What it does is provide a more equitable opportunity to maximize learning.

6. When teachers use instructional practices based on the preferences of the dominant culture, there is a high probability that learners of African American decent with gifts and potential gifts will fail to achieve their potential or actualize their gifts and talents.

7. African American learners with gifts require specifically designed instructional programs to meet their unique and varied cognitive, affective, and creative needs if they are to experience success in school and in life.

8. To maximize achievement or potential for achievement, African American learners with gifts will require a culturally responsive curriculum and an instructional style that is not at odds with their cognitive (learning) styles.

9. Effective teachers of African American learners with gifts recognize and establish programs for diverse levels of ability, differences in learning styles or modes of learning, variations in types and modes of expression, and student interests. They also possess a broad repertoire of teaching skills and techniques and an extensive knowledge of cultural differences.

10. Although heredity and the environment play a significant role in determining intelligence, intellectual ability, or giftedness, research supports the position that the environment has the greatest influence on its development.

Final Comments

The disproportionate representation of African American students in gifted programs is a recurring problem in gifted education. Even though the literature and practical experience embrace the importance of understanding the cultural, linguistic, and socioeconomic backgrounds of African American students, how best to meet the educational challenges of this unique population remains unresolved. I believe identifying the gifts and talents of African American learners is the first step toward reversing the disproportionate representation of these youngsters in gifted programs, and in helping them to maximize their learning potential. A second step entails the development of enriching and challenging programs and experiences that reflect knowledge and respect for their culture, values, language, and beliefs. A third step necessitates a match between the learning styles of African American youngsters and appropriate instructional approaches. And a fourth step involves providing these youngsters, especially those from economically depressed backgrounds, with instruction in various skills (e.g., study skills, test-taking skills, higher-order thinking skills, alternative modes of learning, and the like) proven to maximize learning outcomes. Finally, by incorporating these recommendations, general and special education teachers will have the power to reverse misclassification, underachievement, lack of motivation, and lack of interest in schools. But as long as instructional methodologies continue to be held to the standards of the dominant culture, equal educational opportunity and justice for all will continue to be an illusion for the African American learners with gifts and talents.

Discussion Issues

1. Briefly explain how assessment can contribute to the underrepresentation of African American students in programs for the gifted.

2. Discuss why it is important for teachers to understand the culture, language, customs, and beliefs of African American students.

3. Summarize some specific learner characteristics of African American students.

4. Explain why it is important for teachers to match their instructional styles with the learning and behavioral styles of their students.

5. Analyze how teachers can contribute to the underachievement of African American gifted students.

REFERENCES

Banks, J. A. (1977). *Multiethnic education: Practices and promises.* Bloomington, IN: Phi Delta Kappa Educational Foundation.

Baytops, J. L., & Reed, D. (1997). Making connections: Developing strategies to teach African American gifted learners effectively. *Multiple Voices, 2*(1), 38-42.

Bracey, G. W. (1992). Finding gifted Blacks and Hispanics. *Phi Delta Kappan, 74*(4), 344.

Burnette, J. (1999). *Critical behaviors and strategies for teaching culturally diverse students.* Reston, VA: Council for Exceptional Children. (ERIC Document Reproduction Service No. ED 435 147)

Byrd, H. B. (1995). Curricular and pedagogical procedures for African American learners with academic and cognitive disabilities. In B. A. Ford, F. E. Obiakor, & J. M. Patton (Eds.), *Effective education of African American exceptional learners: New perspectives* (pp. 123-150). Austin, TX: Pro-Ed.

Carbo, M., & Hodges, H. (1988). Learning styles strategies can help students at risk. *Teaching Exceptional Children, 20*(4), 55-58.

Clark, B. (1997). *Growing up gifted: Developing the potential of children at home and at school* (5th ed.). New York: Macmillan.

Cline, S., & Schwartz, D. (1999). *Diverse populations of gifted children: Meeting their needs in the regular classroom and beyond.* Upper Saddle River, NJ: Prentice-Hall.

Dixon, C., Mains, L., & Reeves, M. J. (1996). *Gifted and at risk.* Bloomington, IN: Phi Delta Kappa Educational Foundation.

Dunn, R. (1995). *Strategies for educating diverse learners.* Bloomington, IN: Phi Delta Kappa Educational Foundation.

Ford, D. Y. (1996). *Reversing underachievement among gifted Black students: Promising practices and programs.* New York: Teachers College Press.

Ford, D. Y., & Webb, K. S. (1994). Desegregation of gifted education programs: The impact of Brown on underachieving children of color. *Journal of Negro Education, 63*, 358-375.

Franklin, M. E. (1992). Culturally sensitive instructional practices for African American learners with disabilities. *Exceptional Children, 59*, 115-122.

Frasier, M. M. (1979). Rethinking the issue regarding the culturally disadvantaged gifted. *Exceptional Children, 45*, 538-542.

Frasier, M., Garcia, J. H., & Passow, A. H. (1995). *A review of assessment issues in gifted education and their implications for identifying minority students* (Research Monograph No. 95204). Storrs, CT: National Research Center on the Gifted and Talented.

Gallagher, J. J. (1995). Education of gifted students: A civil rights issue? *Phi Delta Kappan, 76*, 408-410.

Gollnick, D. M., & Chinn, P. C. (1991). *Multicultural education for exceptional children.* Reston, VA: Council for Exceptional Children. (ERIC Document Reproduction Service No. ED 333 620).

Grossman, H. (1990). *Trouble-free teaching: Solutions to behavior problems in the classroom.* Mountainview, CA: Mayfield.

Hale-Benson, J. (1986). *Black children: Their roots, culture, and learning styles.* Baltimore: Johns Hopkins University Press.

Hilliard, A. G. (1976). *Alternative to IQ testing: An approach to the identification of gifted in "minority" children* (Report No. 75175). San Francisco: San Francisco State University.

Johnson, G. M. (1998). Principles of instruction for at-risk learners. *Preventing School Failure, 42*(4), 167-174.

Obiakor, F. E. (1999). Teacher expectations of minority exceptional learners: Impact on "accuracy" of self-concepts. *Exceptional Children, 66*, 39-53.

Obiakor, F. E. (2001). *It even happens in "good" schools: Responding to cultural diversity in today's classrooms.* Thousand Oaks, CA: Corwin.

Patton, J. M., & Baytops, J. L. (1995). Identifying and transforming the potential of young, gifted African Americans: A clarion call for action. In B. A. Ford, F. E. Obiakor, & J. M. Patton (Eds.), *Effective education of African American exceptional learners: New perspectives* (pp. 27-67). Austin, TX: Pro-Ed.

Patton, J. M., & Townsend, B. L. (1997). Creating inclusive environments for African American children and youth with gifts and talents. *Roeper Review, 20*(1), 13-17.

Richert, E. S. (1985). Identification of gifted children in the United States: The need for pluralistic assessment. *Roeper Review, 8*(2), 68-72.

Shade, B. (1997). *Culture, style, and the educative process: Making schools work for racially diverse students* (2nd ed.). Springfield, IL: Charles C Thomas.

Shaklee, B. D. (1992). Identification of young gifted students. *Journal for the Education of the Gifted, 15*(2), 134-144.

Torrance, E. P. (1969). Creative positives of disadvantaged children and youth. *Gifted Child Quarterly, 13*(2), 71-81.

Chapter Nine

Communication Skills of African American Learners With Disabilities

Martha Scott Lue, Cheryl Evans Green,
and Shelia Yvette Smalley

Whereas, numerous . . . studies demonstrate that African American students as a part of their culture and history as African people possess and use a language described in various scholarly approaches as "Ebonics" (literally "Black sounds") or "Pan-African Communication Behaviors," "African Language Systems"; . . . therefore, be it resolved that the Board of Education officially recognizes the existence, and the cultural and historic bases of West and Niger-Congo African Language Systems, and each language as the predominantly primary language of African-American students.

—Oakland, California, Board of Education (1996, p. 1)

anguage is personal and it is interactive. It celebrates who we are and from whence we have come. It develops over time. It separates us from any other species and helps us in defining our special uniqueness. Therefore it is not surprising that the December 18, 1996, resolution passed by the Oakland School Board in California noted the existence of language differences, recognized Ebonics as a second language, and generated a firestorm of controversy.

The resolution went on to affirm that language development would be enhanced when teachers recognize and understand the language structures unique to African American students. The resolution by the Oakland Board of Education acknowledges the complexity of issues related to understanding and appreciating the communication skills of African American learners. As our nation's schools become more diverse, more of these issues will arise. Consider the following:

- McLaughlin and McCleod (1996) asserted that if classroom students were distributed evenly across the nation's classrooms, every class of 30 students would include about 10 students from ethnic or racial minority groups. Of the 10, about 6 would be from language minority families. Of these students, 2 to 4 would have limited English proficiency (LEP); of these, 2 would be from immigrant families. Of the 6 language minority students in the class, 4 would speak Spanish as their native language, and 1 would speak an Asian language. The other language minority student would speak any one of more than 100 languages.
- In 2000, about 1 in 10 United States residents (about 10% of the population) were foreign born. About half of these individuals lived in the central city of metropolitan areas (Lollock, 2001).
- Culturally and linguistically diverse students with disabilities experience general language difficulties (Rodriquez, Parmar, & Signer, 2001).
- African American children may be at considerable risk for misidentification of having a communication disorder because of unfair language assessment methods or methodology (Craig & Washington, 2000; Polloway, Patton, & Serna, 2001).

The U.S. Department of Census (2000) released preliminary population figures for the year 2000. In the United States, there are slightly more than 281 million persons, an increase of 13.2% in the last decade. The greatest population growth in the nation occurred in Arizona, Georgia, Florida, and Texas, with growth ranging from 23% to 44%. These figures included the total number of people in the 50 states and the District of Columbia on census day, April 1, 2000. The report suggested that we had never had so many people and have never had so much diversity.

From these statistics, it is clear that we continue to live, work, and teach in a world that is in constant change. In some classrooms, teachers are educating classes of students whose nationalities, ethnicity, race, gender, social, and economic classification may shift on a weekly basis (Lue, 2001). Understanding and appreciating the communication skills of African American students requires knowledge of their history, from their preslavery existence to the 21st century when African Americans made poetic use of hip-hop and rap music. Therefore it is imperative that any discourse dealing with the African American learner in any detail would certainly warrant some discussion of the communication process used by African American people.

This chapter focuses on communication skills of African American learners, including those with disabilities. Key concepts related to demographic changes, language, culture, language disabilities, African American families, and parent-professional partnerships are highlighted. Finally, culturally responsive strategies that the classroom teacher might use in working with students from diverse cultures are identified.

THE AFRICAN AMERICAN LANGUAGE TRADITION

It is generally agreed that in years to come, general and special educators will be teaching groups of learners who are quite different from any others that they have taught in the past. Moreover, many of these youngsters will come from more diverse cultural and linguistic backgrounds (American Speech-Language-Hearing Association, 2001). In addition, they will exhibit a wide range of language, learning, and behavioral characteristics that may present challenges to educators (Adger & Wolfram, 1993; Craig & Washington, 1994; Craig, Washington, & Thompson-Porter, 1998; Washington & Craig, 1999). Some may be at risk of academic failure and placed in special education settings because of their limited English proficiency, their behavioral characteristics, and their socioeconomic status (Roseberry-McKibbin, 1995; Thomas, Correa, & Morsink, 2001). The challenge for general and special educators is to provide an empowering school culture. Vaughn, Bos, and Schumm (2000) described such a culture as one that promotes gender, racial, and social-class equity; it creates an atmosphere for looking at biases and prejudices, identifying strategies to eliminate them, and substituting opportunities to enhance the positive self-esteem of students. African American students are among those who deserve an empowering school environment that provides opportunities for understanding their traditional cultural and linguistic characteristics and deals with frequent biases and prejudices that they face.

As discussed by Green (1999) in his review of the 1971 work by Robert Hill, a pioneer researcher on Black families in America, African American families have a commitment to a language tradition, African American vernacular English (AAVE), and an appreciation of the skills and subtleties of bilingualism. African American English (AAE) is a term used to describe various ways of speaking by some African Americans. Over the years, a number of different terms have been used to identify how African Americans speak. A number of different speech patterns or dialects of African Americans have been the focus of both linguistic and general-public attention. The terms most frequently used to identify how African Americans speak include Black English, Ebonics, Black vernacular English (BVE), and African American vernacular English. It is important to note that not all African Americans use these varieties of speech patterns and that differences exist among African Americans in phonology, syntax, and conversational discourse (Cole & Taylor, 1990). Examples of differences include deletion of an auxiliary verb (*The rabbit is hopping* = *The rabbit hopping*), substitution of medial and final sounds (*father* = *fava; talked* = *talk*), and, deletion of the possessive suffix (*girl's* = *girl* as in *It is the girl doll*) (Kuder, 1997).

Researchers (Banks, 2001; Hyter, 1998; Wyatt, 1995) have suggested that African American children's communicative patterns are shaped through multiple sources of language input and various sociocultural factors, including (a) the community in which the family lives and the family's dialect, education, socioeconomic status, and social background; (b) the child's community network; and (c) attitudes in the child's community about standard dialects (e.g., among teachers and the general society).

LANGUAGE DIFFERENCE
VERSUS LANGUAGE DISORDER

A discussion on language differences, especially as it relates to African Americans, is extremely important, for numerous reasons:

- Lack of understanding and unfamiliarity with language differences may lead to mis understanding, misinterpretation, and, in some cases, unintentional insult to African Americans (Taylor, 1990).

- Clashes in culture may occur when those persons in authority are not able to recognize or acknowledge that other cultures or languages are indeed legitimate (Van Keulen, Weddington, & DeBose, 1998).

- For some learners, many of whom may be of African American descent, their language use may not be the standard that is often heard in many middle-class families (Lue, 2001).

According to the American Speech-Language-Hearing Association (ASHA) (1983), the national professional, scientific, and credentialing association for speech, language, and hearing professionals, the English language is composed of many linguistic varieties. These linguistic varieties may include Ebonics, Spanish-influenced English, Appalachian English, and standard English. A language difference is not necessarily a language disorder. Each language contains a variety of forms, called *dialects*. Dialects are a variation of a symbol system and reflect our shared regional, social, or cultural and ethnic factors (Committee on Language, Speech, and Hearing Services in Schools, 1982; Turnbull, Turnbull, Shank, Smith, & Leal, 2002). ASHA (1983) further posited that each dialect represents a functional form of English, permitting speakers to communicate adequately while, at the same time, maintaining a "symbolic representation of the historical, social, and cultural background of the speakers" (p. 24). Although some dialect speakers may have a speech or language disorder, the dialect itself is not the disorder. However, the presence of a dialect should not necessarily rule out the possibility that a language disorder might exist (Van Riper & Erickson, 1996).

A language disorder is a problem in understanding or producing meaningful conversation. A language disorder might involve (a) a serious disruption of the language acquisition process; (b) difficulty with following rules of grammar; (c) the inability to understand or use words in correct context; (d) not choosing appropriate language for different situations; and (e) problems of written and spoken language, or other symbol systems (Committee on Language, Speech, and Hearing Services in Schools, 1982; Hardman, Drew, & Egan, 1999). Language disorders may vary in severity, ranging from mild to severe (Polloway et al., 2001). Speech-language pathologists, the professionals who treat speech and language disorders, are trained to distinguish between a language difference (i.e., dialect) and a language disorder. In some cases, it might be helpful for them to become familiar with specific rules that underlie the use of particular dialects (Van Riper & Erickson, 1996).

LEARNERS WITH DISABILITIES: ENVIRONMENT, LANGUAGE, CULTURE, AND PARTNERSHIPS

Research for almost three decades clearly indicates that both language and culture affect learning of students, including African American learners with disabilities (Banks, 2001; Franklin, 1992; Hale-Benson, 1986; Hilliard, 1989; Sileo, 1998; Tharp, 1989). Studies further suggest that similar cultural values, often shared by African American families, influence the learning and interactive patterns of their children with disabilities. Therefore it is critical to form and maintain partnerships that effectively facilitate the continuity of learning that occurs in the home, school, and community environments (see Franklin, 1992; Cummins, 1984).

While the importance of parent-teacher-community partnerships as resources in the education of African American learners with disabilities seems obvious, the literature infrequently examines conditions that affect the establishment and maintenance of such relationships. The types of parent-teacher-community partnerships that are formed and maintained are related to both an understanding of African American students with disabilities as learners and the diverse cultural and linguistic backgrounds of these learners. Several critical factors concerning African American families and their involvement with schools are important to note. First, the participation of African American parents in an educational partnership with school staff members may be affected by their comfort level when dealing with schools. For some African American parents, schools are not often seen as very user-friendly places. If parents feel uncomfortable with the school's conceptualization of their parent involvement, they may choose to abstain from any of the roles made available to them by school personnel (Voltz, 1995). For example, teachers who erroneously believe African American parents are apathetic or uninterested in their children's education may attribute a very marginal role to parents and expect little support or assistance from them. This expectation may result in African American parents believing their participation in the education of their children is neither wanted nor welcomed by the school.

Second, African American parents with limited verbal skills and little experience in negotiating the educational system may find it difficult to identify and to access appropriate educational resources for their children (Sileo, Sileo, & Prater, 1996). Dealing with any bureaucracies, including school systems, can be a frustrating and overwhelming process. African American parents who are dealing with a variety of life challenges may not have the tenacity or ability to be persistent or consistent in seeking out and using services and programs for their children. These parents may rarely have the capacity to participate in educational partnerships, especially when they sense that they are dealing with a system that does not recognize that they suffer from the double-whammy of dealing with both race and disability (Haughton, 1993). And third, if African American parents have had negative experiences themselves with schools, this may present a barrier to their participation as partners in the educational process (Thorp, 1997). Some of these negative experiences may be subtle; other experiences may be more overt. For example, when parents feel that there is little or no attempt in the school curriculum to accurately represent the historical contributions of African Americans, they may be reluctant or even unwilling to form partnerships with teachers and others involved in the education of their children. African American parents, including those who have children with disabilities, usually understand that knowledge of one's racial identity and cultural heritage is a critical factor in promoting positive self-esteem in African American children and in socializing them to effectively cope with racism (McAdoo, 1997). The lack of understanding by teachers of the importance of cultural legacy for African Americans in assisting them to deal with the negative impact of racism on self-esteem and security does not facilitate development of partnerships with parents.

Franklin (1992) noted that teachers' attitudes, perceptions, and interactive styles can be effective in facilitating continuity between their students' school, home, and community environments. Several other observers (Singh, Ellis, Oswald, Welcher, & Curtis, 1997; Voltz, 1994, 1995) suggest that successful school-family-community collaborations appear to be tied to teachers' abilities to be (a) sensitive to their own cultural experiences, attitudes, and values, particularly in relation to working with African American learners with disabilities; (b) knowledgeable about the needs and backgrounds of African American learners with disabilities in the classroom; and (c) skilled in translating this sensitivity and knowledge into teaching strategies that are culturally responsive to, and inclusive of, the communication, curriculum, and instructional needs of African American learners with disabilities.

As Sileo (1998) notes, the quality of parent-professional partnerships depends on the ability of the educator to be sensitive to the diverse needs of learners in their classes as well as the needs of students' parents and other family members. He argued that teacher preparation programs need to play a major role in preparing teachers to be effective in establishing partnerships with parents. To this end, he explained that teachers who have acquired the knowledge, skills, and abilities to work with students and families from diverse backgrounds are professionals who can "go beyond a menu-driven array of general options for family involvement, identify strategies to facilitate participation based on family preferences for their degree of involvement, and tailor family-school interactions to address specific needs and priorities" (p. 513).

CULTURALLY RESPONSIVE TEACHING STRATEGIES

When instructing African American students with speech and language impairments, changes in pedagogy may be required. In addition, these students may need a more realistic format in which lessons are presented. Smalley and Moch (1999) stated that

> all too often, students in general, and inner city, African American students in particular, are expected to learn . . . in ways more appropriate to other learning styles and experiences. It is easier for teachers to rely on abstract paper and pencil tasks to determine mastery, to overuse worksheets, and to use skill and drill. (p. 13)

According to Irvine and Armento (2001), "On most indicators and measures of academic achievement, African American and Hispanic American students' performance lags behind their white and Asian peers" (p. 3). In addition, in the area of mathematics, the National Center for Educational Statistics (NCES; 2001, August) indicated that for the 2000 assessment, White students, in all three grades (4th, 8th, and 12th), had higher scores, on average, than Black or Hispanic students. The report went on to say that these large gaps between subgroups' performances appeared to have been substantial and have remained relatively unchanged since 1990. In the area of reading, results of the 2000 assessment indicated that fourth-grade White and Asian/Pacific Islander students outperformed their black, Hispanic, and American Indian peers (NCES, 2001, March).

Due to frustration in the classroom, some African American students may exhibit behaviors that are disruptive and inappropriate until the general and special education teacher recognizes and appropriately deals with the embarrassment or discomfort these students may have experienced in the past. The teacher must be both knowledgeable about the dynamics of communication and willing to routinely find ways of connecting communication skills to African American students' daily experiences of living. This process must first begin with teachers assessing their own cultural biases, which enables the teacher to be effective in conveying a genuine love of learning (Chisholm, 1994). For example, conventional strategies of rote and routine paper-and-pencil tasks may be the basis for some of this frustration, due to the fact that these types of tasks may not be connected to the students' learning styles and culture.

If many conventional approaches have not worked, what effective strategies can classroom teachers employ while working with African American learners in regular, special, and inclusive settings? General and special education teachers should (a) behave differently from the past as they plan meaningful and exciting ways to teach these students communication skills; (b) motivate African American students to learn and appreciate communication for its relevance to their lives; (c) empower these learners to make meaningful connections between street language and standard American English (SAE); and (d) modify their current language arts curriculum and teaching in order to use examples from real-life situations.

CONCLUSION

Key Points to Remember

Following are 10 key points that general and special educators should remember as they work with African Americans with communication disorders:

1. It is important to develop a genuine relationship with students. When many African American students perceive the teacher-student relationship to be "fake," they may refuse to learn. Conversely, teachers can positively affect these students' achievement when they make a concerted effort to form real relationships with them.

2. Educators must create a learning environment that fosters the use of critical thinking and problem-solving skills. Teachers should display their excitement for teaching communication skills to promote students' growth of positive attitudes toward learning. Modeling the communication behavior they expect of their students is essential. The classroom environment should be structured in such a way that students feel at ease in participating in various instructional arrangements (e.g., large and small groups).

3. Identifying current issues and concerns of African American students and their families is essential in the teaching-learning process. Effective and proactive teachers become familiar with what is meaningful in the lives of their students and the lives of their students' families. Information of this type will assist teachers in identifying and developing suitable, practical examples for use in the classroom.

4. Educators should use storytelling skills to facilitate communication skills. In the African American culture, the passing down of family traditions, values, and beliefs through storytelling is a very rich tradition. Accordingly, these students are inclined to remember a concept or a construct when given a story to make the connection. Details including who, what, when, where, how, and why should be given. After the story, teachers should check the students' comprehension by having them suggest alternative options to produce the same results.

5. Reinforcing skills in diverse ways and settings is essential. After students have been taught concepts and skills, the teacher should engage them in reinforcement activities in diverse ways and across settings. For example, field trips to local historical sites can reinforce students' communication skills. Other ways to reinforce these students' skills may include the use of communication software, games, and brainteasers.

6. Educators must participate in professional development training. To integrate "professional development opportunities for teachers" is one of the objectives of the Goals 2000 Educate America Act (1994, § 231). Professional development training can positively impact teachers because they have the freedom to become learners again in a cooperative and collaborative environment.

7. It is important to use the enrichment activities listed in the language arts teachers' guides as the norm and not the exception. Because enrichment activities are often viewed as too time-consuming and too much extra work, some teachers tend to omit them. Since many of these activities correlate with practical experiences, there is an inherent need to include them within instructional delivery.

8. Technology must be infused into the school curriculum at all levels. Researchers (U.S. Department of Commerce, 2000) measured the extent of digital inclusion and concluded that while African Americans and Hispanics have made impressive gains in Internet access, they still lag behind other groups. For many African American students who have not had the experience or the access to technology in the home, the classroom presents an excellent opportunity for them to develop and enhance their technological skills. When general and special education teachers devise creative ways to teach students, technology can make a great difference in the way students learn (White House, 2000). Creative uses of technology in the classroom can foster students' self-esteem, expand the collaborative efforts of students, teachers, and external resources, and promote increased learning and interest (Smalley & Moch, 1999).

9. To teach African American learners, it is important that general and special educators distinguish between language deficits and language differences. Such an understanding will reduce the misidentification, misassessment, and misinstructing of African American learners.

10. Educators must look at language from a developmental perspective to avoid illusory generalizations and discriminatory expectations.

Final Comments

This chapter addressed the ongoing demographic changes resulting in cultural and language diversity in our nation's classrooms and further described the African American language tradition and communication characteristics. We believe the relationship between language and culture must be explored as well as how language and culture may influence behavior. Making the distinction between language difference and language disorder, particularly as it relates to African American learners with disabilities, must be an imperative to practitioners. We can do this by understanding their learning environment, language, and culture. We must work with parents and see them as partners with equal responsibilities. In the end, we must adopt culturally responsive strategies that will help African American learners to maximize their fullest potential.

Discussion Issues

1. Briefly describe the type of program that you would design for new teachers to assist them in effectively working with African American students with communication problems.

2. Explain why a teacher must distinguish between a language difference and a language disorder when working with African American learners.

3. Identify two different factors that could influence the communication patterns of African American learners. Explain how these factors affect student-teacher communication.

4. Describe resources (e.g., time, money, equipment, expertise, and staff) that are needed to implement two or three culturally responsive teaching strategies for African American learners.

5. Discuss three benefits of establishing partnerships with the family members of African American learners.

REFERENCES

Adger, C. T., & Wolfram, W. (1993, Fall). Language differences: A new approach for special educators. *Teaching Exceptional Children, 26*(1), 44-47.

American Speech-Language-Hearing Association. (1983). Position paper: Social dialects. *ASHA, 25,* 23-24.

American Speech-Language-Hearing Association. (2001, August). *Communicating in a diverse society.* Retrieved February 24, 2002, from asha.org/press/Diverse_society.cfm

Banks, J. (2001). *Cultural diversity and education: Foundations, curriculum, and teaching.* Boston: Allyn & Bacon.

Chisholm, I. M. (1994, Winter). Preparing teachers for multicultural classrooms. *Journal of Educational Issues of Language Minority Students, 14,* 43-68.

Cole, P. A., & Taylor, O. L. (1990). Performance of working-class African American children on three tests of articulation. *Language, Speech, and Hearing Services in Schools, 21*(3), 171-176.

Committee on Language, Speech, and Hearing Services in Schools. (1982). Definitions: Communicative disorders and variations. *ASHA, 24,* 949-950.

Craig, H., & Washington, J. (1994). The complex syntactic skills of poor, urban, African American preschoolers at school entry. *Language, Speech, and Hearing Services in Schools, 25,* 181-190.

Craig, H., Washington, J., & Thompson-Porter, C. (1998). Performances of young African American children on two comprehension tasks. *Journal of Speech, Language, and Hearing Research, 41,* 445-457.

Craig, H. K., & Washington, J. A. (2000, April). An assessment battery for identifying language, impairments in African American children. *Journal of Speech, Language, and Hearing Research, 43*(2), 366-379.

Cummins, J. (1984). *Bilingual and special education: Issues in assessment and pedagogy.* San Diego, CA: College-Hill Press.

Franklin, M. E. (1992). Culturally sensitive instructional practices for African American learners with disabilities. *Exceptional Children, 59,* 115-123.

Goals 2000: Educate America Act (1994), Pub. L. No. 103-227. Retrieved February 26, 2002, from www.ed.gov/legislation/GOALS2000/TheAct/

Green, J. (1999). *Cultural awareness in the human services: A multi-ethnic approach.* Boston: Allyn & Bacon.

Hale-Benson, J. E. (1986). *Black children: Their roots, culture and learning styles.* Baltimore: Johns Hopkins University Press.

Hardman, M., Drew, C., & Egan, M. (1999). *Human exceptionality: Society, school, and family* (6th ed.). Boston: Allyn & Bacon.

Haughton, C. D. (1993). Expanding the circle of inclusion for African Americans with disabilities. *The Black Collegian, 24*(4), 63-68.

Hilliard, A. (1989). Teachers and cultural styles in a pluralistic society. *NEA Today, 7*(6), 65-69.

Hyter, Y. D. (1998). Ties that bind: The sounds of African American English. *Multicultural Electronic Journal of Communication Development, 1*(1). Retrieved March 7, 2002, from American Speech-Language-Hearing Association, www.asha.ucf.edu/hyter.html

Irvine, J., & Armento, B. (2001). *Culturally responsive teaching: Lesson planning for elementary and middle grades.* Boston: McGraw-Hill.

Kuder, S. J. (1997). *Teaching students with language and communication disabilities.* Boston: Allyn & Bacon.

Lollock, L. (2001, January). *The foreign-born population in the United States: Population characteristics* (Current Population Report No. P20-534). Washington, DC: U.S. Census Bureau.

Lue, M. (2001). *A survey of communication disorders for the classroom teacher* (pp. 69-87). Boston: Allyn & Bacon.

McAdoo, H. (1997). *Black families*. Thousand Oaks, CA: Sage.

McLaughlin, B., & McLeod, B. (1996). The Impact Statement on Practice and Knowledge: Educating all our students: Improving education for children from culturally and linguistically diverse backgrounds. In *Final report of the national center for research on cultural diversity and second language learning*. University of California, Santa Cruz. Retrieved March 7, 2002, from www.ncbe.gwu.edu/miscpubs/ncrcdsll/edall.htm

National Center for Education Statistics. (2001, March). *The nation's report card 2000: Fourth-grade reading assessment results*. Retrieved March 7, 2002, from nces.ed.gov/naep3/pdf/main2000/2001513.pdf

National Center for Education Statistics (NCES) *National Assessment of Educational Progress* (NAEP). (2001, August). National Mathematics Assessment Shows Continued Progress for 4th and 8th-Graders [Press release]. Retrieved March 7, 2002, from /nces.ed.gov/Pressrelease/rel2001/8_2_01.asp

Oakland, California, Board of Education. (1996, December). Text of the resolution by the Oakland board of education adopting the report and recommendations of the African American task force. Retrieved February 24, 2002, from www.English.uiuc.edu/English302/obestatement.htm

Polloway, E., Patton, J., & Serna, L. (2001). Strategies for teaching learners with special needs (7th ed.). Upper Saddle River, NJ: Merrill/Prentice Hall.

Rodriquez, D., Parmar, R., & Signer, B. (2001). Fourth-grade culturally and linguistically diverse exceptional students' concepts of number line. *Exceptional Children, 67*(2), 199-210.

Roseberry-McKibbin, C. (1995, Summer). Distinguishing language differences from language disorders in linguistically and culturally diverse students. *Multicultural Education*, pp. 12-16.

Sileo, T. W. (1998). Preparing professionals for partnerships with parents of students with disabilities: Textbook considerations regarding cultural diversity. *Exceptional Children, 64*, 513-529.

Sileo, T. W., Sileo, A. P., & Prater, M. A. (1996). Parent and professional partnerships in special education: Multicultural considerations. *Intervention in School and Clinic, 31*, 145-153.

Singh, N. N., Ellis, C. R., Oswald, D. P., Welcher, H. A., & Curtis, W. J. (1997). Value and address diversity. *Journal of Emotional and Behavioral Disorders, 5*, 24-35.

Smalley, S. Y., & Moch, P. L. (1999, Winter/Spring). Inner-city African American students' street mathematics vs. school mathematics. *Journal of At-Risk Issues, 5*(2), 11-17.

Taylor, O. L. (1990). Cross cultural communication: An essential dimension of effective education. Retrieved February 24, 2002, from www.maec.org/cross/4.html

Tharp, R. G. (1989). Psychological variables and constants: Effects on teaching and learning in schools. *American Psychologist, 44*(2), 349-359.

Thomas, C., Correa, V., & Morsink, C. (2001). *Interactive teaming: Enhancing programs for students with special needs* (3rd ed.). Upper Saddle River, NJ: Merrill/Prentice Hall.

Thorp, E. K. (1997). Increasing opportunities for partnership with culturally and linguistically diverse families. *Intervention in School and Clinic, 32*, 261-269.

Turnbull, R., Turnbull, A., Shank, M., Smith, S., & Leal, D. (2002). *Exceptional lives: Special education in today's schools* (3rd ed.). Upper Saddle River, NJ: Merrill/Prentice Hall.

U.S. Department of Census. (2000, December). *Census 2000 Apportionment News Conference*. Washington, DC: National Press Club.

U.S. Department of Commerce. (2000, October). *Falling through the net: Toward digital inclusion. A report on Americans' access to technology tools*. Washington, DC. Retrieved February 24, 2002, from www.ntia.doc.gov/ntiahome/fttn00/Falling.htm#2.1

Van Keulen, J., Weddington, G., & DeBose, C. (1998). *Speech, language, learning, and the African American child*. Boston: Allyn & Bacon.

Van Riper, C., & Erickson, R. (1996). *Speech correction: An introduction to speech pathology and audiology* (9th ed.). Boston: Allyn & Bacon.

Vaughn, S., Bos, C., & Schumm, J. (2000). *Teaching exceptional, diverse, and at-risk students in the general education classroom* (2nd ed.). Boston: Allyn & Bacon.

Voltz, D. L. (1994). Developing collaborative parent-teacher relationships with culturally diverse parents. *Intervention in School and Clinic, 29*, 288-291.

Voltz, D. L. (1995). Learning and cultural diversities in general and special education classes: Frameworks for success. *Multiple Voices, 1*(1), 1-11.

Washington, J. A., & Craig, H. (1999). Performances of at-risk, African American preschoolers on the Peabody Picture Vocabulary Test-III. *Language, Speech, and Hearing Services in Schools, 30*(1), 75-82.

White House. (2000, February 2). *From digital divide to digital opportunity: The importance of bridging the digital divide*. Retrieved March 7, 2002, from clinton3.nara.gov/WH/New/digitaldivide/digital3.html

Wyatt, T. (1995). Language development in African American English child speech. *Linguistics and Education, 7*(1), 7-22.

Chapter Ten

Developing Self-Empowerment in African American Learners With Special Problems

Festus E. Obiakor

We live in two different Americas. In the ghetto, our laws are totally different, our language is totally different, and our lives are totally different. I've never felt American, I've only felt African American. An American is supposed to have life, liberty, prosperity, and happiness. But an African American is due pain, poverty, stress, and anxiety. As an African American I have experienced beautiful things, but the majority of the things I've experienced are not beautiful. And I don't even have it as bad as most—there are millions of young men and women living the struggle even harder than me. As children, they have to make day-to-day decisions about whether to go to school or whether to go on the corner and sell drugs. As children, they know that there may not be a tomorrow. Why are African American children faced with this dilemma at such an early age? Why must they look down the road to a future that they might never see? What have my people done to this country to deserve this? And yet I am supposed to feel American. I am supposed to be patriotic. I am supposed to love this system that has been detrimental to the lives of my people. It's hard for me to say how I'm an American when I live in a

second America—an America that doesn't wave the red, white, and blue flag with fifty
stars for fifty states. I live in a community that waves a white flag because we have
almost given up. I live in a community where on the walls are the names of fallen com-
rades of war. I live in a second America. I live there not because I chose to, but because
I have to. I hate to sound militant, but this is the way I feel.

—LeAlan Jones (1997, pp. 199-200)

In the quote above, Jones exposed critical elements of disappointment, frustration, and dis-empowerment of many African Americans in the United States. His youthful cry for empowerment appears to go on deaf ears, especially when the frequent response is, "This is America—pull yourself up by the bootstraps." Interestingly, those who prescribe this kind of solution seem to forget that some people do not have boots and straps, and those who strive to have boots frequently need straps to tie them. This confusion has certainly led to the blame game where schools blame parents and parents blame schools, or where everyone blames others without assuming responsibility for the empowerment of children and youth. An analysis of Jones's youthful plea reveals his deep cries for empowering supports from children and youth, their families, schools, communities, and government.

The critical question is, whose job is it to empower African American learners, especially those with special problems? My premise is that to develop self-empowerment in the whole child, a comprehensive support model (CSM) must be employed (Obiakor, 1994, 1996a, 2001). In this approach, several key players including the self must be involved to build a strong foundation. Today, how the self of the African American learner survives in school, family, community, and government has become a critical dimension in general and special educational processes. In other words, the self of the African American learner can be built or destroyed, and the self can be very resilient. In this chapter, I discuss specific and general ways to develop self-empowerment in African American learners with special problems. Embedded in my discussion is how the dynamic power of the self can be developed as it interacts with the family, school, and community.

THE SELF: CONCEPTUAL FRAMEWORK

The role of the self in determining educational success has been overlooked. Obiakor (1996b) and Osborne (1996) noted that the self is a dynamic structure that develops in a way that continuously reconfirms itself. The concept of self is not an entity in itself; it is composed of several constructs such as self-knowledge, self-esteem, self-determination, self-perception, self-ideal, self-empowerment, and self-responsibility. Sometimes educators and researchers use these constructs synonymously, and sometimes they mean different things to them. In all, the power of the self cannot be downplayed. Osborne defined self-concept as the sum total of attributes, attitudes, and values that people believe define who they are. The self may become more or less positive or negative as a person encounters life's successes or failures. It can be holistically or multi-dimensionally viewed. According to Osborne, the self centers on a person's beliefs and how those beliefs influence behavioral actions. As a result, the self can be very active or inactive depending on whom it interacts with (Obiakor, 1992, 1994, 1999, 2001).

The selves of African American learners can be measured, and their potential can be optimized (Obiakor, 1994, 1996b, 1999, 2001). Within general and special education programs, African American learners with special problems are faced with many situations that attempt to damage their selves. In many cases, African American students fall into the mode of self-fulfilling prophecy or learned helplessness because of negative encounters such as misidentification, misassessment, miscategorization, misplacement, and misinstruction. Viewed from such a perspective, their perceptions of themselves become their reality (Osborne, 1996) and are frequently inaccurate (see Obiakor, 1992, 1999). As Osborne pointed out, if students perceive themselves as not being smart or intelligent, they may begin to engage in behaviors that confirm that perception. Students may choose not to complete certain tasks deemed as difficult because they feel not smart enough. Such a negative view yields damaging results for African American students' self-empowerment. Hence the concept of the self must be enhanced if these students are to be prepared to encounter difficult situations and respond appropriately. There are many aspects underlining the development of the self for African American learners with special problems. As indicated, the self is a dynamic entity. A logical extension is that family, school, community, and government entities impact the self. Consider the following mutually inclusive variables of African American learners:

1. When neighborhoods that African American learners come from are misperceived as "bad," there will be a tendency for them to feel a little inferior when they come in contact with those who have been misperceived to come from "good" neighborhoods.

2. When schools that African American learners attend are misperceived as "bad," there will be a tendency for them to feel that they are not getting a quality education. The result is that truly good teachers will find safety in flight.

3. When African American learners are misperceived as intellectually inferior because of their performance on tests that lack reliability and validity, they are misplaced in programs that impede their ability to maximize their potential. This affects how they accurately or inaccurately view themselves.

4. When African American learners are misidentified and misassessed, they are frequently miscategorized, mislabeled, and disproportionately placed in special education programs. As a result, they poorly interpret their own strengths and weaknesses.

5. When African Americans are misplaced, their instructional programs are frequently inferior and low-rated. Consequently, their talents are not maximized.

Based on the aforementioned connections, it is no surprise that African American learners are misperceived as having poor or negative self-concepts. Indeed, their circumstances within the school environments create multidimensional, self-concept destructive tendencies. It is apparent that how others view African American learners is based on perception or gut feeling. Even when popular standardized tests are used, the results are based on the composite interpretation of positive or high and negative or low without considering the specific areas of strengths and weaknesses of students. Ironically, some of these tests have even failed to define self-concept, the construct that they purport to measure. Eight questions deserve some attention:

1. Can African American learners with special problems accurately know who they are when their school programs are loaded with illusory generalizations?

2. Can African American learners value themselves for who they are when they consistently hear how inferior their race is?

3. Can African American learners expend efforts to achieve goals when their efforts are frequently devalued?

4. Can the devaluation of the self (e.g., individual values) affect how African American learners accurately or inaccurately define their self-knowledge, self-esteem, and self-ideal?

5. Can making African American families powerless influence how their children accurately or inaccurately define their self-knowledge, self-esteem, and self-ideal?

6. Can critical school variables (e.g., "good" or "bad" teacher) influence how African American learners accurately or inaccurately define their self-knowledge, self-esteem, and self-ideal?

7. Can critical community variables (e.g., provision or lack of provision of job opportunities and choices) influence how African American learners accurately or inaccurately define their self-knowledge, self-esteem, and self-ideal?

8. Can critical governmental variables (e.g., laws that foster or do not foster civil rights) influence how African American learners accurately or inaccurately define their self-knowledge, self-esteem, and self-ideal?

USING THE CSM TO SELF-EMPOWER AFRICAN AMERICAN LEARNERS WITH SPECIAL PROBLEMS

The critical questions identified above confirm that individual students, their families, their schools, and their communities can affect how they accurately or inaccurately define their personal characteristics, self-valuations, and self-responsibility. To effectively empower African American learners with special problems, the entities in the CSM (e.g., student's self, family, school, community, and government) must work collaboratively.

The Role of the Individual Student

The multidimensional problems that confront African American students with special problems may make it a little far-fetched to involve them in their self-empowerment. In reality, they must be involved in their self-empowerment and self-survival. For instance, growing up in poverty or in a single-parent home may not be an excuse for not realizing one's full potential. African American students must be taught to be resilient, self-determined, and to have a well-defined sense of self. According to Brown, Caston, and Benard (2001), children who are resilient, self-determined, and have a strong sense of self strive to rise above the darkness of life's injustice to the light of life's joys. Through their efforts and characters, these children ultimately define themselves and determine their own destiny (Osborne, 1996; Stipek, 2002).

There have been several cases where African American students with special problems have risen above unfortunate life circumstances to become successful, contributing adults within the society. Consider Case One (Box 10.1).

BOX 10.1 CASE ONE

Paula is an African American young lady who was born in a small rural town in Mississippi. Most of the residents in this town earned a living by picking cotton or peas. There was no running water or indoor plumbing. As she went to school, she often wore the same tattered clothing three times a week. Because of her background, she was labeled as having a learning disability (LD). Her mother was the proud single parent of six children. At 36 years of age, her mother had difficulty meeting the basic needs of her children even while receiving government assistance. Paula would often reflect on how hard a time her mother had rearing her and her siblings. In spite of her academic problems, she started to focus her attention on becoming a lawyer. After many years of study, she accomplished her goal by graduating from one of the best law schools. She is currently practicing law with a major law firm in Memphis, Tennessee.

Case One reveals the power of the self to survive. The conditions and circumstances in which Paula was reared are very similar to how many African American children are being reared today. However, this case illustrates how she was self-determined to change her destiny from that of her mother. Despite her home and school situations, she was resilient. She did not allow those circumstances to determine her fate but used those circumstances as fuel to burn her internal desire to reach her goal and to maximize her potential (Stipek, 2002). In this case, Paula exhibited confidence in her abilities and took steps toward achieving her goal. She did not allow the learning-disabled (LD) label to cloud her view of what she wanted and knew she could become. She did not view poverty as a never-ending cycle but as a state of mind. Although, in the materialistic sense, Paula was poor, her mind was rich with knowledge of self, and her heart was filled with the desire and self-determination to succeed. This is the type of resiliency that schools, parents, and communities must develop in African American learners with special problems.

The Role of the Family

The family plays a unique role in influencing future decisions of their children. Field and Hoffman (1999) confirmed that many children are growing up in substandard living conditions, single-parent homes with limited family resources, and within families operating in the uninvolved parent style. According to Kerka (2000), family functioning and parent-child relationships have greater influence in career development than family structure or parents' educational and occupational status. In addition to family functioning, another major influence is parenting style. The manner in which African American parents rear their children can heavily persuade future decisions their children will make. Kerka described parenting styles as broad patterns of child-rearing practices, values, and behaviors. For families to increase the likelihood of children maximizing their full potential while positively contributing to society as a whole, greater parent-child relationships must be formed. In addition to the need for stronger parent-child relationships, African American families must become more functional.

In their study, Way and Rossman (1996) found that students identified proactive family interactions as engines behind their successful career choices. As Kerka (2000) noted, proactive

---

BOX 10.2   CASE TWO

James is an African American student who was consistently punished by his teacher for one reason or another. He was categorized as having behavior problems. James's parents were poor financially, but they were rich in spirit. They attended parent-teacher organization meetings and made sure they knew what their son was doing in school. Because of the parents' involvement in school, the teachers began to understand that they could not treat James any way they wanted. Before long, James's behaviors began to improve, and he began to be empowered to succeed in his education. He started to perform very well in school and was put in the classroom for students with gifts and talents.

---

families (a) are well-organized, cohesive, and expressive; (b) are extroverted and manage conflict positively; (c) seek out ways to grow; (d) are sociable; (e) make decisions through the democratic process; (f) encourage individual development; and (g) are emotionally engaged. These descriptors are invaluable in helping to develop the self in African American children and helping families to become stronger by becoming more functional. Hence, the role of the African American family in helping their children develop themselves is very important. Consider Case Two (Box 10.2).

Case Two exposes the role that African American parents and guardians can play in empowering their children. James was consistently punished and categorized as having behavior problems. However, the involvement of his parents prevented further destruction of his ability to succeed in school. When parents get empowered, their children get similarly empowered in school programs.

The Role of the School

Each morning, millions of students across the nation enter school walls. These students come from different cultural, racial, and socioeconomic backgrounds. Along with differences in backgrounds are variances in self-interpretations, self-perceptions, and self-views embedded within particular cultures. For example, the concept of self is viewed differently among ethnic groups. To Anglo Americans who make up the majority of those in the teaching force, the concept of self means being independent, while to African Americans, the self is viewed as being interdependent and connected within a social context (Katz, 1993). The recognition of African American students' differences by general and special educators is critical in providing them the necessary skills to maximize their potential (Obiakor, 1994, 1996b, 1999, 2001).

While African American students' motivation may be cultivated at home, one of the most effective avenues for engendering their motivation is a school's environment (Renchler, 1992). The school can increase their motivation by implementing policies that promote (a) goal setting and self-regulation, (b) student choices, (c) student achievements, (d) teamwork and cooperative learning, and (e) self-assessment models rather than social comparisons. In addition, general and special education teachers can enhance students' intrinsic motivation by allowing them to feel in control of their own learning (Dev, 1997). Unfortunately, not all schools implement policies that promote the self. Especially in schools that are located within large urban school districts, there are several factors that impact on African American students' ability to reach their potential. General and special education teachers often form perceptions and judgments about students based on their race, data found in personal records, and the environments where they live. For example, An Anglo American student from an affluent area of town may be perceived as being smart and well-behaved, while an African American student who may come from the poorest area of town may be viewed as not being smart with behavior problems (Obiakor, 2001).

In my other works (Obiakor, 1992, 1994, 1999), I have noted that the aforementioned problems have contributed greatly to unwarranted generalizations, miscategorization, and stereotypical tendencies prevalent in schools and communities. Such perceptions put unnecessary burdens on how African American students view their abilities and self-concepts. Tauber (1998) noted that teachers form expectations and assign labels to students based on their body build, gender, race, ethnicity, name, attractiveness, dialect, and socioeconomic level. A teacher who perceives the student as being smart will expect more work from the child. On the other hand, a teacher who perceives the student as not being smart will expect less from the child. Students who are perceived to be low in ability are rarely given opportunities to learn new materials—they are called on in class less, get little praise, and are provided less informative feedback (Obiakor, 2001). Embedded in such perceptions is the notion that poor students cannot do well in school because they lack the ability. Such beliefs are absorbed within students and contribute to the inaccurate self-knowledge, self-esteem, and self-ideal they form of themselves. While the expectations of teachers are critical, researchers (e.g., Brophy, 1998; Obiakor et al., 2002) have found that teacher expectations usually lead to self-fulfilling tendencies. Thus, teachers are encouraged to assess their own attitudes, beliefs, and expectations as they work with African American learners with special problems.

In today's general and special education programs, poor performance is often attributed to lack of ability and viewed as being irreversible no matter how much effort a person puts forth. Therefore many African American students begin to develop what Brophy (1998) called the "failure syndrome." He contended that students who exhibit failure syndrome tend to approach tasks with low expectations for success and give up when there are early signs of difficulty. However, such behaviors can be reversed and success can be achieved. Consider Case Three (Box 10.3).

Case Three demonstrates that general and special educators can play magical roles in empowering their African American students. Trina grew up "poor" and lived in the projects. Her mother abused drugs, but she never gave up. Additionally, her teachers never gave up on her. They supported and empowered her and she later graduated with honors. What, then, prevents other educational practitioners from behaving like Trina's teacher?

The Role of the Community

Like the family, the community plays a key role in developing the "self." The community may house a wealth of resources that African American learners with special problems can access for academic and social development. In addition to accessing community resources, individuals must take advantage of the many learning opportunities that are available within the community (i.e., library, museum, schools, jobs, and entrepreneurial offers). African American communities are frequently viewed negatively by those who reside in them and outsiders who are ignorant of what happens in them. For instance, in neighborhoods where crime, drugs, prostitution, and unemployment are commonplace, the community may not be viewed as a place of hope for many of its residents or outsiders. However, the desperate conditions that may be

---

BOX 10.3 CASE THREE

Trina is an African American who was born in a housing project in Chicago. She lived in a small, one-bedroom apartment with mother and her three younger siblings. Her mother, who was addicted to drugs, worked at a local McDonald's. The money she earned usually went to support her habit, thereby leaving very little money to buy food and other basic necessities for her children. To help support the family, Trina was forced to get a job. As a result, her grades began to falter—she began to perform poorly in school. Trina's teacher refused to refer her for special education even though some learning and behavioral problems were manifesting themselves—in fact, she continued to support and empower her. Trina graduated with honors, was admitted into college, and was later accepted into medical school in Nashville, Tennessee. Today, she is a medical doctor.

---

present within a particular community should not be used as an excuse for not assisting individual students to maximize their potential. Consider Case Four (Box 10.4).

Case Four demonstrates how communities can empower their members. Facilities such as churches, libraries, and centers can be very helpful to African American at-risk learners. For John, he had excellent support bases and people who believed in him in the community. He participated in community self-empowerment programs that were culturally relevant to him. Surprisingly, many skeptics view financial support for community programs as unnecessary financial waste rather than as future investment.

It is apparent that the community can be a great resource to assist individuals to develop themselves. However, it is also apparent that the community can act as an unwilling agent to destroy the self. Hindrance of access to resources within the community through racist practices seeks to destroy individual self-concept and self-development of African American learners. For instance, police brutality, racial profiling, the disproportionate incarceration of African American males, and the disproportionate representation of African Americans in special education programs can affect accurate or inaccurate self-confidence and self-esteem. In addition, the massive amount of negative advertisement in various media surrounding the less fortunate paints false perceptions in the minds of many Americans. Such negative perceptions turn into attitudes, acts, or practices that seek to destroy the self—these acts and practices may manifest themselves in schools in the forms of low teacher expectations, labeling, and miscategorization (Obiakor, 1994, 1996b, 1999, 2001; Osborne, 1996). The communities' negative perceptions concerning the race and class of people is a reality—many cultures, particularly African American, continue to receive unwarranted criticisms about their state of being in society. However, the negative perceptions of others must not become the perceptions individuals have of themselves. To overcome these barriers, African Americans must develop a strong sense of self and resiliency to injustices they confront. Additionally, they must develop necessary knowledge, skills, and higher expectation to fight the battle and win the war in a community that cares.

One of the most effective ways in which community establishments can assist African American students in becoming more community-minded while helping them develop a sense of self-confidence and pride is by providing them with service learning opportunities (Brown, 1998). Service learning is a work-based learning experience through which students learn, develop, and apply academic and vocational skills to address the real-life needs of their local

---

BOX 10.4 CASE FOUR

John is an African American student who attended an urban school. He was placed in a special education program because of his learning problems. This urban city had facilities like the Boys & Girls Clubs of America and the Urban League, and wonderful libraries. The Urban League facility had a great collection of books. It also had workers who helped at-risk learners with their homework, including John. John began to do well in school. Today, he is a lawyer and very involved in community development programs.

---

communities. During the 1990s, many school districts implemented school-to-work programs in an effort to link what was being taught in the classroom to real-world situations. However, service learning differs from school-to-work programs. While school-to-work programs are more focused on school-based learning and learning about work-related issues, service learning is work-based and actively engages students in the process. However, school-to-work and service learning are both initiatives designed to connect students to their community and give them opportunities to apply learned skills in real-life settings while helping them develop the attitudes, values, and behaviors that will lead them to become contributing members of society.

The Role of the Government

The landmark Supreme Court case of *Plessy v. Ferguson* (1896) mandated that races could be separated as long as facilities for each group were commensurate. This era, known by many as the Jim Crow era, blatantly disregarded the law because institutions were separate but unequal. With a legitimized form of racist exclusionary policies, schools engaged in similar policies that denigrated African Americans. *Plessy v. Ferguson* was ruled unconstitutional with the *Brown v. Board of Education of Topeka* (1954) decision that led the initiative to desegregate public schools. Although schools were being desegregated, it was evident that children from multicultural backgrounds, including African American students with special problems, were being systematically removed from the regular classroom. Through important legislative mandates, for example, the Education for All Handicapped Children Act (1975) and the reauthorization of the 1990 Individuals With Disabilities Education Act (IDEA; 1997), the government attempted to enhance possibilities for a free and appropriate education for all students, including African Americans. Unfortunately, the spirits of these laws have been sometimes missed, and as a consequence, savage inequalities continue to exist in many general and special education programs for African American learners (Kozol, 1991). In addition, even though many of these government laws have guaranteed school funding at local, state, and federal levels, inadequate funding continues to be problematic for African Americans in school programs.

It is essential to note that government initiatives, such as Goals 2000: Educate America Act (1994), have allowed school districts to receive resources at local and state levels to help implement divergent educational programs for all students, including African Americans. In addition, governments have funded and awarded grants to various institutions of higher learning and community organizations that aspire to design innovative programs geared toward bridging educational, economic, and social gaps between people. For instance, institutions such as charter, voucher, and choice schools have been supported at some levels to create opportunities for

---

BOX 10.5 CASE FIVE

Mary is an African American student in a sixth-grade urban school. Her mother rarely participated in her school programs. Coupled with her home circumstances, she had minor learning problems. Before long, she was tested and placed in a special education program like other African American learners in her school district. The government began to probe why many African American learners were disproportionately placed in such programs. As a consequence, Mary was retested and was found to belong in the regular classroom.

African American students. Even with these supposed changes, rarely do government agencies monitor how their policies are put into practice. The important question is, does the government care about how its policies affect self-valuation and self-empowerment of African American learners with special problems? The popular governmental slogan today is, "No child should be left behind." How can no child be left behind when African American learners are discriminately assessed, prejudicially categorized, disproportionately placed, and poorly instructed by disempowering teachers and professionals who are culturally disconnected from them?

In reality, governments can enhance how institutions (e.g., schools) comply with rules and regulations that buttress civil rights of African American families and their children. Consider Case Five (Box 10.5).

Case Five reveals how a minor government probe can result in something good for African American learners. There were similar situations many years ago in California, for example, *Diana v. State Board of California* (1970) and *Larry P. v. Wilson Riles* (1979 & 1986) when tests were used to misidentify, misassess, miscategorize, misplace, and further misinstruct African American and other culturally diverse learners. While race-based governmental remedies might be unpopular, they can be used to empower people of different races and enhance equality of all citizens.

CONCLUSION

Key Points to Remember

Based on the aforementioned details, following are 10 key points to remember:

1. To be self-empowered, African American students must know who they are, love themselves for who they are, and be able to expend efforts to achieve their goals.

2. Although some general and special educators form negative perceptions of African American students, the perceptions that these students have of themselves also affect their learning.

3. Misidentification, misassessment, miscategorization, misplacement, and misassessment force African American learners with special problems to have inaccurate self-concepts of themselves.

4. Rather than focus on positive or high and negative or low self-concept, the focus should be on the accuracy or inaccuracy of self-concept. We need to know the real strengths or weaknesses of African American learners.

5. Expectations of general and special educators affect how African Americans empower themselves in school programs.

6. Poverty does not in any way mean poor zest to succeed in school or in life. In other words, poverty is a myth that can be made real when teachers misuse it to victimize African American learners with special problems.

7. African American students who are resilient exhibit the social competence to form relationships, the metacognition to solve problems, the autonomy to develop a sense of identity, and sense of purpose to plan and hope for the future.

8. When African Americans self-empower themselves, they maximize their fullest potential.

9. Learning environments that respect students' human or civil rights as instituted by the government can empower African Americans to maximize their potential in general and special education settings.

10. Communities that provide after-school resources help to empower African American learners with special problems.

Final Comments

In this chapter, I have focused my attention on how self-empowerment can be developed in African American learners with special problems. The student, school, family, community, and government are critical elements that positively or negatively influence the development of the self. Fostering development of the African American child requires school, family, community, and government collaboration; and creating a healthy and democratic educational community is crucial to the development of self. In fact, the self is the foundation on which the student's development is facilitated. The important step is for African American learners with special problems to believe in themselves as they develop the ability to achieve in the face of adversities. Poverty, poor living conditions, drug-infested neighborhoods, single-parent homes, racism, negative expectations, and prejudicial conclusions are endemic societal problems that deserve our attention. While it has been acknowledged that many of us do not have boots and straps, it has also been acknowledged that most successful people are those who pulled themselves up by their own bootstraps. I strongly believe a strong sense of self is a powerful tool that directly influences the ability of African American learners to succeed not just in school but also in life.

Since the self is dynamic, we must develop success-oriented behaviors in African American learners with special problems. From my perspective, our mission in general and special education must be clear. To be professionally responsible, we must use multidimensional methods to (a) address individual differences, (b) make expectations realistic, and (c) develop self-empowerment in our students. Clearly, we must treat African American students with special problems as we treat other students, yet we must understand that they come to school programs with unique strengths and weaknesses. As we prepare them for life, we must avoid unwarranted labels, derogatory categories, and illusory generalizations that tend to disempower them. I believe self-empowerment is not genetically predetermined. As a consequence, we must make sure that how African American students view themselves is empowering. In addition, we must make sure that their interactions with their families, schools, communities, and government agencies are empowering. In the words of Kleinke (1994),

> A person's self-image is certainly affected by past experience, and it may be of value to explore the process of how one has developed into her or his present self. What is more important, however, is to realize that one's self is not fixed and immutable. First, we have a variety of possible selves we can choose to emphasize to fit particular situations. Second, we are not bound to our perceptions of who we are in the present. The future offers the opportunity for our selves to evolve in whatever direction we choose to follow. (pp. 259-260)

Discussion Issues

1. In your own words, define self-empowerment.

2. Briefly explain how misidentification, misassessment, miscategorization, and misplacement can influence self-empowerment of African American learners with special problems.

3. Describe the roles that schools play in empowering or disempowering African American learners.

4. Evaluate how communities can force African American learners to misinterpret their capabilities or incapabilities.

5. Discuss four ways to develop self-empowerment in African American learners with special problems.

REFERENCES

Brophy, J. (1998, May). Failure syndrome students. *Elementary and Childhood Education*, pp. 1-3.

Brown, B. L. (1998). Service learning: More than community service. *Career Education, 198*, 1-4.

Brown, J. H., Caston, M. D., & Benard, B. (2001). *Resilience education*. Thousand Oaks, CA: Corwin.

Brown v. Board of Education of Topeka, 347 U.S. 483 (1954).

Dev, P. C. (1997). Intrinsic motivation and academic achievement. *Remedial and Special Education, 18*, 12-20.

Diana v. California State Board of Education (1970). No. C-70, RFT, Dist. Ct. No. Cal.

Education for All Handicapped Children Act (1975), Pub. L. No. 94-142, 20 U.S.C. § 1401 *et seq.*

Field, S., & Hoffman, A. (1999). The importance of family involvement for promoting self-determination in adolescence with autism and other developmental disabilities. *Focus on Autism and Other Developmental Disabilities, 14*, 36-42.

Goals 2000: Educate America Act (1994), Pub. L. No. 103-227. Retrieved February 26, 2002, from www.ed.gov/legislation/GOALS2000/TheAct/

Individuals With Disabilities Education Act Amendments (1997), Pub. L. No. 101-476, 20 U.S.C. § 1400.

Jones, L. (1997). Our America. In L. Jones, L. Newman, & D. Isey (Eds.), *Our America: Life and death on the south side of Chicago* (pp. 199-200). New York: Scribner.

Katz, L. G. (1993, August). Self-esteem and narcissism: Implications for practice. *Elementary and Childhood Education*, pp. 1-4.

Kerka, S. (2000). Parenting and career development. *Career Education, 214*, 1-5.

Kleinke, C. L. (1994). *Common principles of psychotherapy*. Pacific Grove, CA: Brooks/Cole.

Kozol, J. (1991). *Savage inequalities: Children in American schools*. New York: Crown.

Larry P. v. Wilson Riles (1979 & 1986). C-71-2270 FRP. Dist. Ct.

Obiakor, F. E. (1992). Self-concept of African American students: An operational model for special education. *Exceptional Children, 59*, 160-167.

Obiakor, F. E. (1994). *The eight-step multicultural approach: Learning and teaching with a smile*. Dubuque, IA: Kendall/Hunt.

Obiakor, F. E. (1996a). Collaboration, consultation, and cooperation: The "whole village" at work. In N. Gregg, R. S. Curtis, & S. F. Schmidt (Eds.), *African American adolescents and adults with learning disabilities: An overview of assessment issues* (pp. 77-91). Athens: University of Georgia, Roosevelt Warm Springs for Rehabilitation Learning Disabilities Research and Training Center.

Obiakor, F. E. (1996b). Self-concept: Assessment and intervention for African American learners with problems. In N. Gregg, R. S. Curtis, & S. F. Schmidt (Eds.), *African American adolescents and adults with learning disabilities: An overview of assessment issues* (pp. 15-29). Athens: The University of Georgia, Roosevelt Warm Springs for Rehabilitation Learning Disabilities Research and Training Center.

Obiakor, F. E. (1999). Teacher expectations of minority exceptional learners: Impact on "accuracy" of self-concepts. *Exceptional Children, 66*, 39-53.

Obiakor, F. E. (2001). *It even happens in "good" schools: Responding to diversity in today's classrooms*. Thousand Oaks, CA: Corwin.

Obiakor, F. E., Algozzine, B., Thurlow, M., Gwalla-Ogisi, N., Enwefa, S., Enwefa, R., & McIntosh, A. (2002). *Addressing the issue of disproportionate representation: Identification and assessment of culturally diverse students with emotional or behavioral disorders*. Arlington, VA: Council on Children with Behavioral Disorders, Council for Exceptional Children.

Osborne, R. E. (1996). *Self: An eclectic approach*. Boston: Allyn & Bacon.

Plessy v. Ferguson, 163 U.S. 537 (1896).

Renchler, R. (1992). School leadership and student motivation. *Educational Management, 71*, 1-5.

Stipek, D. (2002). *Motivation to learn: Integrating theory and practice* (4th ed.). Boston: Allyn & Bacon.

Tauber, R. T. (1998, December). Good or bad, what teachers expect from students they generally get! *Teacher Education*, pp. 1-4.

Way, W., & Rossman, M. (1996). *Learning to work: How parents nurture the transition from school to work*. Berkeley, CA: National Center for Research in Vocational Education.

Part III

Complementing the School Environment

Chapter Eleven

Service Delivery for African American Young Children With Special Needs

Regina L. Enwefa and Stephen C. Enwefa

There have been many expectations and demands placed on our children in schools that are congruent with traditions, behaviors, and values of the middle-class mainstream society. Hence, schools in the United States are designed to prepare middle-class children to participate in their own cultures (Saville-Troike, 1979). The curricula and instructional approaches in schools are organized so that the academic skills that the middle class has learned at home are reinforced and practiced. Thus many middle-class children have significant school-comparable experiences prior to entrance (Heath, 1982). Interestingly, the African American culture often has been viewed by educational institutions as inferior and interfering with the intellectual and emotional development of children of mainstream U.S. culture. Similarly, educational practices based on the assimilationist melting pot philosophy require uniformity that disregards cultural and linguistic differences of African American learners. Instead of reinforcing and using children's diverse cultures and languages, most practices in today's schools seem to either ignore or eradicate real differences that are strengths of students.

Barriers to the provision of quality educational services to young children from the African American culture include ethnocentric attitudes of professionals, low expectations, and negative attitudes toward African American students, their families, and communities; lack of professional training regarding cultural and linguistic diversity; test bias and misdiagnosis; monocultural educational materials and curricula; inadequate and inappropriate instructional techniques; and different disciplinary and reward systems (Campbell, 1986, 1993, 1994; Campbell, Brennan, & Steckol, 1992; Campbell & Taylor, 1992; Ford, 1992; Gay, 1989, 1993; Menyuk & Menyuk, 1988; Ogbu, 1982).

Several scholars (e.g., Cole, 1989; Crowe, 1997; Gollnick & Chinn, 1998; Lynch & Hanson, 1992) have discussed the changing demographics of the United States. They all contend that this country is no longer a melting pot where people come from other countries and blend with everyone; ironically, many cultures work hard to maintain their individual identities. The U.S. Department of Census reported in 1990 that 61 million of the 248 million people in the United States were from culturally and linguistically diverse backgrounds. Thirty-two million Americans spoke one of many languages other than English. Over 6 million school-age children speak a language other than English at home (Hernandez, 1997). In addition, these children come from a variety of family situations, income strata, and cultural backgrounds. It is reasonable to assume that differences in enrollment rates in early childhood special education across levels of poverty indicate different access to this level of education. For example, in 1995, young children from families who were classified as poor were less likely to be enrolled in an early childhood special education program than children from families who were classified as nonpoor (Hernandez, 1997). Children from single-parent families seem more likely to experience early school problems and are less likely to participate in early literacy activities than children in two-parent families (Gollnick & Chinn, 1998).

The definition of family has changed greatly over the last few decades. Today, children live in a variety of family structures associated with different educational outcomes. The effects of family structures are likely to be affected by family income, parents' education level, race and ethnicity, and the amount of time that parents participate in their children's education. Apparently, quality childcare is vital to breaking the cycle of poverty that traps many African American families. The quality of learning experience for children later enhances school success and lowers the high school dropout rate. Reinforcing early educational development diminishes educational failures for children. The focus of this chapter is on service delivery for African American young children with special needs.

EARLY INTERVENTION: WHERE WE ARE

Early intervention or service delivery historically has included children and their families who demonstrate a diversity of strengths and needs. These needs encompass a broad range of developmental, ecological, and health-related issues, resulting in an array of services delivered by a number of professionals from various disciplines (Harry, 1995). Within early intervention are a number of phases in the service delivery process in which teams must function. The teams play a very important role in the early intervention process with the child and family. Major issues in this process include collaboration, professional identity, function and intervention targets, and evaluation of effectiveness. Although these are not new issues, since the 1980s new twists have arisen as practices have become refined (e.g., DEC Task Force on Recommended Practices, 1993).

As stated earlier, children in the United States come from a variety of family situations, income, and cultural backgrounds. As a result, our nation's schools are faced with unique challenges as they strive to provide equal educational opportunities to all students. Factors such as family income, family structure, and educational level of parents have been shown to influence a child's educational opportunities. Of the 4 million babies born annually, nearly 1 out of 8 is born to a teenage mother, 1 out of 4 to a mother with less than a high school education, almost 1 out of 3 to a mother who lives in poverty, and 1 out of 4 to an unmarried mother (Lynch & Hanson, 1996). These conditions have been shown to be associated with children experiencing problems such as repeating a grade, requiring special education services, being suspended, and dropping out of school.

Students from racial and ethnic minority backgrounds and low-income families are more at risk for poor school outcomes and are becoming an increasing part of the student population. Since the mid-1960s, studies have linked the educational disadvantage of minority students to a combination of out-of-school factors, many of which center on family characteristics, such as poverty and the education of parents.

As mentioned above, social background factors such as race and ethnicity, income, limited English proficiency, educational background, and the structure of the family can be associated with many levels of educational access and different educational outcomes. For example, differences in preprimary enrollment, incidence of early childhood academic and behavioral problems, level of student achievement, and the likelihood of dropping out of school or going on to college are affiliated with various social background factors. In addition, poverty is negatively associated with enrollment in early childhood special education. As also mentioned earlier, differences in enrollment rates in early childhood special education across levels of poverty may indicate different access to education. For example, in 1995, 3- and 5-year-olds from families who were classified as poor were less likely to be enrolled in early childhood special education than 3- and 4-year olds from families who were classified as nonpoor (see Lynch & Hanson, 1996).

TEACHERS AND PROFESSIONALS WORKING IN EARLY CHILDHOOD SPECIAL EDUCATION PROGRAMS

Lynch and Hanson (1996) noted that individuals who work in early childhood special education programs are not as diverse as those they serve. Moreover, many early childhood special education professionals have little preparation for working with families from a wide range of cultures and linguistic backgrounds. In many cases, educators and other service providers' lack of experience with, and knowledge of, diverse families makes the development of relationships with them difficult and may contribute to families' underuse of services. These problems are particularly devastating to African American learners with exceptionalities.

Teachers facing the challenge of teaching children from different cultural communities are hard-pressed to decide what constitutes an appropriate curriculum. The cultural diversity of African American learners makes it hard for teachers to assess each learner's developmental status, find common education experiences to promote growth, and measure the achievement of educational objectives. Before children come to school, they have all learned many of the same things. As professionals, we must be cognizant of what we do with children. Teachers must have in place a variety of strategies and techniques when working with African American learners.

PROACTIVE STRATEGIES FOR WORKING WITH AFRICAN AMERICAN YOUNG CHILDREN WITH EXCEPTIONALITIES

To maximize the potential of young African American children with exceptionalities, general and special educators should

1. *Develop a personalized rapport with families.* Families are more likely to develop effective working relationships with professionals they trust (Dinnebeil & Rule, 1994). Gonzalez-Alvarez (1998) and Schwartz (1995) indicated that some families might prefer a more informal, friendly relationship to a more formal relationship with early childhood special education professionals.

2. *Communicate with families in culturally appropriate ways.* It is critical to maintain open, ongoing communication with families from diverse linguistic backgrounds. This type of communication may be in the form of home program notebooks, oral exchanges, or other modes of communication (Obiakor, 2001).

3. *Recruit staff that view diversity as an asset.* It is important to consider hiring staff members who embrace diversity as an asset and demonstrate a willingness to learn about the experiences and traditions of individuals whose backgrounds are different from their own (Harry, 1995).

4. *Create alliances with cultural guides.* It is important to encourage the participation of community leaders as cultural guides to facilitate communication and understanding between professionals (Obiakor, 2001).

5. *Provide professionals with information about community beliefs, values, communication style, and events.* The more the professionals know about students' parents and communities, the more people collaborate, consult, and cooperate (Obiakor, 2001).

6. *Provide ongoing evaluation for young children.* The need for ongoing evaluation of early childhood special education programming is great. Evaluation outcomes can be done through surveys, phone interviews, and questionnaires. Professionals may also consider conducting a needs assessment to identify areas for training and self-evaluation and reflection (Obiakor et al., 2002).

7. *Provide an interpretation of the school's agenda for parents.* School learning occurs when family values reinforce school expectations. Teachers, children, and families must create a shared understanding and new contexts that give meaning to the knowledge and skills being taught. Additionally, teachers should acknowledge the fact that children from different racial and ethnic groups may differ in gestures, actions, and meanings of words (Obiakor, 2001).

8. *Be knowledgeable about formal and informal assessments.* Assessments must be delayed until teachers and other professionals are able to build a set of new meanings for the child. Assessment processes must incorporate materials that reflect the culture of African American children. During these processes, parents must be empowered to advocate for the needs of their families in formal and informal ways (Obiakor et al., 2002).

9. *Seek preservice and inservice education.* Inservice training must incorporate developmentally and culturally appropriate practices as well as social and emotional development of

African American children. Models should be created within your school districts for delivering training to African American early childhood professionals to include the following components: on-site training or training in accessible locations; curriculum designs to meet the cultural and cognitive needs of staff members; and intensive outreach throughout the community. All early childhood special education professionals must be exposed to forms of training that include curriculum design and pedagogical skills that are appropriate for working with African American children.

10. *Create successful learning environments*. Efforts must be made to reduce the amount of overcrowding, provide consistent scheduling, develop group and individual instruction, and encourage children to engage in free exploration (Obiakor, 2001).

A COLLABORATIVE MODEL OF SERVICE DELIVERY FOR AFRICAN AMERICAN YOUNG CHILDREN

Policymakers across the United States are attempting to determine ways to restructure education. Since the number of students with special needs increases as the population increases, their efforts have been geared toward collaborative, consultative, and full inclusive models where the needs of exceptional learners can be met in early childhood special education programs. Over the years, parents and professionals have recognized that the early years are critical to a child's physical, social, emotional, and cognitive development. Furthermore, as mothers of young children are returning to work right after childbirth, greater attention is being paid to promoting the highest quality care for young children.

History has provided evidence of discrimination against minority groups, women, and persons with disabilities. The first public commitment to young children with special needs was Head Start in 1965. The Head Start goal was simply to break the cycle of poverty based on the assumption that the best way to do this is to intervene in the early years. Head Start addressed improvement of health, social and emotional development, self-confidence, and responsibility. Since the establishment of Head Start, there have been more than 11 million children receiving an array of services (day care, medical and dental screenings, nutritious meals, and family support). According to Bailey and McWilliam (1990), there are approximately 1,300 or more Head Start programs serving over 450,000 children. Most of the children are between the ages of 3 and 4 years. Approximately two thirds are children from culturally and linguistically diverse groups, primarily African American and Hispanic (Bailey, Simeonsson, Yoder, & Huntington, 1990). The Handicapped Children's Early Education Assistance Act (1968) created the Handicapped Children's Early Education Program (HCEEP) to establish models for providing early intervention services. At the time, there was no mandate in place for early intervention. By 1991 or 1992, all states were required to demonstrate how they were providing free and appropriate public education to all young children with disabilities. The critical question is, could this goal have been met without the collaborative and consultative efforts of families, schools, communities, and governments?

Major issues in service delivery are collaboration, professional identity, function and intervention targets, and evaluation of effectiveness. Early intervention service delivery historically has included children and families who demonstrate a diversity of strengths and needs. Many in the early intervention discipline have recommended that professionals from discipline-specific developmental areas combine their expertise and collaborate to meet the child and family's needs (Bruder & Bologna, 1993). Collaboration occurs between two individuals as well as between groups of individuals. Earlier, McCollum and Hughes (1988) suggested adopting a team model in which each professional is assigned a role and responsibility. Maddux (1988) defined a team as a group of people whose purpose and function stem from a common philosophy and shared goals. It is imperative for professionals to work in teams in order for the early intervention process to be successful with African American children and their families.

Most of the literature on the use of teams in early intervention has focused on the need to adopt models of collaborative service delivery to ensure effectiveness (Allen, Holm, & Schiefelbusch, 1978; Bruder & Bologna, 1993; Bruder, Lippman, & Bologna, 1994; File & Kontos, 1992; Hanson & Widerstrom, 1993; McCollum & Hughes, 1988; McGonigel, Woodruff, & Rozzman-Millican, 1994). Studies have examined (a) components of team functioning and the level of participation among team members (Bailey, Helsel-DeWert, Thiele, & Ware, 1985; Gilliam & Coleman, 1981); (b) team meeting behaviors in the decision-making process (Bailey, Buysse, Simeonsson, Smoth, & Keyes, 1995; Ysseldyke, Algozzine, & Mitchell, 1982); and (c) training of team members at preservice and inservice levels (Bailey et al., 1990; Courtnage & Smith-Davis, 1987). It is important to understand that teams of professionals are recommended as the preferred service delivery structure within early intervention (Bruder & Bologna, 1993; Garland & Linden, 1994; McGonigel et al., 1994).

Within early intervention, there are many phases in the service delivery process in which teams must function in order to meet the needs of young children and their families. Professionals must consider the culture first before anything else is done in early intervention. They must include language, environment, values, beliefs, religion, and family structure in terms of roles and responsibilities. The child and family assessment should be done both individually and jointly. This part of the teaming function is concerned with the family, household, and community. Early intervention planning teams play a vital role when it comes to the development of the individualized education program (IEP) or individualized family service plan (IFSP). Regardless of the function of the team, professionals must adopt a process that aides in accomplishing goals for service delivery in early intervention of African American young children. Within early intervention, teams have functioned traditionally in multidisciplinary, interdisciplinary, and transdisciplinary fashions (McCollum & Hughes, 1988). These teams do differ both in description and function. In a multidisciplinary team, the professionals represent their own discipline and provide isolated services for assessment and intervention. In an interdisciplinary team, all of the professionals provide discipline-specific assessments and interventions—members of the team must provide their own plan of intervention. The transdisciplinary team approach integrates disciplines into a team—this approach has been recognized as ideal for design and delivery of services for young children with disabilities (Garland & Linden, 1994; Hanson & Hanline, 1989; McGonigel et al., 1994).

Enwefa and Enwefa (2001) articulated a continuum of service delivery models that should be used by all professionals. These models range from pull-out to integrated service delivery. Knowledge about the ways in which integrated programs can meet the needs of children and parents for high quality early childhood education has grown significantly. The active involvement of parents, regular and special education teachers, and administrators is now viewed as crucial in developing successful integrated early childhood special programs. Although the number of people on a team varies according to the needs of the child, the parent must always be a member of the team. Most early childhood and regular and special education teachers believe they are able to meet the needs of children in their classes when intervention is supportive of their expertise. New teaching strategies are being developed that meet the individualized needs of children with disabilities in inclusive classes. The task now before early childhood special education programs is to find the best ways to provide education that is respectful of the talents and needs of African American children, parents, and teachers. Appropriate teaching strategies are an important component of a successfully integrated early childhood program. Although a team approach to early childhood special education seems to be effective, caution is warranted. Many training programs for professionals at the undergraduate and graduate levels neglect to prepare students on collaborative teams (Bailey & McWilliam, 1990; Courtnage & Smith-Davis, 1987).

CONCLUSION

In this chapter, we have addressed ways to provide services for African American young children with special needs. The current trend in early childhood special education highlights parental partnerships and family-centered intervention to meet the needs of African American children. Intervention goals, objectives, and techniques for African American children must reflect their needs and their family's interests, priorities, and values. Activities and techniques that are culturally appropriate and compatible with their learning style, preferences, and orientations must be considered. We believe families transmit and shape cultural attitudes, behaviors, and patterns. Effective home-school partnerships are necessary for meeting the needs of the child, family, and school. General and special education professionals must acknowledge differences in social rules and roles as well as verbal and nonverbal communication rules used by children and their families. Surely, these rules affect interpersonal dynamics. Cultures, communication behaviors, norms, values, assumptions, and beliefs are all integral parts of collaboration, consultation, and cooperation.

The involvement of African American families may span a continuum, with information sharing at one end and family training at the other end. Most families want their children to succeed, even though they may not know how to help. Parents are often unaware of the school demands placed on their child. We believe professionals who know how to include families will have an increased likelihood of success. Families can provide interventionists with information that can enhance the service delivery process for their children. It is time we acknowledged that families have a lot to teach early childhood special education professionals about how best to reach their children. Although parents and professionals may have different perspectives, they can work together to create successful learning environments for African American young children with special needs.

REFERENCES

Allen, K., Holm, V., & Schiefelbusch, R. (1978). *Early intervention: A team approach.* Baltimore: University Park Press.

Bailey, D. R., Jr., Buysse, V., Simeonsson, R. J., Smith, T., & Keyes, L. (1995). Individual and team consensus ratings of child functioning. *Developmental Medicine and Child Neurology, 37,* 246-259.

Bailey, D. B., Jr., Helsel-DeWert, M., Thiele, J. E., & Ware, W. (1985). Measuring individual participation on the multidisciplinary team. *American Journal of Mental Deficiency, 88,* 247-254.

Bailey, D. B., & McWilliam, R. A. (1990). Normalizing early intervention. *Topics in Early Childhood Special Education, 10*(2), 33-47.

Bailey, D. B., Jr., Simeonsson, R. J., Yoder, D. E., & Huntington, G. S. (1990). Preparing professionals to serve infants and toddlers with handicaps and their families: An integrative analysis across eight disciplines. *Exceptional Children, 57*(1), 26-34.

Bruder, M. B., & Bologna, T. M. (1993). Collaboration and service coordination for effective early intervention. In W. Brown, S. K. Thurman, & L. Pearl (Eds.), *Family centered early intervention with infants and toddlers: Innovative cross-disciplinary approaches* (pp. 103-128). Baltimore: Paul H. Brooks.

Bruder, M. B., Lippman, C., & Bologna, T. M. (1994). Personnel preparation in early intervention: Building capacity for program expansion within institutions of higher education. *Journal of Early Intervention, 15*(1), 66-79.

Campbell, L. R. (1986). A study of the comparability of master's level training and certification and needs of speech-language pathologists. *Dissertation Abstracts International, 46,* 10B. (University Microfilms No. 85-28, 727)

Campbell, L. R. (1993). Maintaining the integrity of children's home communicative variety: Speakers of Black English vernacular. *American Journal of Speech-Language Pathology, 2*(1), 11-12.

Campbell, L. R. (1994). Discourse diversity and Black English vernacular. In D. N. Ripich & N. A. Creaghead (Eds.), *School discourse problems* (pp. 93-131). San Diego, CA: Singular.

Campbell, L. R., Brennan, D. G., & Steckol, K. F. (1992). Preservice training to meet the needs of people from diverse cultural backgrounds. *ASHA, 34,* 29-32.

Campbell, L. R., & Taylor, O. L. (1992). ASHA certified speech-language pathologists: Perceived competency levels with selected skills. *Howard Journal of Communication, 3*(3&4), 163-176.

Cole, L. (1989). Multicultural imperatives for the 1990s and beyond. *ASHA, 31,* 65-70.

Courtnage, L., & Smith-Davis, J. (1987). Interdisciplinary team training: A national survey of special education teacher training programs. *Exceptional Children, 53*(5), 451-458.

Crowe, T. A. (1997). *Applications of counseling in speech language pathology and audiology.* Baltimore: Williams and Wilkins.

DEC Task Force on Recommended Practices. (1993). *DEC recommended practices: Indicators of quality in programs for infants and young children with special needs and their families.* Pittsburgh, PA: Division for Early Childhood.

Dinnebeil, L. A., & Rule, S. (1994). Variables that influence collaboration between parents and service providers. *Journal of Early Intervention, 18*(4), 349-361.

Enwefa, R., & Enwefa, S. (2001, January). *Team approach as an effective strategy for service delivery in early childhood special education.* Paper presented at the Seventh National African American Student Leadership Conference, Rust College, Holly Springs, MS.

File, N., & Kontos, S. (1992). Indirect service delivery through consultation. Review and implications for early intervention. *Journal of Early Intervention, 16,* 221-233.

Ford, B. A. (1992). Multicultural education training for special educators working with African American youth. *Exceptional Children, 59,* 107-114.

Garland, C. W., & Linden, T. W. (1994). Administrative challenges in early intervention. In L. J. Johnson, R. J. Gallagher, M. J. LaMontagne, J. B. Jordan, P. L. Hutinger, J. J. Gallagher, & M. B. Karnes (Eds.), *Meeting early intervention challenges: Issues from birth to three* (pp. 133-16). Baltimore: Paul H. Brookes.

Gay, G. (1989). Ethnic minorities and educational equality. In J. A. Banks & C. A. McGee Banks (Eds.), *Multicultural education: Issues and perspectives* (2nd ed., pp. 167-194). Boston: Allyn & Bacon.

Gilliam, J. E., & Coleman, M. C. (1981). Who influences IEP committee decisions? *Exceptional Children, 47,* 642-644.

Gollnick, D. M., & Chinn, P. C. (1998), *Multicultural education in a pluralistic society.* Upper Saddle River, NJ: Prentice Hall.

Gonzalez-Alvarez, L. I. (1998). A short course in sensitivity training: Working with Hispanic families of children with disabilities. *Teaching Exceptional Children, 31*(2), 73-77.

Handicapped Children's Early Education Assistance Act (1968). Pub. L. No. 90-538.

Hanson, M. J., & Hanline, M. F. (1989). Integration options for the young child. In R. Gaylord-Ross (Ed.), *Integration strategies for students with handicaps* (pp. 177-194). Baltimore: Paul H. Brookes.

Hanson, M. J., & Widerstrom, A. H. (1993). Consultation and collaboration: Essentials of integration efforts for young children. In C. Peck, S. Odom, & D. Bricker (Eds.), *Integrating young children with disabilities into community programs: Ecological perspectives on research and implementation* (pp. 149-168). Baltimore: Paul H. Brookes.

Heath, S. B. (1982). What no bedtime story means? Narrative skills at home and school. *Language and Society, 11*, 49-76.

Hernandez, H. (1997). *Teaching in multilingual classrooms: A teacher's guide to context, process and content.* Upper Saddle River, NJ: Prentice Hall.

Lynch, E. W., & Hanson, M. J. (1992). Steps in the right direction: Implications for interventionists. In E. W. Lynch & M. J. Hanson (Eds.), *Developing cross-cultural competence: A guide for working with young children and their families* (pp. 355-377). Baltimore: Paul H. Brookes.

Lynch, E. W., & Hanson, M. J. (1996). Ensuring cultural competence. In M. Mclean, D. B. Bailey, Jr., & M. Wolery (Eds.), *Assessing infants and preschoolers with special needs.* Englewood Cliffs, NJ: Prentice Hall.

Maddux, R. B. (1988). *Team building: An exercise in leadership.* Menlo Park, CA: Crisp Publications.

McCollum, J. A., & Hughes, M. (1988). Staffing patterns and team models in infancy programs. In J. Jordan, J. Gallagher, P. Hutinger, & M. Karnes (Eds.), *Early childhood special education: Birth to three* (pp. 129-146). Reston, VA: Council for Exceptional Children.

McGonigel, M. J., Woodruff, G., & Rozzman-Millican, M. (1994). The transdisciplinary team: Team and family issues and recommended practices. *Infants and Young Children, 1*(1), 10-21.

Menyuk, P., & Menyuk, D. (1988). Communicative competence: A historical and cultural perspective. In J. S. Wurzel (Ed.), *Toward multiculturalism: A reader in multicultural education* (pp. 151-161). Yarmouth, ME: Intercultural Press.

Obiakor, F. E. (2001). *It even happens in "good" schools: Responding to cultural diversity in today's classrooms.* Thousand Oaks, CA: Corwin.

Obiakor, F. E., Algozzine, B., Thurlow, M., Gwalla-Ogisi, N., Enwefa, S., Enwefa, R., & McIntosh, A. (2002*). Addressing the issue of disproportionate representation: Identification and assessment of culturally diverse students with emotional or behavioral disorders.* Arlington, VA: Council for Exceptional Children.

Ogbu, J. (1982). Cultural discontinuities and schooling. *Anthropology and Education Quarterly, 13*(4), 390-397.

Saville-Troike, M. (1979). Culture, language, and education. In H. T. Trueba & C. Barnett-Mizrahi (Eds.), *Bilingual multicultural education and the professional: From theory to practice* (pp. 139-148). Rowley, MA: Newberry House.

Schwartz, W. (1995). *A guide to communication with Asian American families: For parents/about parents.* New York: ERIC Clearinghouse on Urban Education. (ERIC Document Reproduction Service No. ED 396 014).

Ysseldyke, J. E., Algozzine, B., & Mitchell, S. (1982). Special education team decision making: An analysis of current practice. *Personnel and Guidance Journal, 60*, 308-313.

Chapter Twelve

African American Families: Equal Partners in General and Special Education

Loretta P. Prater

There is a vicious misconception circulating among educational circles that African American parents do not care about the education of their children! No doubt, we have all heard it more than once. Statements suggesting that African American families have little concern for general and special educational outcomes of their children have been communicated, through the continuously growing grapevine, by educators, politicians, an array of media sources, business owners, and various other individuals, including some African Americans. If this misconception is continuously repeated, there will be a tendency to presume that it is correct.

If one is to believe the rumor, as indicated above, then one must discount the years African American families have struggled to receive parity in educational opportunities. One must dismiss the accounts reporting descendents of African American family members dying for committing the crime of learning to read and write. Despite the oppression of slavery, some 5% of the 400,000 freed African Americans could read and write (Billingsley, 1992). To believe the rumor, one would have to forget about the mothers and grandmothers who scrubbed floors, cooked meals, washed and ironed clothes, took care of infants, and completed other duties as assigned in the households of White families for five dollars or less a day. Many saved this money to help their offspring get an education in the hope of having a better life. If one is to believe such a rumor, one must believe that Woodson's (1933) and Kozol's (1991) accounts of educational situations impacting African Americans in America are fictional, or that institutionalized polices based on separate but equal were justified. Would one dare to suggest that parents of the nine African American students chosen to integrate Central High School in Little Rock, Arkansas, devalued education (Beals, 1994)? Considering the tremendous historical obstacles African American families have had to overcome to educate their children, how could anyone doubt the intensity with which African American parents value education?

No doubt, there is a deep historical and cultural belief in the efficacy of education among African Americans. As Billingsley (1992) acknowledged, African Americans have sought education in every conceivable manner and at every level. This chapter recognizes this commitment by presenting African American families as equal partners in general and special education.

MYTHS AND REALITIES ABOUT AFRICAN AMERICAN FAMILIES AND EDUCATION

In the opinion of some skeptics, African American families are the single entity responsible for the lack of school achievement for their children. Although family background may be a factor, it may only partially explain the level of academic achievement attained (Adams & Singh, 1998). Interestingly, when African American children succeed in school, it is rare that family members are given credit. In those instances, it was because of the wonderful school environment. This seems to be especially true if the school is in a predominately White neighborhood. For example, the program A Better Chance identifies academically talented minority students and supports their enrollment at predominantly White independent preparatory schools. Reports are that 90% of these students go on to college (Griffin, 1999). It is understandable that one would assume that students have opportunities to receive a better education in schools located outside of inner city America. By all standards, such as money spent on buildings, textbooks, and personnel, inner city schools fall short (Ayers & Klonsky, 1994; Kozol, 1991). Thousands of teachers in Illinois failed at least one of the tests required to be certified to teach in Illinois (Associated Press, 2001). Furthermore, it was indicated that teachers with the worst exam records were about five times more likely to teach in low-performing, low-income, high-minority schools than in schools with high income and achievement levels and fewer minority students. The critical question is, if these teachers with low scores are placed in high-minority schools, why should African American families alone be falsely accused for the failure of their children? Admittedly, it is difficult to cite one factor responsible for African American families' designation as the scapegoat for low school achievement among their children, but the influence of the Moynihan report (Harry, Allen, & McLaughlin, 1995) was certainly significant. The report identified the structure of the African American family as a primary culprit.

IMPOSED ASSUMPTIONS ABOUT AFRICAN AMERICAN FAMILIES

Much attention has been specifically focused on African American children and their families because these children seem to be overwhelmingly prevalent among those not succeeding in schools, based on socially acceptable and imposed criteria. African American students are reported to be at a disadvantage in preschool attendance, grade retention, academic achievement, drop-out rates, parental involvement, educational aspirations, labor market outcomes, and adult literacy patterns (U.S. Department of Education, 1994). With a prediction of failure like this, one wonders how any African American child succeeds in school. If the self-fulfilling prophecy applies in this case, African American families are doomed. A logical extension is that if children are African American, they are destined to become members of America's underclass.

As it appears, there is a presumption that people have accurate information about African American families based on what is showcased on television or through other media sources. Although the institution of the family is dynamic, and single females with children represent the fastest growing family form in America (Danziger & Farber, 1990), some scholars have reported statistics specifically related to the structure of African American families. Female-headed households are becoming the norm among African American youth (Bankston & Caldas, 1998; Bianchi, 1995). Many of these single-parent families resulted from teenage pregnancies (Prater, 1995). Earlier, Staples (1994) reported that having a child out of wedlock and failing to marry accounts for 41% of all African American households headed by women. Of importance to this discussion is the fact that correlations have been identified between children living in single-mother families and school outcomes. For example, research has reported that students from one-parent households have significantly lower grades and test scores than do students from two-parent households, and that the percentage of single-mother families in schools is a powerful predictor of levels of school violence and discipline problems (Bankston & Caldas, 1998; Mulkey, Crain, & Harrington, 1992). According to Bankston & Caldas, two thirds of African American students attended segregated schools during the 1990s, and these students go to schools with disruptive, unsafe environments. Furthermore, the majority of these students are from single parent households. Being surrounded by schoolmates from female-headed families had the second largest negative association with the academic achievement of African Americans, greater than the association of academic achievement with individual family structure.

Some scholars (e.g., Acock & Kiecolt, 1989) link negative associations between family and schooling outcomes with being poor. African American families are still noted because they are disproportionately represented among the numbers of those living in poverty in America. A significant number of children from these families are among those labeled at risk (Bright, 1996; Gavin & Greenfield, 1998; Kotlowitz, 1991; Thornburg, Hoffman, & Remeika, 1991). For instance, Kotlowitz estimated that one in three children in the inner city is living in poverty. Bright reiterated that in some neighborhoods in the African American community, as many as 45 percent of preschool-age children live in poverty. Although this number is alarming and is a disgrace in the "land of plenty" and has serious repercussions, one must acknowledge that the majority of African Americans live above the poverty level and that African American families do not constitute the majority of families on public assistance, more commonly referred to as welfare. There is diversity within African American cultures (Dillon, 1994; Townsend & Patton, 2000). Regardless of their economic status, many African Americans believe the broad stroke of racism makes no economic class distinction in regard to educational opportunities. The African American experience includes memories of doors being closed to schooling, even when one had the money to pay tuition.

MYTH OR REALITY OF "BLACK BELT" AND POVERTY

When reviewing the economic status of African American families, one sees some geographical patterns of poverty and schooling worth noting. Kusimo (1999) reported some disturbing findings related to African American residential patterns, poverty, and educational status in the south. In the 1990s, over 90% of rural African Americans lived in the south and continued to suffer high poverty rates and low educational attainment. After *Brown v. Board of Education of Topeka* (1954) abolished laws permitting segregation in 21 states, integration was achieved primarily by closing schools in African American neighborhoods and busing African American students, a practice that some African American parents are now rejecting. Many communities addressed the integration mandate by withdrawing support from public schools and opening private, segregated academies. Other schools accomplished maintaining the segregated status quo by resegregation in the name of ability grouping. They determined that African American and White children were of different abilities and, therefore, would be assigned to different classrooms. As recently as 1998, 53% of African Americans still lived in the South, and 91% of rural African Americans lived there. Most lived in the "black belt" comprising Alabama, Arkansas, Florida, Georgia, Louisiana, Mississippi, North and South Carolina, Tennessee, Texas, and Virginia. When one pairs the high poverty rate in the black belt with the fact that 54% of African Americans aged 25 or older residing there do not have a high school diploma, alarming future implications surface (Kusimo, 1999).

Even if parents are below the poverty line, that is not an indication that they care little about their children's education. Parents with high aspirations for their children may not be able to translate these aspirations into motivation and achievement orientation among their children (Ogbu, 1990). For example, after interviewing 58 mothers and fathers of low-income African American fifth-grade children, Bright (1992) found that these parents cared deeply about their children's education and were intimately involved with their children's school experiences, including attending evening school events. In further research of African American families, Bright (1992) reported that 95% of parents said that learning to read, write, and do arithmetic was very important for their children. Also, a substantial percentage reported the following as important: (a) thinking creatively and trying new activities; (b) getting along well with the teacher and other children in the classroom; (c) getting good grades or excellent report cards; (d) going to college; (e) making a good living as an adult; (f) having a safe learning environment; (g) having before- and after-school care, tutors for homework, and assistance with discipline and disruptive behavior on the school bus; and (h) getting more male teachers as role models. Do these expressions mirror parents who care little about their child's education?

SCHOOLS' VIEW OF CHILDREN OF AFRICAN AMERICAN FAMILIES

In school settings, the children of African American families are overrepresented in special education or remedial programs (Kusimo, 1999; Patton, 1998; Sexton, Lobman, Constans, Snyder, & Ernest, 1997). Is this a coincidence, or is this placement by design? This is the question African American families tend to ask. One might assume that because children are assigned to a special education classroom, they are appropriately placed. This might not necessarily be the situation. It is understandable that African American families may develop a sense of distrust of school officials, considering that their children continue to be overrepresented in programs for mental retardation and serious emotional disturbance and underrepresented in special education programs for children with gifts and talents (Chinn & Hughes, 1987; Oswald, Coutinho, & Best, 1999). According to Harry and Anderson (1994), African American youth may be falsely labeled. This practice of placing African American students in low tracks, even if their scores suggest otherwise, can have a long-lasting and negative impact on self-concept and achievement motivation (Campbell-Whatley & Comer, 2000).

Many educators interpret the behavior of African Americans based on their outsider assumptions (Patton, 1998). School professionals may use the same type of rubric for labeling students. Consider the following experience. I saw a guidance counselor label students in a high school setting where I taught. The school was in a predominately White, upper-middle-class community. Very few minorities were in attendance and, of those who were, most were bused to the school. There was a school enrollment of 1,200, and only approximately 2% were African Americans. In situations where minority students transferred from another school, especially during midyear, this particular guidance counselor would automatically place them in special education classes until their records arrived. After the arrival of the records, if documentation warranted being placed in a regular class, then she would move them. Sometimes weeks passed before the transition occurred. The African American special education teacher confronted her with a complaint regarding this practice and reported it to the principal, although no appreciable change in her behavior was realized. Her assumption was that if the students came from an inner-city school, their level of achievement and performance was probably at the special education classification level. Because of residential patterns in that city in the Southeast, most of the African American transfer students lived in urban neighborhoods and had attended an urban school. The guidance counselor's behavior is a perfect example of Patton's (1998) theory of outsider assumptions. Furthermore, according to the special education teacher, the guidance counselor did not place White students in her special education class while awaiting arrival of their records. Based on her behavior, the guidance counselor appeared to always assume that White students were in regular or accelerated classes prior to their transfer to the school.

On further investigation of the practice of identifying increased numbers of African American students for remedial education, it is apparent that African American male children tended to be among those especially tracked in special education programs (Adams & Singh, 1998; Harry & Anderson, 1994). These are also students most likely to be labeled as troublemakers and to be kicked out of class, or worse, suspended or expelled from school (Horgan, 1995). This overrepresentation of males in these situations has far-reaching and negative consequences for African American families, impacting dynamics of family well-being for years into the future. For example, there are historical and social pressures that produce racial variations in family structures resulting in a predominance of female-headed families among African Americans (Bankston & Caldas, 1998). If males are uneducated or undereducated and unable to secure jobs to adequately support their families, they and their families will likely get caught up in the cycle of poverty. The profile of African American males developed in recent decades is dismal, identifying plights of negative consequences, such as being unemployed, incarcerated, uneducated, an abuser of drugs, or the victim of a homicide before age 30. In fact, African American males have been declared an endangered species (Gibbs, 1988). When this is coupled with a previously established welfare system with rules that punished two-parent families living in poverty, survival may have been the motivator for single-parent households being established in great numbers in African American families. Public assistance was available if single and unavailable if married. In another translation, if the husband is not employed and lives in the household with his family, the children may not eat. If he leaves the household, termed desertion, the children can eat.

Tragically, people occupying business or government positions, who have the authority to make decisions to improve this situation, may believe the accusations that African American men do not love their children, do not want to work, or are all criminals. This is a vicious cycle, especially when these men are not receiving the education required by society for employment in occupations with good salaries. Even for those with a good education, there are reported instances of unfair labor practices resulting in lower salaries for African American men in comparison to their White counterparts. Collectively, all these factors may influence whether or not African American males remain in the homes with their children. This presence is significant to this discussion, because a father residing in the home can have a positive impact on school achievement (Bright, 1996).

THE FAÇADE ON FAMILY INVOLVEMENT

Family involvement is a certainty for parents of children in special education programs. This involvement is mandated. Parents of children in special education programs are legally required to participate in the child's individualized educational plan. However, this involvement of African American parents is usually evident in their signing a consent form rather than in active participation in policy making (Harry et al., 1995). The involvement is formal and one-way communication from school to home (Henderson, Marburger, & Ooms, 1986). These limiting opportunities for involvement can serve to disempower parents to believe that their views have little value, based on subtle and overt messages from professionals. The consequence of these feelings of powerlessness is that parents may allow intimidation to prohibit them from asking important questions on their child's behalf (Prater & Ivarie, 1999). To empower parents and increase their involvement to a level of significance, Harry (1992) proposed that parental involvement should include such roles as advocates and policymakers.

The process of educating children begins before children enter school. The importance of early childhood education has been recognized and addressed. For example, Head Start is one program targeted to this concern. Family participation is a significant component of Head Start. Parental involvement in Head Start makes a significant contribution to children's school adjustment (Gavin & Greenfield, 1998). More precisely, Reynolds (1992) reported that parental involvement was important to the academic success of at-risk minority children.

Later research by Taylor and Machida (1994) cited that parental involvement in early childhood interventions has been associated with increased cognitive and social skills in children. The term parental involvement has been applied rather loosely. Many African American children do not reside with biological parents. For example, African American children represent about 70% of children placed in long-term, family foster care (Tatara, 1992). This presents a challenge for professionals working in the field. Early interventionists must view each child and family within a framework that encompasses the entire political, social, economic, cultural, and spiritual experience that shapes the identity and behavior of the families and children with whom they work. The one-size-fits-all approach is a gross oversight in the helping profession. It is a manifestation of institutionalized racism that lumps African Americans into one pile and takes no consideration of the individual needs of children and their families (Dillon, 1994). These same considerations must be applied in school settings.

CULTURAL DISCONNECT
BETWEEN PROFESSIONALS
AND AFRICAN AMERICAN FAMILIES

There is an ongoing debate regarding what, if any, is the impact of the cultural and ethnic background of teachers and other school personnel who work primarily with African American schoolchildren. As recently as 1995 to 1996, African American teachers made up only 7.3% of the teaching force in public schools (Kusimo, 1999). Moreover, when exclusively viewing classrooms for instruction of students in special education programs, one finds a continuous decline of African American personnel for years (Sexton et al., 1997). Does this matter? According to King (1993), low-achieving African American students benefit most from relationships with African American teachers. King's view corresponds to that of Delpit (1988), who expressed the significance of a common culture between African American children and their educators. Although decreasing in numbers, there are African American early interventionists working with African American families. What, if any, is the impact of this situation? Sexton and colleagues (1997) reported that Black interventionists had somewhat less favorable perspectives on family-interventionist interactions with African American children and their families. The researchers further surmised that this conclusion could result from the fact that African American professionals shared similar cultural values, beliefs, and preferences with African American families. Cultural empathy may have enabled them to appraise more realistically how accomplished they and their colleagues were in their multicultural practices with African American families.

Society is becoming more diverse, not less diverse. Professionals working in early intervention must embrace differences and respect the unique cultural backgrounds of families with whom they work. Possibly, the cliché "You don't know what you haven't been taught" would apply in this situation. Sexton and colleagues (1997) noted that 75.6% of professionals working in early intervention had never taken a course for credit on multicultural education, and 62.2% had never attended a workshop on the topic. To further stratify the results from a racial perspective, it was found that 80% of Whites and 66.7% of African American interventionists had never taken a multicultural college course and did not receive workshops on this topic. This is definitely a problem, compounded by the fact that there is a lack of administrative support for early intervention practices focused on multicultural concerns (Sexton, et al., 1997). How can these concerns be addressed using preventive measures rather than reactive ones?

Institutions preparing professionals to enter careers focused on early intervention and early childhood education must bear some of the responsibility. For example, there is a serious lack of preparation for future teachers in preservice training regarding multicultural issues. While working in a previous role as a professor in a college of education, I witnessed some problems related to the lack of multicultural education for students planning to be teachers in early childhood classrooms. For example, a White female student expressed to me a fear of going into an urban school setting to do her practice teaching. This student was from an upper-middle-class family and neighborhood. Although she claimed to have never visited any inner-city neighborhoods, she felt certain that she would be robbed, raped, or worse. Ironically, a school located in the inner city is most likely where she would eventually find employment. This same student reported to me later that she was treated very well by students and teachers, and she expressed surprise that she had very positive experiences at the school. Conversely, an African American male shared with me negative practice-teaching experiences he encountered at his placement in an all-White elementary school. He reported that he was walking down the hall toward his classroom, and a female student was at the water fountain and noticed him. When she saw him approaching, she started screaming in fear and running in the opposite direction while shouting, "It's a Black man." He said that he was not treated well and that most of the teachers would not even speak to him. He was the only African American at the school. In all likelihood, he would not be employed in an all-White school within a small all-White community. In fact, upon his graduation, he returned to his hometown and began teaching in the elementary school he attended as a child. This example represents only a brief snapshot of the consequences of avoiding inclusion of instruction on multicultural issues. Interestingly, African American teachers of young children, when compared with their White counterparts, consistently reported a greater need for multicultural education (Rashid, 1990). Teacher preparation institutions must stop pretending that all is well and address this educational deficit in their programs.

In accepting the established assumption that there are two sides to every story, we must consider the position of both educators and parents. What are some varying views expressed by educators that contrast with those of African American parents regarding the status of parental participation? Teachers say that parents are welcome to come to the school and that they are invited to join the school's parent and teacher organization. In addressing this matter, Gavin and Greenfield (1998) reported that teachers' encouragement of parents' involvement in specific activities resulted in a higher level of involvement in these activities, in comparison with teachers using the strategy of general encouragement. For example, if parents are invited to work in a specified booth at the annual school carnival on Saturday afternoon, participation is more likely than if the teacher merely states that the school has an open-door policy for parent participation. Teachers, like everyone else, may tend to avoid situations in which they perceive rejection as the outcome. Sensing negative reactions from parents, there could be instances in which teachers are more passive in seeking parental involvement because they fear an unsuccessful result. Becker and Epstein (1982) explained that teachers who did not prejudge parents were more likely to involve them in school activities. In additional research, Epstein (1986) found that when schools support parental involvement, in addition to merely inviting involvement, parents were more likely to participate and reported a higher level of satisfaction with the school. Support could be evidenced in actions such as providing on-site child care for school events or scheduling activities at times more convenient for working parents. In establishing a support system for parent involvement, Gavin and Greenfield (1998) suggested that school personnel become familiar with the school's community in order to determine those activities more likely to solicit parental involvement.

BEYOND ASSUMPTIONS AND MYTHS: DOING WHAT WORKS FOR AFRICAN AMERICAN FAMILIES

Some general and special educators have discovered the right formula for success in securing school participation of African American parents. One model family and school partnership was reported by Morris (1999). He investigated the pattern of family participation at Fairmont Elementary School in a predominately African American community in St. Louis, Missouri. The student body was 100% African American, and 95% of these students qualified for free or reduced meals. In his opinion, Fairmont's school climate and culture approximated those of segregated African American schools before the *Brown v. Board of Education* (1954) decision, when neighborhood schools were stabilizing forces in the community. Morris (1999) found that Fairmont served this purpose for its students and families. Physical and emotional barriers limiting parental involvement at other schools were not present at Fairmont. Parents lived in the community, could walk conveniently to the school, and felt genuinely welcomed on their arrival. The African American principal and teachers (of which 85% were African American) had a close, personal relationship with parents and students. The percentage of turnover among school faculty and staff was very low. Some of the teachers had been there long enough to have taught more than one generation of family members. In some instances, teachers still lived in the community. Morris described a friendly, affectionate school atmosphere where all seemed to know one another. Parents knew teachers on a personal level and vice versa. Families expressed a belief that school personnel sincerely cared about the education of their children rather than merely being there to earn a paycheck. As one indicator of family interest, attendance at Fairmont's PTA meetings was described as "jam packed," including the presence of parents, grandparents, uncles, and aunts of the students. Fairmont's relationship between school and parents is an illustration of Siddle-Walker's (1996) communal-bonds theory. The success of Fairmont's level of parental involvement is in total opposition to the assumption that one has to have money to be an active participant in the education of one's child.

Some may simply express that it would be "nice" if more African American parents participated in schooling their children. It is more than nice; it is critical to continue to seek and secure involvement and form partnerships with parents, especially since the school occupies only 9% of children's lives (Murphy, 1993). In inquiring as to why the apparent lack of involvement of parents, as defined by school professionals, scholars, and parents alike has identified a complexity of issues. First of all, there is an underlying issue of power that must be explored. African American parents have a lack of ability to mobilize power and resources; this is especially true for the not-so-well educated. These parents have few avenues by which they can challenge curriculum choices, instructional strategies, or course placement decisions (Kusimo, 1999). African American parents reported feelings of isolation, alienation, disengagement, intimidation, and an array of other negative feelings regarding interaction with personnel at their child's school (Harry, 1992). Overwhelmingly, they are treated like second-class citizens, based on what Harry described as a deficit or pathological view of African American families. Predictably, these families responded in much the same way as others would, given the same set of circumstances (i.e., they withdraw). We have long been socialized to seek rewarding, pleasant circumstances and avoid those that punish or cause hurt and pain. Furthermore, whether or not parents attend a noon meeting at school could be a symptom of other problems rather than a signal that they do not care about their child's education. Harry (1992) identified trust, parental apathy, logistical constraints, stressful life circumstances, or parents' disagreement with special education classifications as factors to consider in understanding the level of parental involvement.

Instead of criticism and constant indictments on what they are doing wrong, African American parents need support and encouragement to continue what they are doing right. For example, the fact that many African American families exist within an extended household or family kinship networks should be viewed as a strength and not a weakness (Taylor, Chatters, Tucker, & Lewis, 1990). Schools can best improve the academic achievement of African American children when they work in partnership with parents (Kusimo, 1999). It would be beneficial for schools to use Obiakor's (1994) comprehensive support model, which illustrates strategies of family inclusion for the success of minority students from pre-K through college. Earlier, Harry (1992) suggested that we need qualitative, intervention-oriented research that investigates ways to change the imbalance of power between professionals and African American families with low incomes. More than a decade ago, Delpit (1988) was very explicit in stating the importance of involvement of parents of minority children. According to Delpit, appropriate education for poor children and children of color can only be devised in consultation with adults who share their culture. What group of adults most shares their culture? Obviously, parents are the group of adults who must be allowed to participate fully in the discussion of what kind of instruction is in their children's best interest. Moreover, students gain in personal and academic development if their families are continually involved and emphasize the importance of schooling (Epstein, 1991).

As educational professionals, we must ask why we continue to repeat those behaviors that are not working. As it appears, we continue to exclude families, devalue their suggestions, primarily use the ideas of experts, and value more the opinions of those who have possibly never even met the students. Prater and Tanner (1995) completed a case study report that detailed the tragedy of such practices and the subsequent result of sabotaging parental aspirations and curtailing educational opportunities for youth in special education programs. Relying on the ideas of experts and ignoring the real people, the families, is a mistake (Sexton et al., 1997). Academic achievement is a function of schools, parents, and students operating synchronously and synergistically (Adams & Singh, 1998). This suggestion highlights Prater and Ivarie's (1999) discussion of the family system as it applies to empowering parents and integrating parental involvement into the instructional plans for special education students. In the words of Gavin and Greenfield (1998), we need more research on involvement of African American parents, with issues of cultural sensitivity in mind. I tend to agree completely.

CONCLUSION

Certain themes clearly emerge. Wake up America! We have an educational system that is failing the masses. We are wasting talent by the nondevelopment of potentially great minds, while applying sophisticated-sounding labels to students and their families to justify our actions. When will this injustice end? How far must this country fall behind in order for this madness to be stopped? These are questions that must be addressed. As the demographic population continues to change, there will be fewer and fewer White, middle-class children to be chosen for educational opportunities. The tragedy on September 11, 2001, in New York and Washington highlights the fact that our educational programs must focus on understanding the world's cultures at all levels. This understanding should not be one-sided. All citizens of the world must learn to value other people's cultures whether they are American or foreign. A logical extension is that when working with parents of all cultures, our educational programs must be culturally responsive.

Exclusionary practices communicate to African American parents that they can contribute to the education of their child's schooling only by special invitation from educators and only in limited, carefully selected activities. Educational systems establishing general and special education programs must nurture a web of support for students. Students, parents, educators, employers, lawmakers, and other community entities must be totally focused on an integrated goal of educating all. We use cute slogans such as, "No child will be left behind," but, in actuality, few children are moving forward. My final thought is that we must restructure the school environment for the 21st century. To accomplish this task, ideas significantly embedded in our psyches will need to be challenged. Elements to change could include the school schedule, where schools are physically located, the role of parents, and an instructional methodology that should match learning styles. Decades of research have been completed with outcomes to suggest strategies that will work. There are examples of successful techniques. One only has to examine the variables in schooling students with successful educational outcomes and compare them with variables in miseducating African American children with low incomes to determine what works and what doesn't work. We know what works. An inclusive instructional structure, focused on families as partners rather than enemies, should serve as the model for changing general and special education programs.

REFERENCES

Acock, A. C., & Kiecolt, J. K. (1989). Is it family structure or socioeconomic status? Family structure during adolescence and social adjustment. *Social Forces, 68,* 553-571.

Adams, C. R., & Singh, K. (1998). Direct and indirect effects of school learning variables on the academic achievement of African American 10th graders. *Journal of Negro Education, 67,* 48-66.

Associated Press. (2001, September 7). Chicago Sun-Times report: Thousands of state teachers fail competency tests. [Charleston, IL] *Times-Courier,* p. A3.

Ayers, W., & Klonsky, M. (1994). Navigating a restless sea: The continuing struggle to achieve a decent education for African American youngsters in Chicago. *Journal of Negro Education, 63,* 5-18.

Bankston, C. L., & Caldas, S. J. (1998). Family structure, schoolmates, and racial inequalities in school achievement. *Journal of Marriage and the Family, 60,* 715-723.

Beals, M. P. (1994). *Warriors don't cry: A searing memoir of the battle to integrate Little Rock's Central High.* New York: Pocket Books.

Becker, H., & Epstein, J. (1982). Parent involvement: A survey of teacher practices. *Elementary School Journal, 83,* 86-102.

Bianchi, S. M. (1995). The changing demographic and socioeconomic characteristics of single parent families. *Marriage and Family Review, 20,* 71-97.

Billingsley, A. (1992). *Climbing Jacob's ladder: The enduring legacy of African American families.* New York: Simon & Schuster.

Bright, J. A. (1996). Partners: An urban Black community's perspective on the school and home working together. *New Schools, New Communities, 12,* 32-37.

Brown v. Board of Education of Topeka, 347 U.S. 483 (1954).

Campbell-Whatley, G. D., & Comer, J. P. (2000). Self-concept and African American student achievement: Related issues of ethics, power, and privilege. *Teacher Education and Special Education, 23,* 19-31.

Chinn, P. C., & Hughes, S. (1987). Representation of minority students in special education classes. *Remedial and Special Education, 8,* 41-46.

Danziger, S., & Farber, N. (1990). *Adolescent pregnancy and parenthood.* Ann Arbor, MI: University of Michigan, ERIC Clearinghouse on Counseling and Personnel Services. (ERIC Document Reproduction Service No. ED 315 704).

Delpit, L. D. (1988). The silenced dialogue: Power and pedagogy in educating other people's children. *Harvard Educational Review, 58,* 280-298.

Dillon, D. (1994). Understanding and assessment of intragroup dynamics in family foster care: African American families. *Child Welfare, 73,* 129-139.

Epstein, J. (1986). Parents' reactions to teacher practices of parent involvement. *Elementary School Journal, 86,* 277-294.

Epstein, J. (1991). Effects on student achievement of teachers' practices of parent involvement. In S. Silvern (Ed.), *Literacy through family, community and school interaction* (pp. 24-36). Greenwich, CT: JAI Press.

Gavin, K. M., & Greenfield, D. B. (1998). A comparison of levels of involvement for parents with at-risk African American kindergarten children in classrooms with high versus low teacher encouragement. *Journal of Black Psychology, 24*, 403-417.

Gibbs, J. T. (Ed.). (1988). *Young, black, and male in America: An endangered species.* Dover, MA: Auburn House.

Griffin, J. B. (1999). Human diversity and academic excellence: Learning from experience. *Journal of Negro Education, 68,* 72-79.

Harry, B. (1992). Restructuring the participation of African American parents in special education. *Exceptional Children, 59*, 123-131.

Harry, B., Allen, N., & McLaughlin, M. (1995). Communication versus compliance: African American parents' involvement in special education. *Exceptional Children, 61*, 364-377.

Harry, B., & Anderson, M. (1994). The disproportionate placement of African American males in special education programs: A critique of the process. *Journal of Negro Education, 63,* 602-619.

Henderson, A., Marburger, C., & Ooms, T. (1986). *Beyond the bake sale: An educator's guide to working with parents.* Columbia, MD: National Committee for Citizens in Education. (ERIC Document Reproduction Service No. ED 270 508).

Horgan, D. D. (1995). *Achieving gender equity: Strategies for the classroom.* Boston: Allyn & Bacon.

King, S. (1993). The limited presence of African American teachers. *Review of Educational Research, 63*, 115-149.

Kotlowitz, A. (1991). *There are no children here.* New York: Anchor.

Kozol, J. (1991). *Savage inequalities: Children in America's schools.* New York: Crown.

Kusimo, P. A. (1999). Rural African Americans and education: The legacy of the Brown decision. *ERIC Digest.* Washington, DC: Office of Educational Research and Improvement. (ERIC Document Reproduction Service No. ED 425 050).

Morris, J. E. (1999). A pillar of strength: An African American school's communal bonds with families and community since Brown. *Urban Education, 33,* 584-605.

Mulkey, L. M., Crain, R. L., & Harrington, A. J. (1992). One-parent households and achievement: Economic and behavioral explanations of a small effect. *Sociology of Education, 65,* 48-65.

Murphy, J. (1993). What's in? What's out? American education in the nineties. *Phi Delta Kappan, 74,* 641-646.

Obiakor, F. E. (1994). *The eight-step multicultural approach: Learning and teaching with a smile.* Dubuque, IA: Kendall/Hunt.

Ogbu, J. U. (1990). Minority education in comparative perspective. *Journal of Negro Education, 59,* 45-57.

Oswald, D. P., Coutinho, M., & Best, A. M. (1999). Ethnic representation in special education: The influence of school-related economic and demographic variables. *The Journal of Special Education, 32,* 194-206.

Patton, J. M. (1998). The disproportionate representation of African Americans in special education: Looking behind the curtain for understanding and solutions. *Journal of Special Education, 32,* 25-31.

Prater, L. P. (1995). Never married biological teen mother headed household. In S. M. Hanson, M. C. Heims, D. Julian, & M. Sussman (Eds.), *Single parent families* (pp. 305-323). New York: Haworth.

Prater, L., & Ivarie, J. (1999). Empowering culturally diverse parents in special education programs. In F. E. Obiakor, J. O. Schwenn, & A. F. Rotatori (Eds.), *Advances in special education: Multicultural education for learners with exceptionalities* (pp. 149-166). Stamford, CT: JAI Press.

Prater, L. P., & Tanner, M. P. (1995). Collaboration with families: An imperative for managing problem behaviors. In F. E. Obiakor & B. Algozzine (Eds.), *Managing problem behaviors: Perspectives for general and special educators* (pp. 178-206). Dubuque, IA: Kendall/Hunt.

Rashid, H. M. (1990). Teacher perceptions of the multicultural orientation of their preservice education and current occupational settings. *Educational Research Quarterly, 14,* 2-5.

Reynolds, A. J. (1992). Comparing measures of parental involvement and their effect on academic achievement. *Early Childhood Research Quarterly, 7,* 441-462.

Sexton, D., Lobman, M., Constans, T., Snynder, P., & Ernest, J. (1997). Early interventionists' perspectives of multicultural practices with African American families. *Exceptional Children, 63,* 313-328.

Siddle-Walker, E. V. (1996). *Their highest potential: An African American school community in the segregated south.* Chapel Hill, NC: The University of North Carolina Press.

Staples, R. (1994). Changes in Black family structure: The conflict between family ideology and structural conditions. In R. Staples (Ed.), *The Black family: Essays and studies* (pp. 11-19). Belmont, CA: Wadsworth.

Tatara, T. (1992*). Characteristics of children in substitute and adoptive care based on FY82 through FY88 data.* Washington, DC: American Public Welfare Association.

Taylor, A. R., & Machida, S. (1994). The contribution of parent and peer support to Head Start children's early adjustment. *Early Childhood Research Quarterly, 9,* 387-405.

Taylor, R. J., Chatters, L. M., Tucker, M. B., & Lewis, E. (1990). Developments in research on Black families: A decade review. *Journal of Marriage and the Family, 52,* 993-1014.

Thornburg, K., Hoffman, S., & Remeika, C. (1991). Youth at risk: Society at risk. *Elementary School Journal, 91,* 199-207.

Townsend, B. L., & Patton, J. M. (2000). Reflecting on ethics, power, and privilege. *Teacher Education and Special Education, 23,* 32-33.

U.S. Department of Education. (1994). The condition of education: 1994. Washington, DC: U.S. Government Printing Office.

Woodson, C. G. (1933). *The mis-education of the Negro.* Philadelphia: Hakim.

Chapter Thirteen

African American Community Resources: Essential Education Enhancers for African American Children and Youth

Bridgie Alexis Ford

We read a story about how eagles can fly even when they are raised by chickens. I learned that I don't have to be afraid to be who I am; I can do math and I get to learn more about math in this program.

—Response of a fourth-grade, African American girl about what she learned in a Saturday program sponsored by a nonprofit African American community organization.

I work full-time, and there are some things I can't do. I want him to succeed in school, go to college. This program can reinforce him, help him meet other goal-oriented children, help him to stay on track and make right choices and be confident in himself, have good self-esteem.

—Comments of a parent about her fifth-grade son's participation in
an African American organization program for youth.

He came into the classroom very excited this morning. He shared with me the things you did at the Project Well-Being program last Saturday. He still has the name strip with his positive characteristics you gave him, taped to his desk. He is talking more in class now. Your program has made him feel part of the group. Will the program run during the summer?

—Communication from a special education classroom teacher of students
with mild mental retardation to the directors of Project Well-Being,
a collaborative decision-making program designed for
African American adolescents.

Across the nation, the demand for greater accountability and equal access to quality public education is being proclaimed. Spearheaded by the publication of *A Nation at Risk* (National Commission on Excellence in Education, 1983), varied reform groups put forth strategic actions to improve the educational outcomes for students at risk. School-community partnerships have consistently become one of the recommendations. Various terms, such as *integrated, collaborative, coordinated,* or *school linked* are used to describe services for the present-day school-community movement (Rigsby, 1995; Wang, 1997). This current combining-of-resources paradigm is based on the premise that schools alone cannot adequately address the multitude of complex problems and needs confronted by today's youth and their families, especially those who reside in urban, low-socioeconomic locales. These problems include poverty; poor health; hunger; physical, mental, or substance abuse; unemployment; teen pregnancy; and violence. These out-of-school, noneducational problems serve as constant barriers to students' academic achievement and warrant systemic, comprehensive attention. Unfortunately, schools are lacking in both the professional expertise and fiscal resources necessary to provide social services on behalf of children and their families (Abrams & Gibbs, 2000: Rigsby, 1995). In order to directly address these very real challenges to the schooling process, there is a need for the involvement of others (outside the school) who have a direct stake in what happens to youth (e.g., parents and community). To this end, a primary goal of the school-community movement is the creation of learning environments that support learning success by focusing on meeting the physical and social wellness needs of students and their families. Simply put, this is accomplished by bringing together (linking) existing social and health agencies, schools, and other educational institutions (Rigsby, 1995; Wang, 1997). Proponents of the school-community movement advocate a comprehensive approach.

To underscore the importance of collaboration, federal agencies and states have compiled policies to serve as guidelines for local education agencies. In addition, granting sources now require documentation of collaboration as criteria for funding. A large percentage of school-community collaborative programs are instituted in urban areas, with the recipients being economically poor, ethnic minority youth who are at risk for school failure. Wang, Haertel, and Walberg's (1995) investigation of the effectiveness of collaborative school-linked services indicates that there is no single school-community collaborative model. They identify the following three models that guide programmatic services:

1. *Curriculum-based programs.* These programs provide knowledge to recipients (e.g., remedial instruction in basic skills for drop-out programs, programs to prevent teenage pregnancy, programs that teach parents about their children's developmental stages, and programs that teach about refusal and coping skills to impact drug usage).

2. *Services-based programs.* These programs provide health and mental health care, recreation, housing, day care, substance abuse treatment, and transportation to appointments.

3. *Curriculum- and services-based combined programs.* These programs incorporate curricula and services provided to reduce problems confronting students.

The three models described above incorporate specific kinds of services that can be effectively used to address the multifaceted needs manifested by students in at-risk contexts, including African Americans. However, given the persistent deficit paradigm afforded African American families by public organizations (including the school system), precautions should be taken to help ensure that the delivery of needed services is done within a positive and culturally responsive framework. Kemper, Spitler, Williams, and Rainey (1999) interviewed African American adults about the important characteristics and criteria that African American youth needed in order to be successful. Nine success-promoting themes were identified: healthy self concept, success expectations, religion, reframing obstacles as challenges that can be met, goals, education, personal characteristics and traits, appropriate behaviors, and connectedness. Kemper and associates (1999) concluded that these nine themes were consistent with findings of literature concerning resiliency, protective factors, and coping skills on the part of adolescents. Using these criteria, Kemper and associates examined program offerings of public agencies that provided services for African American youth. Their findings revealed that the agency representatives viewed favorably the success criteria (nine themes). However, little explicit information existed about how these criteria actually were incorporated into their programs.

Based on monitoring school-community integrated services from a culturally responsive perspective, we are required by the acute school failure of African American youth with and without disabilities to ask a critical question: What other innovative, educationally affirming strategies on behalf of African American youth need to be embraced and linked to the schooling process? In this chapter, I propose that, in addition to the three aforementioned models, a fourth must be included. When working with African American youth, if educators are serious about instituting a comprehensive approach in linking youth (and families) with community resources that optimize their outcomes, an additional program model is essential. I term this program model *student cultural systems*. This student cultural systems program model places African American children at the core of community services and program offerings by significant, nonprofit African American groups and organizations. The student cultural systems model embodies

1. *Student.* The individual African American child and student is the focus or center. This frame of reference is manifested throughout the whole process.

2. *Culture.* Values, beliefs, affirmations, and socialization are reflected in the programmatic themes, topics, activities, strategies, materials, communication styles, guest speakers, program location, and parental involvement in this model.

3. *Systems.* Systems in nature are composed of subsystems and are themselves subsystems of some larger system. A view of a system requires understanding the whole in terms of interacting component subsystems, boundaries, inputs and outputs, feedback, and relationships (National Research Council, 1996). To this end, *systems* in student cultural systems refers to the varied and separate, yet connected, groups of significant organizations, agencies, clubs, religious groups, and individuals that make up the African American communities that target African American youth as a priority.

Historically and at present, African American organizations develop and deliver programs conscientiously designed to motivate and prepare African American youth for life. (Examples of common program offerings are discussed later in this chapter. A sample program is also outlined.) Two decades ago, Witty (1982) noted that African American parents and community organizations must be identified to provide support for the schools to realize their goal. Epperson (1991) called attention to the need for collaboration among public schools, African American communities, and parents as essential to the enhancement and development of African American youth. The argument which supports Epperson's viewpoint is that through collaboration of these three social forces, African American youth will learn to develop and pursue aspirations, positive directions in their lives, and reduce the likelihood of their pursuing detrimental alternatives that would negatively impact their health and well-being. In a recent interview, Ervin (personal communication, October 8, 2001), Chairman of the National Educational Policy Committee of the 100 Black Men of America remarked to me,

The African saying, "It takes a village to raise a child," comes out of a deep understanding of the importance of socialization: that is, the appropriate nurturing and development of the spiritual nature of children (not to be confused with religion, although it may be a part of the socialization process). It is a recognition that spiritual growth takes precedence over, and gives guidance to, the child's utilization and application of cognitive achievements. Spirit permits humans to connect in meaningful ways; behaviors and thoughts are constructively focused on mutual benefit to community because the community is spiritually connected to self. Mentoring the 100 Way (programs and services designed to address the varied needs of African American youth and their families) concentrates on development of the whole child, strengthening the spiritual connection between self and community, and, above all, [encouraging participants] to know themselves and their relationship and responsibilities to their community. As Asa Hilliard states, "Those who know themselves are not intimidated by those who claim cultural supremacy and hegemony."

FUNCTIONALIZING SIGNIFICANT AFRICAN AMERICAN COMMUNITY RESOURCES FOR SCHOOL PERSONNEL

"The people who do these program see Black kids in a different light. This program brought out my son; he has come a long way." This comment was made by an African American mother about her 10-year-old son's participation in an enrichment program sponsored by a nonprofit African American organization.

Several legislative mandates to reform and restructure educational policies and practices have been promulgated for all students' benefits, in particular those who historically were given inequitable opportunities. The Civil Rights Act (1964), the Education of All Handicapped Children Act (1975), the Americans With Disabilities Act (1990), the Individuals with Disabilities Education Act (IDEA) (1997), and the Goals 2000: Educate America Act (1994) were enacted to help optimize equitable learning opportunities. In spite of the recommendations advocated within school reform documents and gains made from legislative mandates, the educational state of affairs for many African American youth with and without disabilities remains dismal. Nationwide, parents of African American youths witness the low performance reported by the local school districts. This alarming, persistent failure is most evident in poor urban areas. The high school graduation rate for African American females and males is 77.2% and 76.7% as compared to 84.2% and 84.3% for White females and males respectively (U.S. Census, 2000). African American youth remain disproportionately represented in special education programs for students with cognitive and behavioral difficulties while having limited access to services for learners with gifts and talents (Artiles & Trent, 1994; Artiles & Zamora-Duran, 1997; Chinn & Hughes, 1987; Ford, Obiakor, & Patton, 1995; Harry, 1994; Obiakor, 1999).

In this new millennium, race of students and their families continues to make a difference in the manner in which school personnel interact with them (Lareau & Horvat, 1999). For instance, Obiakor (1999) noted that low and inappropriate teacher expectations toward African American students remain problematic. Clearly, a reframing and restructuring of the school's traditional organizational structure, paradigms, and policies has become imperative for school districts where African American youth, with and without disabilities, and their families continue to be subjected to ineffective educational services. IDEA (1997) mandates an increase in parental involvement. While this requirement is to be applauded, mandates do not automatically ensure or guarantee that all parents are accorded equal opportunities to become involved. Many African American parents have a history of negative experiences with the school and consequentially are reluctant and intimidated to take advantage of their legal rights (Harry, 1995; Marion, 1980). For those African American parents, a neutral mechanism is needed to help them become knowledgeable about their rights and then exercise them. As discussed by Ford (1995, 1998), a defining attribute of many programs sponsored by African American organizations is participation by local residents (e.g., parents). To this end, significant African American community resources (SACR) have the potential to help encourage and train parents to become empowered and more involved in the schooling process (Banks, 1997; Brandt, 1989, 1998; Deslandes, Royer, Potvin, & Leclerc, 1999; Educational Research Services, 1997; Epperson, 1991; Rueda, 1997).

The establishment of productive school-community partnerships has been strongly recommended by general and special educators at all levels as an essential element in any strategic model or framework designed to promote equitable, quality educational opportunities (Banks, 1997; Comer, 1989; Deslandes et al., 1999; Educational Research Services, 1997; Ford, 1998; Giles, 1998; Hatch, 1998; Telesford, 1994). Many African American scholars (e.g., Byrd, 1995) have elaborated on the importance of school personnel gaining personal experiences with the communities of African American learners and schools, facilitating partnerships with respected community leaders to help optimize the schooling process for African American youth with disabilities. Comer, (1989), Cummins (1986), the Ford Foundation and John D. and C. T. MacArthur Foundation (1989), Hatch (1998), and Wang et al. (1995) documented that collaborative school-community initiatives are important components of schools that make a difference. These measurable differences include parent involvement, academic gains, attendance, and reduced behavior problems.

The importance of the school-community relationship to educational outcome for African American students with and without disabilities demands that general and special educators respond to a pivotal question: How do we systemically refocus educational paradigms, policies, and practices to impact the professional development of preservice level trainees and practicing teachers and administrators, such that we are equipped with the necessary professional knowledge, skills, and attitudes to accept and use the educational strengths of SACR? It is vital that general and special education teachers working with African American youth possess a comprehensive repository of educational strategies. Awareness and usage of SACR that supplement the schooling process for African American learners should be a part of professional practices. Because of the multidisciplinary needs of some youth with disabilities, special education teachers often possess some knowledge of public service providers (e.g., medical and mental agencies, social services, and juvenile service). This knowledge usually does not include nonprofit SACR. Obviously, preservice and inservice training about school-community collaboration is highly needed. Colleges and universities and school districts have an awesome role to play in preparing future and practicing general and special education teachers and administrators to establish linkages with SACR.

Garcia (1991) explained that public schools are a community affair; they are made up of children from the community surrounding the school and, with minor exceptions, reflect their human communities. He noted that a school's community consists of varied social groups who interact with each other, developing cooperative and interdependent networks of relationships. Schools, however, are more likely to extend and participate in the critical cooperative and interdependent networks with social groups who are not poor or from African American backgrounds. Ford and Reynolds (2000) identified six critical questions and concerns that can be used to guide the formation of effective school partnerships with African American communities: (a) Who are the school personnel that must act in leadership roles? (b) What leadership roles should key school personnel undertake? (c) What school initiatives should be used to prepare school personnel and community constituencies for authentic relationships with significant African American community resources? (d) What does school collaboration with the African American community mean in terms of the balance of power and decision-making processes? (e) Which African American community resources should be considered significant enough for inclusion in the school-community partnership? (f) Who makes this decision?

From a broader perspective, the term *community* is a multifaceted concept that includes all groups, individuals, and institutions that are touched by the school. It refers to groups, individuals, and institutions within communities of local schools (Garcia, 1991; Mahan, Fortney, & Garcia, 1983). For instance, Garcia (1991) asserted that the school's community in a small, rural school district is easy to define, but in some large cities, the school's community is not so easily defined. Due to reasons such as desegregation, busing, and traditional changes and shifts in population, urban communities tend to change continuously. Presently, over one third of the students in the nation's schools are likely to be from multicultural backgrounds. The three fastest growing groups are Hispanic Americans and Latinos, African Americans, and Southeast Asian Americans (Grossman, 1995). Currently, 23 of the 25 largest school systems in the United States are heavily composed of students from multicultural backgrounds. It has been well documented that daily and episodic crises plague the nation's public school systems and leave a detrimental impact on the schooling of African American learners. These crises include widespread poverty, inadequate health care, increased school violence, continued low school performances, persistent distrust between many parents and communities with local schools, and increased identification of youth with severe social and emotional problems. Furthermore, despite recent changes in many teacher education programs to include issues of diversity and multicultural education, teacher candidates are still inadequately prepared and seldom choose to teach in schools with large numbers of African American youth, especially those with high rates of poverty (Ford & Bessent-Byrd, 2001; Valli & Rennert-Ariev, 2000; Voltz, 1995). The third recommendation of the 1996 Education Commission of the States was to make parental involvement a top priority, which accentuates the importance of schools connecting with significant community resources (Brandt, 1998). Unfortunately, as discussed above, administrators and special and general education teachers usually lack competence in school-community collaboration, in general, and specifically, in connecting with SACR.

Another phenomenon affecting school districts nationwide but more pronounced in large urban areas is the significant decline in the number of teachers and administrators from African American and other multicultural backgrounds. Wald (1996) noted the diminished supply of teachers from multicultural groups (with 86% of the teachers being White, 10% Black, 2% Latino, and 2% other). Combined with this is a large female teaching force (68%). Further compounding the situation is the realization that the majority of these teachers and administrators do not reside in the communities of the African American students they serve. The potential for a disconnectedness between the school and the community becomes heightened. Ironically, this decline in African American teachers is occurring at a time when African American students, in some geographic locations, constitute a large percentage of the student population. While this shortage of African American administrators and teachers will be a tremendous loss to all students, African American students will more acutely feel it. Historically, African American school personnel served in various critical capacities (e.g., as leaders, role models, mediators, and mentors for students). To this end, educational delivery models that include mechanisms to assist school personnel to reach out and collaboratively connect with primary stakeholders (family members, guardians, and community resources) must be used. Schools connecting students and families with SACR is one way to supplement the loss of those important role models.

Although school-community involvement is presently being advocated as a primary means to address the multidimensional problems faced by students with and without disabilities, it is not a new remedy. The ideals and program components embedded in the 1960s alternative social programs and community empowerment education approaches illustrated the centrality of community involvement. However, the alarming educational achievement reports during the 1980s, for example, *A Nation at Risk* (National Commission on Excellence in Education, 1983), declining fiscal resources in the 1990s, and the spilling over of problems faced by youth and children have made it imperative to institute collaborative models of school-community services (Rigsby, 1995; Wang et al., 1995). Ford (1995, 1998) defined African American significant community resources as not-for-profit service or social organizations, sororities, fraternities, clubs, agencies, religious groups and churches, and individuals that local community residents perceive as providing valuable (significant) services. These services may include educational, advocacy, financial, legal, and empowerment assistance. An important component of significant African American community resources is participation by local residents (e.g., parents). These familiar, significant community resources have established mutually trusting relationships with residents. SACR generally offer numerous types of services and programs to support the various developmental needs of African American (and other multicultural) youth. See Figure 13.1 for a diagrammatic representation of SACR.

Figure 13.1 Significant African American Community Resources (SACR)

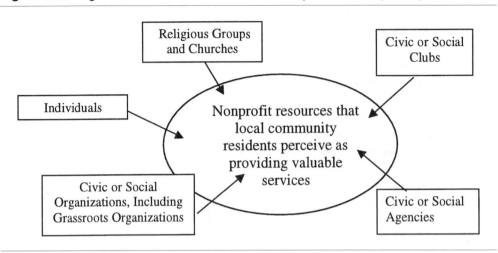

SOURCE: Ford (1995, 1998); Ford & Reynolds (2000).

NOTE: Services may encompass educational, advocacy, financial, legal, and empowerment assistance.

Resources and programs that adequately address the specific needs and concerns of African American youth, as perceived by families, must be the primary criterion for determining significance. For example, within many segments of the African American community, the African American church remains an important leadership institution (Billinsley & Caldwell, 1991). It extends a host of outreach programs to support educational levels ranging from early childhood to adulthood. In addition, African American fraternities and sororities, professional organizations, civic and service organizations (e.g., National Association for the Advancement of Colored People, National Council of Negro Women, and 100 Black Men of America), numerous local social clubs, and grassroots organizations offer a multitude of community-based programs to foster the healthy development of African American youth, including those deemed as at risk, those with disabilities, and those with gifts and talents. The growing population of African American youth in public schools and the continued failure of too many of these youth require a restructuring of the educational system such that positive connections with SACR become the rule rather than the exception.

Another strategic component of the recent reform and restructure movement is site-based school management whereby the locus of decision making shifts from centralized bureaucracies to local district and school levels (Cook, Weintraub, & Morse, 1995). Consequently, under this organizational arrangement, general and special education teachers will be required to take on new leadership roles and make decisions that affect the entire school. Given the current priority of improving school-community relationships, this will be a major decision-making issue. The general and special educators in their new role must see themselves as advocates. According to Compton and Galloway (1984), an advocate is a person who supports the rights of vulnerable populations to obtain benefits and services to which they are entitled. In their role as advocates, they must rethink and respond to the ways in which they can further enhance complementary service delivery for African American students.

SACR: BENEFITS TO AFRICAN AMERICAN LEARNERS WITH EXCEPTIONALITIES

Specifically, numerous SACR benefits to African American learners with exceptionalities include these:

1. Because of their cumulative effects, SACR provide resilience-enhancing resources (Ford, 1998; Ford & Reynolds, 2000; McLittle-Marino & Ford, 1991).

2. The SACR reinforce school-related skills. For example, when students become unmotivated to complete tasks, their parents and significant adults from the community can be involved (Ford, 1995, 2001). In addition, adults within SACR may present school material in a personal and culturally functional manner for African American youth, thereby increasing its relevancy.

3. The SACR expose African American students to real-world experiences. These experiences can involve (a) academic motivation, tutoring, and test-taking skills; (b) self-development of values and cultural group identity; (c) decision-making skills; (d) goal setting; (e) rites of passage; and (f) information networks for students and parents.

4. The SACR create avenues for sensitivity toward culturally responsive school programming. Face-to-face encounters by administrators and teachers with African American families and community resource persons are necessary to promote culturally responsive interactions (Brand, 1996; Harry, Torguson, Katkavich, & Guerrero, 1993).

5. The SACR create accessibility opportunities for adult role models, mentors, and advocates. The more connected students are to a healthy caring parent or supportive adult outside the family, the better (Karen, 1990; Kauffmann, Grunebaum, Cohler, & Gamer, 1979; Rutter, 1983; Werner & Smith, 1983).

6. The SACR lead to increased parental involvement and empowerment. The positive aspects of parental involvement have been well documented (Banks, 1997; Brandt, 1989; Croninger, 1990; Cummins, 1986; Epperson, 1991; Giles, 1998; Harry et al., 1993; Mannan & Blackwell, 1992).

7. The SACR reduce negative attitudes and create community-friendly school environments. Visible and genuine linkages with SACR send an important message to those involved. The U.S. Department of Education (1994) has compiled a variety of literature and materials that school systems may use to promote friendly family and community school environments.

8. The SACR assist in the dissemination and collection of information. Marion (1980), more than two decades ago, listed the need for information for African American parents. This need has become increasingly urgent today. Communication remains the key.

Table 13.1 outlines a sample session of a SACR program for third- to fifth-grade students.

Table 13.1   Sample Session of a SACR Program for Third- Through Fifth-Grade Students

- Icebreaker: Large group activity to get youth interacting with each other
- African American history activities corresponding to session's theme: proverbs and people
- Direct instruction in test-taking and mathematical problem-solving strategies
- Session's guest speaker, African American male author of African American children's literature: interactive presentation and workshop focusing on the theme "follow your dreams"
- Self-affirming chant and quote for the day corresponding to the above theme
- Closure activities: (a) journal writing, (b) dissemination of student materials and parental information (e.g., program, upcoming field trips, and community information), (c) preview of next program's session, and (d) interactive self-esteem game
- Lunch with SACR adults and attending parents and guardians

SOURCE: Program, *Akron Kids Achieving,* designed and implemented by Alpha Kappa Alpha Sorority, Inc., Akron, Ohio, October 2001.

PROFESSIONAL TOOLS FOR SCHOOL-AFRICAN AMERICAN COMMUNITY LINKAGES

The type of linkages between school and the African American community that are described throughout this chapter require (a) the support and commitment of all major stakeholders (e.g., school administrators, certified and licensed school personnel, nonlicensed staff, and the targeted significant community resources); and (b) the adequate preparation of school personnel. A foundational step is the commitment of persons to be involved in the school-community linkages. Using Epstein's (1995) action team format, individual school buildings can formulate a Student Cultural Systems model as part of the school's collaborative plan.

> The action team guides the development of a comprehensive program of partnership. . . . The action team takes responsibility for assessing present practices, organizing options for new partnerships, implementing selected activities, evaluating next steps, and continuing to improve and coordinate practices. (p. 7)

Ford and Reynolds (2000) also described a building-level approach that can be used during the formative stages of the process.

Ford (1995, 1998) outlined a three-phase training model designed to prepare preservice level trainees and practicing school personnel to productively connect and collaborate with SACR. The three phases are

Phase One: Reshaping Attitudes and Personal Redefinitions

Phase Two: Development of Accurate Knowledge Base
    A. Examination of historic and present school-community partnerships and activities
    B. Creation of a comprehensive and inclusive database of significant African American community resources

Phase Three: Productive School-Community Network
    A. Establishment of inclusive school-community connections
    B. Use of significant community resources to affect student outcomes

Table 13.2 Corresponding Knowledge, Skills, Attitudes

Knowledge	Skills	Attitudes
Definition and types of SACR	Examining past and current school-linkage practices with SACR	Personal reflections about African American communities served by the school
Diversity across and within African American communities	Communicating with SACR	Personal reflections about the parents of African American students served by the school
Characteristics of SACR and awareness of directories that provide information about SACR	Sharing information about SACR with other administrators and teachers	Personal reflections and expectations about African American youth with and without disabilities served by the school
Current school practices for linking with SACR	Sharing information with parents about relevant SACR	Personal reflections about the role of SACR in school-community linkages
Differences between public organizations and agencies and nonprofit SACR	Observing and participating in SACR programs	
Programmatic goals and objectives of SACR	Incorporating into the classroom environment education-enhancing knowledge, content, strategies, and resources used in SACR program activities	
Benefits of SACR to students, teachers, and parents	Documenting changes in students' school performance and behavior as a result of participation in SACR programs	
Types of parental involvement in SACR	Sharing with other teachers and parents changes in students' school performance and behavior as a result of participation in SACR programs	
Nature of student involvement in SACR	Sharing with SACR about impact of programs on students' school behavior	
School and building-level procedures for disseminating information about SACR to teachers, parents and students	Determining the kinds of SACR programs appropriate for incorporation into the school's learning environment	
How to incorporate relevant SACR program activities and resources into the classroom environment		

From my perspective, significant African American community resources must be used to aid African American youth and their families. For this comprehensive approach to work, there must be corresponding changes in knowledge, skills, and attitudes of school personnel. (See Table 13.2.)

CONCLUSION

The contemporary school-community models (curriculum based, service based, or both) can be used to combat the multidimensional educational and noneducational problems confronting African American children and youth today. However, they may not provide African American youth with the needed cultural socialization and self-affirming frames of reference that set the stage for optimal performance. As a result, given the continued school failure by large numbers of African American youth with and without disabilities, an additional school-community model, the student cultural systems model, must be seriously considered and adopted. This model requires school personnel to establish authentic linkages with significant resources within African American communities. Special training is needed to help school personnel to work collaboratively with significant resources in African American communities. I have proposed using a three-phase training model, specific knowledge, skills, and attitudes that support effective linkages with SACR and positive outcomes for students and their families. To put my proposal into action, follow these important guiding principles:

- Forging authentic linkages with significant African American community resources is an essential reality for maximizing outcomes for African American youth.
- School personnel must understand the varied benefits of African American youths' participation in programs offered by SACR.
- School personnel's involvement in SACR promotes a more positive and holistic understanding of children and families served by the school.
- School personnel must incorporate community experiences, knowledge, and resources into the school's learning environment.

REFERENCES

Abrams, L. S., & Gibbs, J. T. (2000). Planning for school change: School-community collaboration in a full-service elementary school. *Urban Education, 35,* 79-103.

Americans With Disabilities Act (1990), Pub. L. No. 101-336, 104 Stat. 327.

Artiles, A., & Trent, S. (1994). Over-representation of minority students in special education: A continuing debate. *The Journal of Special Education, 27,* 410-437.

Artiles, A. J., & Zamora-Duran, G. (1997). *Reducing disproportionate representation of culturally diverse students in special and gifted education.* Reston, VA: The Council for Exceptional Children.

Banks, C. A. M. (1997). Parents and teachers: Partners in school reform. In J. A. Banks & C. A. M. Banks (Eds.), *Multicultural education: Issues and perspectives.* Boston: Allyn & Bacon.

Billinsley, A., & Caldwell, C. H. (1991). The church, the family and school in the African-American community. *Journal of Negro Education, 60,* 427-440.

Brand, S. (1996). Making parent involvement a reality: Helping teachers develop partnerships with parents. *National Association for the Education of Young Children, 51*, 76-81.

Brandt, R. (1989). On parents and schools: A conversation with Joyce Epstein. *Education Leadership,47*(2), 24-27.

Brandt, R. (1998, May). Listen first. *Educational Leadership*, 25-30.

Byrd, H. B. (1995). Issues regarding the education of African American exceptional learners. *Multiple Voices, 1,* 38-46.

Chinn, P. C., & Hughes, S. (1987). Representation of minority students in special education classes. *Remedial and Special Education, 8*(4), 41-46.

Civil Rights Act of 1964, Pub. L. No. 88-352, 42 U.S.C. § 2000 *et seq.*

Comer, J. P. (1989). The school development program: A psychosocial model of school intervention. In G. L. Berry & J. K. Asaman (Eds.), *Black students: Psychosocial issues and academic achievement* (pp. 264-285). Newbury Park, CA: Corwin.

Compton, B., & Galloway, B. (1984). *Social work processes* (3rd ed.). Homewood, IL: Dorsey Press.

Cook, L., Weintraub, F., & Morse. (1995). Ethical dilemmas in the restructuring of special education. In J. Paul., H. Rosselli, & D. Evans (Eds.), *Integrating school restructuring and special education reform* (pp. 119-139). Fort Worth, TX: Harcourt Brace.

Croninger, B. (1990). African American parents . . . Seeing them as colleagues, neighbors, and friends? *Equity Coalition for Race, Gender and National Origin, 1*(2), 8-9.

Cummins, J. (1986). Empowering minority students: A framework for intervention. *Harvard Educational Review, 56*(1), 18-35.

Deslandes, R., Royer, E., Potvin, P., & Leclerc, D. (1999, Summer). Patterns of home and school partnership for general and special education students at the secondary level. *Exceptional Children, 65,* 496-506.

Education for All Handicapped Children Act (1975), Pub. L. No. 94-142, 20 U.S.C. § 1401 *et seq.*

Educational Research Services. (1997). *Getting parents meaningfully involved.* Arlington, VA: Author.

Epperson, A. I. (1991). The community partnership: Operation rescue. *Journal of Negro Education, 60,* 454-458.

Epstein, J. L. (1995). School/family/community/partnerships. *Phi Delta Kappan, 76*, 701-712.

Ford, B. A. (1995). African American community involvement processes and special education: Essential networks for effective education. In B. A. Ford, F. E. Obiakor, & J. M. Patton (Eds.), *Effective education of African American exceptional learners: New perspectives* (pp. 235-272). Austin, TX: Pro-Ed.

Ford, B. A. (1998). Productive school and community partnerships: Essentials to improve educational outcomes for ethnic minority students. In A. Freeman, H. Bessent-Byrd, & C. Morris (Eds.), *Enfranchising urban learners for the twenty-first century* (pp. 91-113). Kearney, NE: Morris.

Ford, B. A., & Bessant-Byrd, H. (2001). Reconceptualization of the learning disabilities paradigm: Multicultural imperatives. In L. Denti (Ed.), *New ways of looking at learning disabilities.* Denver, CO: Love.

Ford, B. A., & Clark, S. (2001). Collaboration and communication. In T. Stephens, R. Weaver, M. Landers, & E. Joseph (Eds.), *A practical guide for educational administrators who have a responsibility for administering special education programs.* Dayton, OH: State Superintendent Task Force for Special Education, School of Education.

Ford, B. A., Obiakor, F. E., & Patton, J. (Eds.). (1995). *Effective education of African American exceptional learners: New perspectives.* Austin, TX: Pro-Ed.

Ford, B. A., & Reynolds, C. (2000). Connecting with multicultural community resources: New approach for multicultural youth with mild disabilities. In C. Utley & F. E. Obiakor (Eds.),

Special education, multicultural education, and school reform: Components of a quality education for students with mild disabilities. Springfield, IL: Charles C Thomas.

Ford Foundation & John D. & C. T. MacArthur Foundation. (1989). *Visions of a better way: A Black appraisal of public schooling.* Washington, DC: Joint Center for Political Studies. (ERIC Document Reproduction Service No. ED 312 320)

Garcia, R. L. (1991). *Teaching in a pluralistic society: Concepts, models, strategies.* New York: Harper Collins.

Giles, H. C. (1998). *Parent engagement as a school reform strategy.* (ERIC Document Reproduction Service No. ED 419 031)

Goals 2000: Educate America Act (1994), Pub. L. No. 103-227. Retrieved February 26, 2002, from www.ed.gov/legislation/GOALS2000/TheAct

Grossman, H. (1995). *Special education in a diverse society.* Boston: Allyn & Bacon.

Harry, B. (1994). *The disproportionate representation of minority students in special education: Theories and recommendations.* Alexandria, VA: National Association of State Directors of Special Education.

Harry, B. (1995). African American families. In B. A. Ford, F. E. Obiakor, & J. M. Patton (Eds.), *Effective education of African American exceptional learners: New perspectives.* (pp. 211-233). Austin, TX: Pro-Ed.

Harry, B., Torguson, C., Katkavich, J., & Guerrero, M. (1993, Fall). Crossing social class and cultural barriers in working with families: Implications for teacher training. *Teaching Exceptional Children,* pp. 48-51.

Hatch, T. (1998). How community contributes to achievement. *Educational Leadership,* pp. 16-19.

Individuals With Disabilities Education Act Amendments (1997), Pub. L. No. 101-476, 20 U.S.C. § 1400 *et seq.*

Karen, R. (1990, February). Becoming attached. *Atlantic Monthly,* pp. 35-39, 42, 44-50, 63-70.

Kaufmann, C., Grunebaum, H., Cohler, B., & Gamer, E. (1979). Superkids: Competent children of psychotic mothers. *American Journal of Psychiatry, 136,* 1398-1402.

Kemper, K. A., Spitler, H., Williams, E., & Rainey, C. (1999). Youth service agencies: Promoting success for at-risk African American youth. *Family and Community Health, 22,* 1-15.

Lareau, A., & Horvat, E. M. (1999). Moments of social inclusion and exclusion: Race, class, and cultural capital in family-school relationships. *Sociology of Education, 72,* 37-53.

Mahan, J. M., Fortney, M., & Garcia, J. (1983). Linking the community to teacher education: Toward a more analytical approach. *Action in Teacher Education, 5,* 1-10.

Mannan, G., & Blackwell, J. (1992). Parent involvement: Barriers and opportunities. *The Urban Review, 24,* 219-226.

Marion, R. L. (1980). Communicating with parents of diverse exceptional children. *Exceptional Children, 46,* 616-623.

McLittle-Marino, D., & Ford, B. A. (1991, November). A community collaboration program. *Journal of the American Public Health Association,* p. 268.

National Commission on Excellence in Education. (1983). *A nation at risk.* Washington, DC: U.S. Department of Education.

National Research Council. (1996). *Science Education System Standards.* Washington, DC: National Academy Press.

Obiakor, F. E. (1999, Fall). Teacher expectations of minority exceptional learners: Impact on "accuracy" of self-concepts. *Exceptional Children, 66,* 39-53.

Ogbu, J. (1978). *Minority education and caste.* San Francisco: Academic Press.

Rigsby, L. C. (1995). Introduction: The need for new strategies. In L. C. Rigsby, M. Reynolds, & M. Wang (Eds.), *School/community connections* (pp. 1-18). San Francisco: Jossey-Bass.

Rueda, R. (1997, January). *Fiesta educativa: A community-based organization.* Paper presented at the Council for Exceptional Children Multicultural Symposium, New Orleans, LA.

Rutter, M. (1983). Stress, coping, and development: Some issues and questions. In N. Garmezy & M. Rutter (Eds.), *Stress, coping, and development in children* (pp. 49-74). New York: McGraw Hill.

Telesford, M. C. (1994, Summer). Tips for accessing and involving families of color in a significant way. *Focal Point*, p. 11.

U.S. Census Bureau. (2000). *Statistical abstract of the United States*. Washington, DC: Author.

U.S. Department of Education. (1994). *Strong families strong schools*. Washington, DC: Author.

Valli, L., & Rennert-Ariev, P. L. (2000, January/February). Identifying consensus in teacher education reform documents: A proposed framework and action implications. *Journal of Teacher Education, 51,* 5-17.

Voltz, D. L. (1995). Learning and cultural diversities in general and special education classes: Frameworks for success. *Multiple Voices, 1,* 1-11

Wald, J. L. (1996). *Culturally and linguistically diverse professionals in special education: A demographic analysis.* Reston, VA: National Clearinghouse for Professions in Special Education.

Wang, M. C. (1997). Next steps in inner-city education: Focusing on resilience development and learning success. *Education and Urban Society, 29,* 255-276.

Wang, M. C., Haertel, G. D., & Walberg, H. J. (1995). The effectiveness of collaborative school-linked services. In C. Rigsby, M. Reynolds, & M. Wang (Eds.), *School/community connections* (pp. 283-309). San Francisco: Jossey-Bass.

Werner, E., & Smith, R. (1983). Vulnerable but invincible. In N. Garmezy & M. Rutter (Eds.), *Stress, coping, and development in children* (pp. 69-82). New York: McGraw Hill.

Witty, E. P. (1982). *Prospects for black teachers: Preparation, certification, employment.* Washington, DC: ERIC Clearinghouse on Teacher Education. (ERIC Document Reproduction Service No. ED 213 659)

Chapter Fourteen

Transitioning African American High School Students With Disabilities

Bertina H. Combes and Beth A. Durodoye

No greater planning priority exists for African American students with disabilities than that of transition planning. Successful transitioning from school to adult life is the ultimate indicator of the outcome of education and services received (Berkell & Gaylord-Ross, 1989). The term *transition* is used throughout the life span of individuals receiving special education services and conveys the action of moving from one life space to another. Ysseldyke, Algozzine, and Thurlow (2000) identified three categories of transition: transition into school, transition during school, and transition beyond school. This chapter focuses on the third category, specifically the transition planning for those individuals in high school and those moving from high school to postsecondary educational options or employment. We begin by providing some transition fundamentals, including an overview of the legislative history of transition. Elements essential to successful transition are then addressed, followed by a discussion of transition options and school personnel responsible for making transition happen. Within these sections, we address cultural and ethnic factors that should be considered when transitioning African American high school students with disabilities.

TRANSITION FUNDAMENTALS: DEFINITION, HISTORY, AND LEGISLATION

The term transition has a rich history of origin that spans many years and includes work-training programs, vocational education, special education, and career education. Even so, the African American population has not been equitably included in the transition discourse. Will (1983) has served as the Assistant Secretary for the Office of Special Education and Rehabilitative Services (OSERS) and is often cited as the catalyst for the focus on transition that began in the early 1980s and continues in legislation and practice today. Spurred by research on employment and life outcomes of youth who had received special education services, transition became a major priority for the administration. Results revealed that students with disabilities moving into adult life left high school to face unemployment, underemployment, dependence on family and friends for living accommodations, and social isolation. These discouraging results prompted professionals in the fields of special, career, and vocational education; individuals with disabilities and their families; and public policy makers to request, develop, and support better transition services. In a 1983 report, Will shared a definition of transition and a conceptualization of how building a bridge from high school to employment with appropriate services can lead to better life outcomes for individuals with disabilities. As she pointed out, transition is a period that includes high school, the point of graduation, additional postsecondary education or adult services, and the initial years in employment. Transition is a bridge between the security and structure offered by the school and the opportunities and risks of adult life. Any bridge requires both a solid span and a secure foundation at either end. The transition from school to work and adult life requires sound preparation in the secondary school, adequate support at the point of school leaving, and secure opportunities and services, if needed in adult situations (p. 2).

Will's (1983) conceptual framework depicts three bridges from school to work, with a range of supports: transition without special services; transition with time-limited services; and vocational rehabilitation, postsecondary vocational education, and ongoing services that allow persons with disabilities to take advantage of work opportunities. These services were depicted as bridges that allowed individuals with disabilities to move from high school to employment. The model was developed to assist states and local education agencies in designing programs and services that (a) focused on all students with disabilities, (b) addressed the complexity of postschool services, and (c) had as a goal employment immediately after school or after a period of postsecondary education or vocational services.

The Education for All Handicapped Children Act (EAHCA; 1975) mandated a free appropriate public education (FAPE) in the least-restrictive environment (LRE) for all children with disabilities (see Table 14.1). The law stipulated that services are to be designed in collaboration with parents and detailed in an individual education program (IEP). Furthermore, the law defined and ensured related services to assist students with disabilities in benefiting from special education. Amendments (EAHCA, 1983) authorized $6.6 million to develop and support school-to-work transition services for youth with disabilities through model demonstrations, research, and personnel preparation projects (Neubert, 2000). Halloran (1989) noted that EAHCA amendments (1986) reflected the result of those outcome studies for youth with disabilities. The various amendments drew attention to the need for improvement in the scope and quality of transition services and planning. EAHCA amendments (1986) also authorized funding to investigate postsecondary outcomes for students with disabilities who had dropped out of school. As noted by Neubert (2000), EAHCA amendments (1983, 1986) did not mandate transition services for

Table 14.1 Progress of Transition Initiatives from EAHCA to IDEA

1975 IDEA (PL 94-142)	1983 IDEA (PL 98-199) Reauthorization	1990 IDEA (PL 101-476) Reauthorization	1997 IDEA (PL 105-17) Reauthorization
Ensure FAPE for children with disabilities	Focused on self-determination for students and families in transition planning	Federal funds were provided to demonstrate transition models	Transition services are defined in legislation
Outlined due-process procedures	Focused on short- and long-range goals rather than objectives within the IEP	OSERS transition model was developed	Legislation included a statement of needed transition services in the IEP for each student age 16 or younger
Established an IEP planning process for each child with a disability	Focused on student planning and participation in the general education curriculum	Transition outcomes were specified in legislative language	Promoted educational planning focused on postschool goals
	Focused on integrating transition planning within the process of educational planning starting at age 14 years		

SOURCE: R. Stodden (1998).

students with disabilities, although they served as the foundation for the significant changes that were to come.

Major revisions to EAHCA resulted in renaming the law the Individuals With Disabilities Education Act (IDEA; 1990). Among the major revisions were a definition of transition, a focus on planning for life after secondary education, the requirement that students be included in transition planning, and the stipulation that IEPs include a statement of needed transition services by age 16, younger if appropriate. Transition services were defined as

A coordinated set of activities for a student, designed within an outcome oriented process, which promotes movement from school to postschool activities, including postsecondary education, vocational training, integrated employment, including supported employment, continuing adult education, adult services, independent living or community participation. The coordinated set of activities must (a) be based on the individual student's needs; (b) take into account student's preferences and interest; and (c) include instruction, community experiences, the development of employment and other postschool adult living skills and functional vocational evaluation. (IDEA, 1990, § 602, 20 U.S.C. § 1401)

IEPs that did not include the services described above were required to document why and on what basis transition was not addressed. As in the past, IEPs were to be reviewed annually and based on assessment of the student. When appropriate, the IEP team was to include professionals from the community (e.g., employers) and adult service agencies (e.g., rehabilitation counselors), as well as parents or guardians, appropriate school personnel, and the student. When outside public agencies were determined necessary to the student's postsecondary success, their responsibilities and linkages to the student prior to exiting the school system were to be described in the IEP (IDEA, 1990).

IDEA amendments (1997) relating to transition further established the importance of secondary planning for postsecondary success. Although there was no change to the definition, the concept of related services was expanded to include support services such as speech and language therapy, occupational therapy, social work, counseling, and recreational services, as well as related services such as transportation. Under the new amendments, students would also have a statement of needed transition services beginning at age 14. As in IDEA, 1990, the goals were to be updated annually; however, their absence did not require explanation or justification in the IEP. It appears that the transition movement has devoted much needed attention to definitions, legislation, policy, and the development of models and curricula. However, aside from mentioning the importance of viewing all factors in a cultural context, little has been written or researched specifically on transitioning as it relates to African American students. As the overrepresentation of students from culturally diverse backgrounds in special education continues to be a major issue, it would seem logical that some attention be devoted to effective transition of this population.

ESSENTIALS OF EFFECTIVE TRANSITION FOR AFRICAN AMERICAN LEARNERS

Implementation of legislation and resulting policy have helped to identify factors that are essential if students are to successfully transition from secondary to postsecondary life. Barriers and pitfalls to transition have also been identified to include (a) failing to plan at the appropriate level, (b) confusing means with ends, (c) failing to involve all relevant educational partners, (d) selecting programs before identifying program destinations, (e) failing to consider evolving future realities in the community, (f) being unaware of the process elements of strategic planning, and (g) assuming that all systematic planning approaches are basically the same (Smith, Edelen-Smith, & Stodden, 1995). Successful transition planning is student centered, involves the family, and is community referenced. It is imperative that the goals of transition are considered from cultural perspectives. The mainstream culture may view a successful transition as one in which individuals live independently, with minimal family and outside support. This view shapes transition planning by teachers as well as the expectation of families for their students, and the students for themselves. Geenen, Powers, and Lopez-Vasquez (2001) argued that the goal of independence may be antithetical to a youth's background. It is important to remember that for many African American students and their families, ethnic identity, and one's identification as a person with a disability (as well as numerous other identifications) are highly intertwined, and this awareness will lead to more effective transition planning.

Student-Centered Planning

Student-centered planning focuses on what is best for the student. More specifically, students' needs in all areas (i.e., academic, self-help, vocational, and independent living), as well as their desires, are considered. In order to ensure that transition planning is student centered, African American students should be involved and their needs appropriately assessed. Documentation of the importance of these factors has been established in transition literature (Kohler, 1998; Thoma, Rogan, & Baker, 2001; Wehman, 1996; Wehmeyer, 1998). However, frequently, the involvement of youth and young adults with disabilities in their own planning is said to be non-existent or passive (Morningstar, Turnbull, & Turnbull, 1996; Van Rusen & Bos, 1990). This may be especially so for African American students, as some report that students and their families have been less likely to be involved in IEP and other planning meetings (Clark & Kolstoe, 1995; Harry, 1995; Marion 1979).

Despite the suggestion that presence of a disability makes participation difficult, individuals with varying levels and types of disabilities have participated successfully in their own transition planning (Brinckerhoff, 1996; Sitlington, Clark, & Kolstoe, 2000; Thoma et al., 2001). A more common reason that African American youth and young adults are not involved in their planning is that they are unfamiliar with the planning process and procedures. Wehman (1996) offered several ways that students can become involved in the transition process and be taught to voice their concerns: (a) by their families, (b) through peer groups, and (c) by having teachers include IEP objectives that teach them how to participate. Parents play an important role by teaching and modeling self-advocacy and assertiveness. They can build confidence in their children by reminding them to express their desires to teachers and other school professionals. By speaking often about transition and future planning, parents or guardians can reinforce the importance of transition in the student's mind. In addition, they can assist their children by following up with the school to see that their own concerns and those of their child or young adult are addressed. Logically, peer groups of friends with disabilities can be arranged for students to discuss transition goals. These groups can meet with or without professional guidance. Students can be encouraged to discuss where they want to live and work and how they want to manage their lives. Finally, teachers can provide instruction using curricula and training programs that have been designed to facilitate student involvement. Many programs include an assessment component to determine what skills the student needs to address and at which point in the curriculum the student should begin. These programs provide instruction in a variety of areas including self-advocacy, self-awareness, self-evaluation, self-efficacy, goal setting, making choices, conflict resolution, community awareness, and career development. Collectively, these concepts can be grouped under the rubric of self-determination.

Family Involvement Planning

Families are critical to the successful transition of youth and young adults with disabilities (Geenen et al., 2001; Morningstar et al., 1996). Hanley-Maxwell, Pogoloff, and Whitney-Thomas (1998) noted that the family provides both foundation and context for decisions made during this time period. As part of the foundation, families influence the career development of adolescents and young adults. Choices made during the transition time period are made within the context of past and current influences that the family has on the individual. Families influence directly and indirectly the values students hold about work, independence, and education. For these reasons, it is essential that African American families be involved in transition planning.

Kohler (1998) detailed reasons for involving parents, guardians, or other family members in transition planning. First, the lives of students and their families are most impacted by transition-focused education and services. Students and their families will have ongoing service needs before and after high school and have knowledge about the true nature of the needs. Second, families can provide insight into students' interests, abilities, histories, and preferences. This may especially be the case for students with more severe disabilities. Third, families may be the most consistent source of support for students after they leave school by remaining in close contact or serving in supportive roles. Families are sustaining factors as school personnel fade away and are replaced by adult service providers or, in some cases, no service provider at all. Last, students whose families have higher levels of involvement are more successful than students with little or no family involvement.

Students with disabilities recognize for themselves the importance of family involvement in the transition from school to adult life. Morningstar et al. (1996) found that students with varying disabilities (emotional and behavioral disorders, learning disabilities, and mild mental retardation) were able to identify areas in which families were instrumental in the planning process. First, both immediate and extended families helped students create a vision for their future and influenced their career aspirations. Second, families participated formally and informally in the planning process. Parents were able to supplement or plan when IEP planning was ineffective or nonexistent. Finally, families were involved in helping facilitate self-determination. Although family participation is viewed as important and critical to the success of transition planning, families may participate at varying levels. This is especially so among African American families. Although lack of, or limited, participation may be viewed as lack of interest, there are many reasons that African American families may not participate in transition planning. They include

1. Belief that education is the responsibility of teachers and other school personnel

2. Issues related to time and resources to attend meetings or conferences

3. Belief that school personnel do not understand or respect their culture

4. Relative importance of transition planning to other more pressing and immediate family issues

5. Past negative interactions with school regarding their adolescent or young adult

6. Past negative interactions with school regarding their own educational experiences

7. Difficulty accepting disability or limitations of their adolescent or young adult

8. Feelings of inadequacy about understanding the school culture and the language of education

9. Insecurities about value of family contribution to the transition process

10. Fear of negative and unexpected information about their adolescent or young adult

11. Feelings of hopelessness about the future of their adolescent or young adult

It is important that school personnel respect what African American parents are able to provide and that they encourage them to participate when and how they can. Without creating stereotypes, school personnel should seek to understand the interactions between adolescents with disabilities and their parents, as well as the importance of family dynamics on the design and delivery of services (Trapani, 1990). Greene (1998) proposed that school personnel build rapport with culturally and linguistically diverse (CLD) families (e.g., African American families) as a means of empowering them in the transition planning process. Specifically, school personnel should

1. Be cognizant of numerous factors of culture and cultural diversity when interacting with CLD families and take precautions not to interact with them in stereotypic ways

2. Use genuine, open-ended ways of finding out what CLD families believe

3. Establish a personal relationship with the family prior to conducting formal transition assessment

4. Visit the student in the home or in a community setting and identify shared interests or family practices

5. Determine the following:
   A. Home language
   B. Family norms for personal and social development
   C. Residential and work-related goals for the youth with disabilities
   D. Family views on disabilities and effects on treatment of youth with disabilities
   E. How the family is conceptualized
   F. Family child-rearing practices
   G. Parent knowledge of legal rights and advocacy

Community-Referenced Planning

For transition planning to be successful, it must not only focus on the student and involve the family, it must also consider the community in which the student lives and will work. Concern for how well students transitioned into the community served as an impetus for the transition movement in the 1980s. Unacceptable numbers of students with disabilities were found to be unemployed or underemployed, dependent on parents or families, socially isolated, and, in general, ill-prepared for life in their communities. A National Council on Disability (NCD; 1989) study on public education reported a number of findings regarding the transition of youth and young adults with disabilities. Among them were

1. "Upon leaving school students with disabilities and their families often have a difficult time accessing appropriate adult services and/or postsecondary education and training" (p. 40).

2. "Graduates with disabilities are more likely to be employed following school if (a) comprehensive vocational training is a primary component of their high school program and (b) they have a job secured at the time of graduation" (p. 42).

3. "There are insufficient partnerships between the business community and schools for the purpose of enhancing employment opportunities for students with disabilities" (p. 43).

Such findings and previously discussed legislation have encouraged general and special educators to find solutions that will yield better results for students and their families prior to their leaving high school. Better access to adult services and postsecondary education and training can be ensured if students and their families are connected to these services prior to leaving high school.

For African American youth and their families, especially those living in the African American community, there may already be a natural connection between the school and the community. Ford (1995) noted that regardless of the economic status, African American communities have a conglomerate of immediate or at-large resources that can support families. These assets include African American religious institutions, professionals, volunteer grassroots organizations, social and service clubs, businesses, and community-based social agencies. Although African American high school students and their families may operate outside the immediate community, connection with the immediate community may serve as a pathway to a broader community. School personnel need to become familiar with resources in the African American student's community as they facilitate transition planning, and parents are often one of the best sources of information about their communities.

TRANSITION OPTIONS FOR AFRICAN AMERICAN LEARNERS

There is a variety of postsecondary options available to African American students with disabilities transitioning from high school. For purposes of this discussion, these options are limited to transition to employment and transition to postsecondary education. The choices students and their families make about transition options vary, based on type and severity of disability, personal and professional goals of the student, readiness of the student for transition, and availability of support systems and resources.

Transition to Employment

Sitlington et al. (2000) agreed that the eventual goal of all transition efforts is to transition to employment. The participation rate of the general labor force for people 18 to 64 years old was approximately 83%; the participation rate of individuals with disabilities, including youth, was 52% (NCD, 1999). For individuals with disabilities from diverse cultures, the participation rate was 38.6%, while the rates for individuals with severe disabilities from diverse cultures was significantly lower. When transition to employment is the immediate goal following high school, the transition planning should take on a focus that is work-based and hands-on. Although the curriculum for transition to work should span the educational career of a student, much of it will be delivered and experienced during the latter years of schooling. The career development and transition education model proposed by Sitlington et al. reflects "critical student outcomes across age/developmental levels, transition exit points for students as they move from one educational level to the next, and the education and service systems needed to deliver transition education and transition services" (p. 26). Nine knowledge and skill domains (communication and academic performance, self-determination, interpersonal relationships, integrated community participation, health and fitness, independent/interdependent daily living, leisure and recreation, employment, and further education and training) cross the developmental life phases and exit points. Preparing students for transition to work requires instruction in the knowledge and skills domain as well as instruction in occupational awareness, employment-related knowledge and skills, and specific vocational knowledge and skills (see Sitlington et al.). In addition to instruction, students need opportunities to put their knowledge and skills to use in real settings. Quality hands-on, work-based experience is a critical predictive factor to transition success when transitioning to work.

Models proposed by scholars such as Sitlington et al. (2000) often serve as the foundation on which schools build transition programs. Earlier, Jackson and Roberts (1996) noted that career development models and inventories are based on White, middle-class, American males and may not be as relevant for minority individuals. As school personnel prepare African American students to transition into work through career awareness and development, they must consider cultural factors that affect students' vocational choices and aspirations. Although ethnicity and socioeconomic status act as confounding variables, researchers must highlight the adverse effects that socioeconomic barriers have on the career development of African American students (Bobo, Hildreth, & Durodoye, 1998; Herr & Cramer, 1992; Murry & Mosidi, 1993). Students tend to aspire to careers and jobs with which they have had experience or to which they have been exposed. This may limit students to stereotypic or lower-paying jobs. School personnel must ensure that African American students are exposed to a wide variety of work-based experiences so that they have opportunities to explore jobs outside their own experiences. African American families may need assistance in broadening their expectation of job placements for their student.

Assessment is an important part of the career development process. A variety of instruments are used to assess students' interest and aptitude or skills for specific jobs. Appropriate attention needs to be paid to selecting devices that are technically sound. When interpreting and using results of the instruments, school personnel must consider both the cultural and economic backgrounds of the student. In addition, they must include in the curriculum strategies to assist African American students to deal with racism and discrimination in the workplace. Ideally, students expect work settings that are welcoming and open to diversity; however, this will not always happen. Racism and discrimination must be discussed with students who have the ability to cognitively understand these concepts. Additionally, they must be empowered with skills to manage their work environment when they feel they are encountering racism or discrimination.

Transition to Postsecondary Education

Transition to postsecondary education is increasingly becoming an option for students with disabilities. Postsecondary education can include vocational and technical programs, community colleges, or 4-year colleges and universities. Data on the participation of adolescents and young adults with disabilities who choose to transition into postsecondary education varies. However, the group tends to be less likely to participate in postsecondary education when compared with their peers without disabilities. Data from Heath Resource Center (2001) revealed that 6% of first-time, full-time, first-year students entering 4-year institutions in 2000 reported that they had a disability. Students reported hearing, speech, orthopedic, learning, and health-related disabilities, as well as partial or total blindness. Results indicated that students were more likely to

- Be from White families
- Be 19 years of age or older
- Be from families whose annual income exceeded $100,000
- Have parents who were college graduates
- Have earned C or D averages in high school

- Anticipate that they will need special tutoring or remedial work in English
- Consider majoring in arts and sciences
- Rank themselves lowest on math ability, intellectual self-confidence, academic ability, and writing ability

As compared to the 1998 report, freshmen in the 2000 class were more likely to be students of color. African Americans represented 11% of the total population with equal representation between males and females. Slightly more than half of the individuals attended pubic institutions (54%). Another 42% attended independent colleges and universities. Students who attended historically black colleges and universities (HBCUs) represented 4% of those surveyed.

When preparing African American high school students with disabilities to transition into postsecondary options, especially 2- or 4-year colleges, the preparation should have a more academic focus. Students need strong content area (reading, math, and science) foundations to ensure that they are prepared for higher-level work in college. Therefore participation in general education is more likely to yield a solid academic foundation. Hildreth and Ford (1998) noted that placement of African American students in more restrictive environments leads them to (a) attend fewer general education classes, (b) be more dependent on teachers, (c) have difficulty with test-taking and organizational and study skills, and (d) not participate in extracurricular activities, and know less about career options requiring postsecondary education. These factors have tended to be predictive of college attendance and success. If African American students with disabilities are going to attend college, school personnel must facilitate placement, as much as possible, in general education settings.

Strong academic skills are essential for African American high school students going to college. However, school personnel and students' families must focus on the development of self-determination, organization, and self-management skills. Although these skills have been organized to be taught in school curricula, parents must work on developing skills at home by expecting and modeling them. Several books assist individuals with disabilities who are preparing for college (see Box 14.1).

African American students may choose to transition into vocational or technical schools as postsecondary options. Vocational-technical education is education geared toward employment that requires specialized education but not a bachelor's degree. Vocational-technical training can be obtained in 2-year community or junior colleges or in single-specialty schools in a variety of areas including cosmetology, animal health, child care and development, automotive maintenance, and law enforcement and criminal justice. African American students transitioning into such programs will benefit from hands-on and work-based transition planning and curricula in high school.

A VISION FOR THIS CENTURY

Kohler (1998) reported that transition takes more than the secondary special education teacher or a transition specialist. Transition and transition planning are the responsibility of the school community and may include special, vocational, and regular education teachers; transition specialists; school and rehabilitation counselors; community agency personnel; school district administrators; parents or guardians; and others.

Effective transition of African American high school students with disabilities requires that school personnel wear different hats from those that they usually wear. This might entail changing roles from teacher, administrator, transition specialist, or counselor to others such as

---

BOX 14.1 BOOKS FOR TRANSITIONING INTO
POSTSECONDARY EDUCATION

J. Cobb (2001). *Learning How to Learn: Getting Into and Surviving College When You Have a Learning Disorder.* Washington, DC: Child Welfare League of America Press.

M. Koehler & M. Kravets (1998). *Counseling Secondary Students With Learning Disabilites: Ready-to-Use Guidelines, Techniques and Materials to Help Students Prepare for College and Work.* West Nyack, NY: Center for Applied Research in Education.

C. T. Mangrum II & S. Strichart (Eds.) (1997). *Colleges With Programs for Students With Learning Disabilities or Attention Deficit Disorders.* Princeton, NH: Peterson's.

J. Mooney & D. Cole (2000). *Learning Outside the Lines: Two Ivy League Students With Learning Disabilites Give You the Tools for Academic Success and Educational Revolution.* New York: Simon & Schuester.

J. M. Taymans, L. West, & M. Sullivan (Eds.) (2000). *Unlocking Potential: College and Other Choices of People with LD and AD/HD.* Bethesda, MD: Woodbine House.

---

advocate, friend, confidant, or mediator. In order to facilitate more effective transition planning, school personnel must also pay attention to the cultural and historical factors that impact African Americans. Additionally, they must be sensitive to their own personal awareness, ethnic-group knowledge, and skills in transition planning to effectively work with the African American population.

Self-Awareness

It is imperative that school personnel be aware of their personal biases as they relate to working with African American high school students with disabilities. They should also be aware of who they are culturally and ethnically. Attention must be given to attitudes toward themselves and others regarding disabilities. Before school personnel can work effectively with this designated population, they must understand how these issues relate to their own life circumstances. Failure to take a personal inventory regarding attitudes and beliefs about these matters may translate into interactions that serve to interfere with the ability to appropriately connect with the students and their families.

In efforts to personally evaluate self in relation to work with African American students with disabilities, special and general educators might ask themselves critical questions such as the following:

1. What do I think and feel about people with backgrounds different from my own (particularly as this relates to ethnicity and disability)?

2. How comfortable am I working with African American students with disabilities?

3. What are my strengths in working with this population?

4. In which areas do I need to improve regarding this population?

5. How can I go about counteracting any stereotypes that I might have regarding this group?

A thorough examination of one's attitudes, values, and beliefs can prove helpful in the enhancement of the relationship between the educator and the student. General and special educators who convey an attitude of sensitivity, reassurance, and patience provide enrichment opportunities for the concerned parties (Bowen & Glenn, 1998).

Ethnic Group Knowledge

General and special education personnel must have knowledge about the general cultural characteristics of African Americans. A focus on this area places the African American student with disabilities in an ethnic context that can guide educators as they work to understand an African American worldview. Conversely, they must remain mindful that African Americans are not monolithic—each African American student is unique. African American culture focuses on values and beliefs best understood as adaptive strengths in the face of historical and social experiences in the United States (Gibbs, 1998). Gibbs identified religion, kinship, family role flexibility, and education as four primary values in African American society. The legacy of Africa includes a strong religious and spiritual orientation for large numbers of African Americans. Traditionally, churches in the African American community have been the hub of social, political, and economic activity. Involvement in the church has shaped family ideas concerning "marital relationships and divorce, abortion, adoption, child rearing practices, and so on" (p. 177). School personnel can benefit from a knowledge of African American religious and spiritual influences through an increased understanding of attitudes that might affect transitioning decisions. With family consent, for example, school personnel may find that a family's minister can be a resource in helping the family deal with changing family dynamics that can arise as the result of one member transitioning from high school to young adulthood.

There is an African adage that says, "I am, because we are; and since we are, therefore, I am" (Mbiti, 1969, pp.108-109). The meaning conveyed is that of a view toward collectiveness. It is important for many African Americans to maintain close ties with an extended family network and the broader community. This network is not restricted to blood relatives but may also embrace neighbors, ministers, and others who are considered integral to the functioning of that particular family. The knowledge of kinship patterns may be valuable to school personnel who may need to mobilize a support system for the transitioning student. The African American family has been described as being flexible, although patterns vary depending on socioeconomic status and rural or urban residence. Responsibilities tend to be based on optimal household functioning rather than on traditional male and female roles. Both male and female children are encouraged to be independent. A successful family role structure may see a child assuming parental responsibilities in nurturing and competent fashion. As school personnel interact and assess the families of African American students with disabilities, they may need to interpret male and female behaviors through this cultural lens.

In fact, contrary to one popular American stereotype, African Americans place high importance on educational achievement. Despite historical oppression, African American parents have remained expectant that their children will pursue careers that bring security and social mobility. But as Gibbs (1998) pointed out, "The impetus for higher education has slowed down" (p. 178). This may be attributed to the social marginalization of poor, inner-city African Americans, the changing economy, and affirmative-action backlash. The resulting and sharpening divide separates middle-class African Americans who can access educational opportunities and poor African Americans who do not have that same access.

Transition Skills

The transitioning of African American high school students with disabilities requires that general and special educators design interventions to facilitate student success in the options they have chosen. School personnel need knowledge about best transition practices and research, as well as the skills to implement transition programs. Traditional teaching, training, administration, or counseling duties, for example, may be supplanted by the roles of consultant, referral source, and advocate (Bowen & Glenn, 1998). The need for flexibility and versatility, as well as knowledge about transition history, models, and curricula, will assist school personnel as they become involved in the transition process for African American learners with disabilities.

CONCLUSION

The relationship between effective transition planning and postsecondary outcomes for young adults with disabilities has been well established. In this chapter, we have provided an overview of transition with special attention to the needs of African American high school students with disabilities. For students to recognize postsecondary success, they and their parents must be involved in their planning. Additionally, the planning must be community referenced. Those involved in the planning should keep in mind the role that culture plays in choices that African American students and their families make as well as how they may respond to transition planning and implementation.

REFERENCES

Berkell, D., & Gaylord-Ross R. (1989). The concept of transition: Historical and current developments. In D. E. Berkell & J. M. Brown (Eds.), *Transition from school to work for persons with disabilities* (pp. 1-21). New York: Longman.

Bobo, M., Hildreth, B. L., & Durodoye, B. A. (1998). Changing patterns in career choice among African American, Hispanic, and Anglo children. *Professional School Counseling, 1*(4), 37-42.

Bowen, M. L., & Glen, E. E. (1998). Counseling interventions for students who have mild disabilities. *Professional School Counseling, 2*, 16-25.

Brinckerhoff, L. C. (1996). Making the transition to higher education: Opportunities for student empowerment. *Journal of Learning Disabilities, 29*(2), 118-136.

Clark, G. M., & Kolstoe, O. P. (1995). *Career development and transition education for adolescents with disabilities* (2nd ed.). Boston: Allyn & Bacon.

Education for All Handicapped Children Act (1975), Pub. L. No. 94-142.

Education for All Handicapped Act Amendments (1983), Pub. L. No. 98-199.

Education of the Handicapped Act Amendments (1986), Pub. L. No. 99-457.

Ford, B. (1995). African American community involvement processes and special education: Essential networks for effective education. In B. A. Ford, F. E. Obiakor, & J. M. Patton (Eds.), *Effective education of African American exceptional learners: New perspectives* (pp. 235-272). Austin, TX: ProEd.

Geenen, S., Powers, L. E., & Lopez-Vasquez, A. (2001). Multicultural aspects of parent involvement in transition planning. *Exceptional Children, 67*(2), 265-282.

Gibbs, J. T. (1998). Black American adolescents. In J. T. Gibbs & L. N. Huang (Eds.), *Children of color: Psychological interventions with minority youth* (2nd ed., pp. 171-214). San Francisco: Jossey-Bass.

Greene, G. (1998, November). *Empowering culturally and linguistically diverse (CLD) families in the transition planning process.* Paper presented at a conference of the Council for Exceptional Children, Division for Culturally & Linguistically Diverse Exceptional Learners, Washington, DC.

Halloran, W. (1989). Foreword. In D. E. Berkell & J. M. Brown (Eds.), *Transition from school to work for persons with disabilities* (pp. xiii-xvi). New York: Longman.

Hanley-Maxwell, C., Pogoloff, S. M., & Whitney-Thomas, J. (1998). Families: The heart of transition. In F. R. Rusch & J. G. Chadsey (Eds.), *Beyond high school: Transition from school to work* (pp. 234-264). Belmont, CA: Wadsworth.

Harry, B. (1995). African American families. In B. A. Ford, F. E. Obiakor, & J. M. Patton (Eds.), *Effective education of African American exceptional learners: New perspectives* (pp. 211-233). Austin, TX: Pro-Ed.

HEATH Resource Center. (2001). *College freshmen with disabilities: A biennial statistical profile.* Washington, DC: American Council on Education, National Clearinghouse on Postsecondary Education for Individuals With Disabilities.

Herr, E. L., & Cramer, S. H. (1992). Career development and counseling of special populations. In C. Jennison (Ed.), *Career guidance and counseling through the life span: Systematic approaches* (pp. 238-283). New York: Harper Collins.

Hildreth, B. L., & Ford, B. A. (1998, November). *Optimum high school transition planning for African American students with learning disabilities.* Paper presented at a conference of the Council for Exceptional Children, Division for Culturally & Linguistically Diverse Exceptional Learners, Washington, DC.

Individuals With Disabilities Education Act (1990), Pub. L. No. 101-476.

Individuals With Disabilities Education Act Amendments (1997), Pub. L. No. 105-17.

Jackson, L. K., & Roberts, K. (1996, January). *Career counseling with African Americans: How far have we really come?* Paper presented at a conference of the Southwest Educational Research Association, New Orleans, LA.

Kohler, P. D. (1998). Implementing a transition perspective of education: A comprehensive approach to planning and delivering secondary education and transition services. In F. R. Rusch & J. G. Chadsey (Eds.), *Beyond high school: Transition from school to work* (pp. 179-205). Belmont, CA: Wadsworth.

Marion, R. L. (1979). Minority parent involvement in the IEP process: A systematic model approach. *Focus on Exceptional Children, 10*(8), 1-16.

Mbiti, J. S. (1969). *African religions and philosophy.* Oxford, UK: Heinemann.

Morningstar, M. E., Turnbull, A. P., & Turnbull, H. R. (1996). What do students with disabilities tell us about the importance of family involvement in the transition from school to adult life? *Exceptional Children, 62*(3), 249-260.

Murry, E., & Mosidi, R. (1993). Career development counseling for African Americans: An appraisal of the obstacles and intervention strategies. *Journal of Negro Education, 62,* 441-447.

National Council on Disability. (1989). *The education of students with disabilities: Where do we stand?* Washington, DC: Author.

National Council on Disability. (1999). *Lift every voice: Modernizing policies and programs to serve a diverse nation.* Washington, DC: Author.

Neubert, B. A. (2000). Transition education and services guidelines. In P. L. Sitlington, G. M. Clark, & O. P. Kolstoe (Eds.), *Transition education and services for adolescents with disabilities* (pp. 39-69). Boston: Allyn & Bacon.

Sitlington, P. L., Clark, G. M., & Kolstoe, O. P. (2000). *Transition education and services for adolescents with disabilities.* Boston: Allyn & Bacon.

Smith, G. J., Edelen-Smith, P. J., & Stodden, R. A. (1995). How to avoid the seven pitfalls of systematic planning: A school and community plan for transition. *Teaching Exceptional Children*, *27*(4), 42-47.

Stodden, R. (1998). School to work transition: Overview of disability legislation. In F. R. Rusch & J. G. Chadsey (Eds.), *Beyond high school: Transition from school to work* (pp. 60-76). Belmont, CA: Wadsworth.

Thoma, C. A., Rogan, P., & Baker, S. (2001). Student involvement in transition planning: Unheard voice. *Education and Training in Mental Retardation and Developmental Disabilities*, *36*(1), 16-29.

Trapani, C. (1990). *Transition goals for adolescents with learning disabilities*. Boston: Little, Brown.

Van Rusen, A. K., & Bos, C. S. (1990). IPLAN: Helping students communicate in planning conferences. *Teaching Exceptional Children, 22*(4), 30-32.

Wehman, P. (1996). *Life beyond the classroom: Transition strategies for young people with disabilities*. Baltimore: Brooks.

Wehmeyer, M. L. (1998). Student involvement in transition-planning and transition-program implementation. In F. R. Rusch & J. G. Chadsey (Eds.), *Beyond high school: Transition from school to work* (pp. 206-233). Belmont, CA: Wadsworth.

Will, M. (1983). *OSER programming for the transition of youth with disabilities: Bridges from school to working life*. Washington, DC: Office of Special Education and Rehabilitative Services.

Ysseldyke, J. E., Algozzine, B., & Thurlow, M. L. (2000). *Critical issues in special education*. Boston: Houghton Mifflin.

Chapter Fifteen

Teacher Preparation for African American Exceptional Learners: A Cultural-Historical Approach

Stanley C. Trent

For many years, African American students have been overrepresented in certain categories of special education (Artiles & Trent, 2000) and underrepresented in programs for the gifted and talented (Ford, 1998). "Typically, ethnic minority (particularly African American and Latino), poor, and male students are most affected by disproportionality" (Artiles & Trent, 2000, p. 513). According to Artiles and Trent, there are several explanations for why this problem exists. These include (a) educators' overreliance on a deficit-based model where, for the most part, weaknesses are believed to reside within students; (b) culturally biased eligibility and placement criteria; and (c) lack of understanding about the role of culture in human development. Other explanations include efficacy of instructional practices, racism and discrimination, failure to consider minority students' perspectives, and lack of alternative services (e.g., effective prereferral models).

As an African American teacher, educator, and researcher in special education, I believe that the aforementioned factors contribute to the poor school performance among significant numbers of African American students and their disproportional enrollments in special education and gifted education programs. Moreover, I believe only comprehensive and complex reforms will yield substantive and sustainable results. One area of focus must be the preparation of pre-service special, gifted and talented, and general education teachers from a cultural-historical perspective (Kea, Trent, & Davis, in press). According to Trent, Artiles, Fitchett-Bazemore, McDaniel, and Coleman (in press), cultural-historical activity theory (CHAT)

> views human development and learning as culturally and historically situated and dialogically based (Bahktin, 1981; Engeström, 1999). Currently, researchers have begun to use this theory to document the discourse, actions, and use of tools within activity systems that lead to transformations in practice (Engeström, 1999). These systems are not seen as static and short-lived, with a discrete beginning, middle, and end. Instead, they are seen as, "systems that *produce* events and actions and evolve over lengthy periods of socio-historical time." (Engeström, 1994, p. 45)

In addition, CHAT focuses on the importance of historicity. Historicity is "understood as concrete historical analysis of the activities under investigation" (Engeström, 1999, p. 25). Engeström notes further that when the subject of an activity system engages in collaborative work, "Differences in cognition across cultures, social groups, and domains of practice are commonly explained without seriously analyzing the historical development that has led to those differences" (p. 26). Viewing the activity system from this perspective may result in the perpetuation of hierarchical relationships where power is amassed and maintained by some and denied to others based on characteristics that have historically relegated individuals and groups to dominant or subordinate status (e.g., race, gender, disability, social class) (p. 7).

As Figure 15.1 depicts, elements of CHAT include the subject, the object, outcomes, mediating artifacts (tools), rules, community, and the division of labor. The subject constitutes "the individual or subgroup whose agency is chosen as the point of view in the analysis" (Engeström, 1994, p. 45). In this case, the subject is the teacher education program, which will consist of professors and administrators. The *object* refers to the "raw material" or "problem space" at which the activity is directed and which is molded or transformed into *outcomes* (see Engeström). In this case, the object includes the evolving teacher preparation program designed to prepare teachers, as agents of equity and social justice, and the students enrolled in the program. "The outcomes represent the goals established for the object by the subject. These outcomes may be influenced by demands and expectations of external activity systems such as state departments of education, parents, and advocacy groups" (Trent et al., in press). "The rules refer to the stated and unstated regulations, procedures, and norms that guide the discourse and actions within the activity system" (Trent et al., in press). Within the teacher preparation program, commitment to each other, to all students and to equity and social justice are some rules that might be adopted. "The community comprises individuals and groups (stakeholders) who also have a shared interest in the object" (Trent et al., in press). In the teacher preparation program, the larger community may include K-12 students, administrators, teachers, paraprofessionals, parents, university faculty from departments outside education, and community advocates or agencies (e.g., community centers, religious institutions). The division of labor refers to both the horizontal division of tasks between the members . . . and to the vertical division of power and status (Engeström, 1994). Finally, mediating artifacts created to accomplish identified outcomes include, but are not restricted to, discourse, reflection, dialogue journals, clinical experiences, syllabi, technology,

Figure 15.1 Intended Structure of the Teacher Education Program's Activity

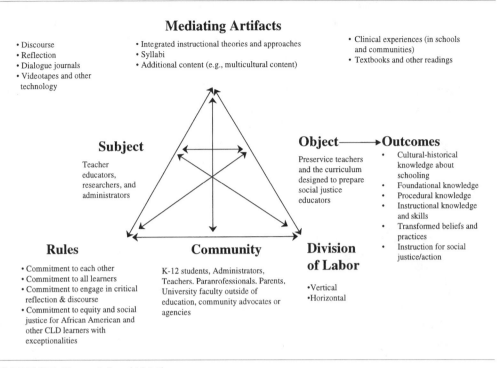

Mediating Artifacts

• Discourse
• Reflection
• Dialogue journals
• Videotapes and other technology

• Integrated instructional theories and approaches
• Syllabi
• Additional content (e.g., multicultural content)

• Clinical experiences (in schools and communities)
• Textbooks and other readings

Subject

Teacher educators, researchers, and administrators

Object——►Outcomes

Preservice teachers and the curriculum designed to prepare social justice educators

• Cultural-historical knowledge about schooling
• Foundational knowledge
• Procedural knowledge
• Instructional knowledge and skills
• Transformed beliefs and practices
• Instruction for social justice/action

Rules

• Commitment to each other
• Commitment to all learners
• Commitment to engage in critical reflection & discourse
• Commitment to equity and social justice for African American and other CLD learners with exceptionalities

Community

K-12 students, Administrators, Teachers. Paraprofessionals. Parents, University faculty outside of education, community advocates or agencies

Division of Labor

•Vertical
•Horizontal

SOURCE: Engeström (1994).

instructional theories and approaches, multicultural content, textbooks, and other readings (Artiles & Trent, 2000).

Thus CHAT does not focus solely on content within a teacher education program (TEP) but also on the process whereby collaboration over time results in improved and transformed outcomes for all members of the activity system. In the remainder of this chapter, I present information that elucidates the importance of viewing preservice teacher education for African American students with exceptionalities from a CHAT perspective. First, I describe the early years of my formal education in segregated and integrated schools and how this historicity has influenced my teaching. Second, based on this brief biography and CHAT, I identify some of the artifacts or tools that must be incorporated into courses and programs designed to prepare teachers to work more effectively with African American students with exceptionalities. Finally, I provide implications for research and practice. Although the primary focus of this chapter is African American learners, the issues addressed herein can be applied to all learners.

MY REFLECTIONS AS AN AFRICAN AMERICAN EDUCATOR

I received my formal, public school education in rural Chesterfield County, Virginia, where I attended two segregated elementary schools and one integrated, combined junior-and-senior high school. I attended Union Branch Elementary School from first through half of third grade and Dupuy Elementary School from the remainder of third grade through sixth grade. At this point, the freedom of choice plan initiated by the school system was abolished and mandatory integration was implemented throughout the county. These were very interesting times! I lived through them but really did not spend too much time thinking about them until I became a teacher educator. After engaging in extensive critical reflection, I became more consciously aware of how these experiences had influenced my personal, intellectual, spiritual, and professional development. Moreover, I have become more aware of the preeminent focus we have historically placed on a deficit perspective in education, particularly for economically disadvantaged African American children, whether they are served in general or special education. Furthermore, many of these early, formal, educational experiences have influenced significantly my evolution as a teacher educator committed to equity and social justice. Themes emanating from these experiences are imbedded in this biographical sketch and are elucidated in subsequent sections.

Union Branch Elementary School

First and Second Grade

I loved my first 2 years at Union Branch Elementary School where Mrs. Audrey Charity was my first and second grade teacher (she taught a first- and second-grade combination class). Mrs. Charity was an excellent teacher who knew how to make learning fun, meaningful, and relevant. She knew many of our extended family members; in fact, she had taught some of our parents and many of our aunts, uncles, and older cousins. She helped us understand why we needed to know certain skills and processes and she used multiple instructional approaches to help us master content. For example, it was Mrs. Charity who taught us the difference between the sight reading approach and the phonics approach in a very explicit and meaningful way.

After completing the first book in the *Dick and Jane* series, Mrs. Charity praised us for the intensive effort put forth to accomplish our goals. After distributing the second book, she told us to read the first story while she worked with the second graders at their table. We were excited. We were up for the challenge. In fact, many of us, especially those at the "smart" end of the table, did not believe it would be a challenge. Quentin and I, considered the smartest students in first grade, pulled out our new, yellow, soft-back books and began reading tenaciously. Little did we know, however, that we were about to be trammeled by a three-letter word on the very first page—T-O-M. I will never forget the discomfort I felt when my eyes met this word. My fluency came to a screeching halt. I had no idea what it was and, suddenly, I felt the frustration experienced at home when I attempted to read the Bible or other text written significantly beyond my comfort level. I turned to Quentin. He would know. After all, he was the smartest student in first grade. I was number two. "What's that word? I can't figure it out," I asked. Shrugging his shoulders, Quentin replied, "I don't know. I was just gettin' ready to ask you." So we became word sleuths and used strategies that Mrs. Charity had taught us, namely, context clues and illustrations. We identified all the T-O-Ms on the first page and read the words before and after them to see if we could break the code. As we searched the pictures, we saw that there was a boy and a bicycle wheel. This boy, who didn't resemble Dick in any way, was rolling the wheel with a stick. After applying these strategies, Quentin and I decided that the word must be "wheel." Shortly after we had made our decision, several classmates came to our end of the table, pointing and asking the same question we had asked ourselves earlier, "What is this word?" We told them it was wheel and based on what followed, I suspect they returned to their seats and read *wheel* every time they saw the word T-O-M. We started reading the story silently, all the while feeling insecure about our choice. All too soon, Mrs. Charity made her way back to our side of the room and sat at the end of the table with the low achievers. She tapped the student sitting next to her and said, "James, I want you to begin reading the very first story in our new book. Take your time and remember everything you've learned." James struggled, but managed to read, "This is wheel. See wheel run. Wheel can run fast."

When asked to read, all my other classmates followed James's lead, and I noticed that every time someone read wheel, the puzzled look on Mrs. Charity's face became more distinct. Finally, she burst into laughter, shook her head, held out her hands, and said, "Hold it, people! Why in the world are you *all* calling T-O-M wheel?" Suddenly, all eyes were on Quentin and me, number one and number two. Janet Jones pointed her index finger in our direction and declared, "That's what Quentin and Stanley told us to call it." Still chuckling, Mrs. Charity asked us why we thought the word was wheel. By this time, we both had turned three shades of red; however, despite our embarrassment, we told her that we had used context clues and the pictures to figure out the word. Mrs. Charity shook her head in the affirmative and began her teacher-directed lesson:

> Ok, people, I can see how you came up with wheel. Sometimes, if you don't know a word, you *can* use the pictures and figure out what it is. You can also use context clues by reading the words before and after the ones that you can't figure out. I've also taught you how to read by the sight word approach. You learn how the word looks, and then you practice reading it until you memorize it. These are good skills to have, but you also need more; you need to know phonics. If you know phonics, you can figure out just about any word. Let me show you.

Then she stood, walked over to the chalkboard, and began her formal teaching of this thing called phonics. I never forgot these experiences; and years later, when I was a novice teacher, I tried to incorporate them into my instructional repertoire.

Third Grade

Then came third grade with Mrs. Brown. According to rumor, she was past retirement age, but no one could convince her that it was time to move on. We trudged into class every morning to find her sitting at her desk with a chalkboard full of assignments created to take us through the entire day with very little teacher-directed instruction. For the most part, we worked individually at our desks. The schedule often looked something like this:

9:00 – 9:30: Handwriting—Copy the weather report from the chalkboard.

9:30 – 10:30: Reading—Read "Space Station" and answer questions 1-5 on page 38.

10:30 – 10:45: Bathroom Break.

10:45 – 11:30: Spelling—Write each spelling word five times each.

11:30 – 11:45: Wash hands for lunch.

11:45 – 12:15: Lunch.

12:15 – 12:45: Recess.

12:45 – 2:00: Math—Complete problems 1-25 on page 54 in your math books.

2:00 – 2:45: Music with Mrs. Robinson.

2:45 – 3:00: Copy homework assignments from the board.

3:00 – 3:15: Prepare for dismissal.

Often, Mrs. Brown fell asleep at her desk while we completed the barrage of busywork she assigned day after day after day. Some students could not even read the directions, let alone complete the tasks without assistance. Needless to say, behavior became an issue in our classroom. The noise level increased, spitballs flew from one side of the room to the other, and, occasionally, some of us would break up the monotony with a game of tag. Eventually, a loud thump, a yell, or a screech would arouse Mrs. Brown from her midmorning nap. Anyone she spotted "misbehaving" was summoned to her desk for the usual punishment, a hand spanking with a stack of Smokey the Bear rulers held together by a thick rubber band. And so, that place called school became boring, painful, and monotonous, and was so very different from what I had experienced for 2 years with Mrs. Charity. Around the end of October, I decided that I could no longer remain in this insipid environment. I wanted out, so every morning, I arose with a stomachache. After about 3 days of this malingering, my mother scheduled a doctor's appointment and was told by Dr. McElwayne in my presence, "As far as I can see, there's nothing wrong with this boy. He just doesn't want to go to school. You need to whip his hind parts and make him go back." This is exactly what she did when I arose the next morning with yet another stomachache!

Though my parents were upset and disappointed by my behavior, they were well aware that I was truly bored and was losing my zest for learning. In fact, other parents within the Union Branch catchment area were complaining about the poor quality of instruction provided by some of the other teachers at Union Branch. They did not believe their children were being prepared for that "great gettin' up morning" when the insidious walls of segregation would come "tumblin'" down, never to rise again. There was some talk of my going back to Mrs. Charity's class to complete third grade, but in the end, due to a long-term illness endured by my mother, my parents decided to send me to live with my aunt who was the teaching principal at Dupuy Elementary School. These schools were miles apart both geographically and instructionally.

Dupuy Elementary School

In addition to the 2 years I spent with Mrs. Charity, it was at Dupuy that I received the strong academic foundation that contributed much to where I am today. Dupuy was an outstanding school. It was within walking distance of Virginia State University (VSU), a historically black university located on the border of Chesterfield County and the city of Petersburg. Some of my classmates' parents were VSU professors, administrators, and staff. The strong social networks that connected these learning communities resulted in many enrichment activities that took place at our school and on VSU's campus. For example, VSU professors and students frequently visited our school to share their talents, knowledge, and skills. I remember string quartets, orchestra concerts, and science and math demonstrations. I remember Dr. Edgar Toppin, a nationally recognized historian, coming to talk with us during Negro History Week about the contributions made by Negro Americans. Also, several times during the year, we boarded our yellow school buses to attend operettas, choir and orchestra concerts, plays, and poetry readings, many of which featured the works of African American writers and musicians.

Though Dupuy was racially homogeneous, it was more socioeconomically diverse than was Union Branch, and on average, the educational level of the parents was higher. There were more members of the middle class, many of whom lived in College Park, a new subdivision of mostly split-level houses that was located across the street from VSU. There was also a group of students much like me. Our parents were skilled laborers who lived across the tracks, out in the rural areas. Then there were those students who lived in extreme poverty and relied on public assistance for housing, food, and medical care.

Many of the same activities I experienced at Union Branch were also in place at Dupuy (e.g., holiday plays, music, Negro History Week). However, after much reflection, I concluded that the teachers at Dupuy were better prepared and were always working together to improve their practice. My cousin and I did not ride the school bus but instead rode to school with my aunt every day. Consequently, we had to stay after school when there were faculty meetings, workshops, or parent-teacher conferences. On fair-weather days, we enjoyed complete ownership of the basketball court, the monkey bars, and the merry-go-round. However, during inclement weather, we had to stay in the building, where we completed homework assignments or listened to teachers' discussions about curricular and instructional issues. Representatives from publishing companies would come by to conduct orientation workshops, sometimes using my cousin and me as guinea pigs. Hence, we often knew about new instructional programs and approaches before they were introduced to the other students.

At Dupuy, teachers would also have discussions about the implementation of instructional models, use of materials, and appropriateness of the curriculum. I remember how some of them, like my sixth grade teacher, Mrs. Tucker, never embraced a new program wholeheartedly, disregarding everything else she had ever learned. She would say something like, "Well, I'll use the new programmed reading materials, but I'm not going to stop using my basal readers. You just can't let children work on their own all the time. They need to be taught. Otherwise, why are we here?" She, along with many of the other teachers, was very much like Mrs. Charity. They used several instructional approaches to promote skill mastery and comprehension. There was much direct instruction (DI), along with group work, independent work, discovery learning, the incorporation of music and art, and activities that today's educators would refer to as *constructivist*. There was also a major focus on learning for understanding. For example, I remember how our Virginia history textbooks often stated that most slaves were treated fairly and were well taken care of by their masters. Most slaves were satisfied with how they lived. I remember how Mrs. Tucker and other teachers always had us read this information and then discuss it as a class. "Let's talk about what you just read. Do you really think Negroes were satisfied being slaves? Did the Hebrews enjoy being slaves?" We learned from these questions to think critically, to question the experts when what we heard or read was inconsistent with beliefs, morals, and values that emanated from our community culture.

Matoaca High School

When mandatory full integration began, we were all transferred to Matoaca High School, a combination junior-and-senior high school. Many of us experienced a great deal of anxiety, some of which was experienced by most students making the transition from elementary to junior high school. I asked myself, "How will I find my way around that big school without getting lost? Will I be able to get from one class to another in 4 minutes? Will I be able to memorize the combination to my locker, open it, grab the appropriate materials, and get to class before the tardy bell rings?" In addition to these questions, many of us understood that we were making history, moving into a world where we had never been before. For the first time, we would be the minority in our formal educational setting. Most or all of our teachers, guidance counselors, and administrators would be White. We would attend schools alongside students who were taught to hate us, who had been told for years that they were better than we were. We were told by our teachers at Union Branch and Dupuy that we would have to work hard to keep up with the White students and that we always had to be better. Conversely, many of our parents told us that these children and their parents were nothing more than poor white trash (PWT), and we should never accept their beliefs about our inferiority and their superiority. As I have written elsewhere (Trent, 1993),

> I could not understand why such hatred existed between human beings that had never once had the opportunity to engage in a civil, sincere interchange. From my observations, I knew that little colored boys and little white boys liked to do some of the same things. I saw them zooming down freshly paved sidewalks on their flashy bikes equipped with red and white streamers, mirrors, reflections, and wired baskets. Though our bikes were not as fancy (we sometimes built them ourselves), we simply lived to ride them. (pp. 20-21)

Now I understand that this separation had been handed down from generation to generation and was spawned and perpetuated by ignorance and hatred. Furthermore, this legacy of inequality and systemic oppression resulted in negative outcomes for many African American students. For example, at the end of the 1st year, I discovered that most of us from Dupuy passed seventh grade, many of us holding honor roll status for most or all of the year. However, only a few students from Union Branch achieved this status. Most of these students, including Quentin, were retained but administratively placed in eighth grade to avoid accusations of racism and discrimination. Needless to say, sometimes, I tremble when I think about this sequence of events. Quentin failed seventh grade and eventually dropped out of high school. *It could have been me!*

TEACHER PREPARATION FROM A CULTURAL-HISTORICAL PERSPECTIVE

Many components needed in teacher preparation programs designed to meet the needs of African American students are embedded in the summary of my early formal educational experiences. Due to space constraints and the focus of this book, I provide more specific information about some of the mediating artifacts or tools that may help preservice teachers develop a comprehensive understanding of what constitutes effective teaching for African American students and other culturally and linguistically diverse (CLD) students with exceptionalities. These include, but are not limited to, knowledge about (a) one's own beliefs and frames of reference, (b) instructional theories and integrated instructional approaches, (c) additional content such as multicultural education, and (d) creating and sustaining positive school, home, and community relations.

Continuous Evaluation of Beliefs and Frames of Reference

Just as I observed among my elementary school teachers, other teacher educators and researchers have emphasized the need for teachers to engage in continual reflection about their beliefs and practices and to engage in collaborative discourse, reflection, and teaching-learning activities with their colleagues (Cochran-Smith, 1995; Zeichner, 1994). This understanding about the evolution of an activity system may lead to deeper insights about individual cultural-historical experiences that influence beliefs, actions, and the ability of the subject of an activity system (e.g., teacher education faculty) to engage in creative, substantive problem solving.

For example, Cochran-Smith (1995) and her colleagues developed a teacher education program that encourages prospective teachers, experienced teachers, and teacher educators to

> examine much of what is usually unexamined in the tightly braided relationships of language, culture, and power in schools and schooling. This kind of examination inevitably begins with our own histories as human beings and as educators; our own experiences as members of particular races, classes, and genders; and as children, parents, and teachers in the world. (p. 500)

To evaluate beliefs and personal frames of reference, student teachers maintained personal narrative essays "about their lives and the experiences that have shaped their views of race, culture, and diversity" (Cochran-Smith, 1995, p. 500). This activity will not only be beneficial to students at the individual level but also at the group level. For instance, in the program Cochran-Smith noted, some African American student teachers confronted inner conflicts about both escaping and embracing their heritages. Conversely, some European American student teachers developed a deeper understanding of how, by virtue of their race, class, and education level, they and their offspring enjoyed privileges that were, in some instances, denied others who were different (e.g., in race, religion, or ability-disability status). Among other benefits, discussions about these insights helped student teachers to understand how oppression affects both the oppressor and the oppressed and how these issues of power and privilege must be acknowledged and confronted consciously in the everyday reflections and actions of teachers. From my perspective, I believe that only through these types of experiences can teachers develop a more substantive understanding of themselves and their colleagues as they attempt to meet the needs of African American exceptional learners. This focus must occur throughout the preparation process in courses, practica, and student teaching experiences (Obiakor, 2001; Utley & Obiakor, 2001).

Instructional Theories and Integrated Instructional Approaches

Another theme that emerged from my biography was that effective teachers use more than one instructional approach to teach children whose cultural experiences (i.e., verbal and non-verbal language patterns, language differences, and learning styles) may be different from those of the mainstream culture. According to Kea, Trent, & Davis (in press):

> Clearly, due to our increasingly diverse school population, preservice teachers—particularly in special education—must be prepared to implement instruction emanating from theories including behaviorism, cognitive psychology, and social constructivism. Even more importantly, in their coursework and practical experiences preservice teachers must have opportunities to appropriate these tools in an integrated manner based on ongoing assessment of their practice and student performance. (p. 11)

Englert, Tarrant, and Mariage (1992) identified four principles of social constructivism, namely: (a) embed instruction in meaningful and purposive activities, (b) promote a classroom dialogue for self-regulated learning, (c) maintain instruction that is responsive to students, and (d) establish a classroom community for learning. Entrenched within these four principles are instructional approaches emanating from both reductionist and constructivist theories. For instance, when promoting a classroom dialogue for self-regulated learning, "teachers involve students in classroom dialogues about cognitive processes rather than rely on seatwork and independent practice to develop students' ability to self-regulate" (p. 72). This process is not confined to, but might include, the use of DI, cognitive behavior modification, and metacognitive strategies that, in combination, lead to internalization and self-regulated learning. Incorporating this approach in general and special education classrooms may result in the resolution of many students' academic and learning problems at the prereferral level and result in fewer special education referrals.

Additional Content Such As Multicultural Education

My teachers incorporated content about African Americans into the curriculum that was not crafted from a Eurocentric perspective. This content not only focused on the contributions made by African Americans but also presented multiple perspectives and pushed students to think critically, question the experts, and take action when confronted with injustice. Though they did not identify specific terminology to articulate and explain the approaches they used, artifacts designed to address multicultural issues were akin to the four approaches to multicultural education identified by Banks (1998). These four approaches include the *contributions* approach, "in which content about ethnic and cultural groups is limited primarily to holidays and celebrations" (p. 30); the *additive* approach, where "cultural content, concepts, and themes are added to the curriculum without changing its basic structure, purposes, and characteristics" (p. 30); the *transformation* approach, which "changes the canon, paradigms, and basic assumptions of the curriculum and enables students to view concepts, issues, themes, and problems from different perspectives and points of view" (p. 31); and the *social-action* approach, which "extends the transformative curriculum by enabling students to pursue projects and activities that allow them to take personal, social, and civic actions related to concepts, problems, and issues they have studied" (p. 32). These approaches are developmental and move from a factual level (i.e., contributions and additive approaches) to a more analytical level of understanding (i.e., transformative and social-action approaches). These levels should not be considered mutually exclusive but can be strategically embedded within the integrated instructional approaches discussed above.

Preservice teachers can learn about the importance of the above approaches and how they can be used to teach basic skills, higher-order thinking skills, and civic responsibility. For example, in one of my courses, I use a video clip that highlights the work of three teenaged girls, two Hispanic and one African American, who are seeking an injunction to halt the building of schools on toxic-waste sites. Using cooperative learning, I ask my students to develop a unit that will incorporate all four of Banks's approaches within this case study. Some activities and ideas include incorporating the contributions of African Americans and Hispanic Americans to the United States across the curriculum, especially in math and science (contributions approach) and inviting guest speakers who share similar concerns about school construction (additive approach). They also incorporate texts and activities that elucidate both pro and con perspectives (transformative approach); and activities that emphasize the importance of civic responsibility, for example, establishing a group of parents, students, and teachers who will address issues of environmental racism within the school and community settings (social-action approach). In addition, my students have incorporated integrated instructional approaches such as DI and constructivism to accomplish desired outcomes (e.g., using DI to teach scientific information about the effects of toxic substances on humans and, at the same time, using constructivist activities to help students connect prior knowledge and experiences to this new content).

Creating and Sustaining Positive
School, Home, and Community Relations

Many of my teachers lived in our community, attended local churches, and were actively involved in community activities. Also, they were well aware that there were different types of parent involvement and strategically planned how to solicit the support of parents. For example, before integration, our teachers always included student performances in the Parent Teacher Association meetings. This, undoubtedly, encouraged more parents to attend the meetings. Other researchers who have studied African American parent involvement retrospectively have cited this strategy (Walker, 1993). It appears, then, that teachers should be aware of the different types of parent involvement and continually assess their beliefs about parents and communities through a cultural-historical lens. For example, Edwards (1990) reviewed the literature on African American parent involvement and concluded that historically, many school personnel view these parents negatively. Negative perceptions included "poor literacy skills, language deficits, inability to implement suggestions, cultural distance between school and community, unwillingness or inability to attend meetings, and the inability to recognize their importance to their children's achievement" (p. 223). However, Edwards also found that these parents "are deeply concerned with getting an effective and relevant education for their children. They want the educational system to reflect their values and way of life, and they feel they ought to influence and exercise control over their children's education" (p. 223).

Based on the aforementioned findings, it is imperative that teacher educators develop activities that illuminate the cultural-historical origins of these opposing beliefs (e.g., slavery, racism, and discrimination) and encourage the creation of sustainable models that define parental and community involvement more broadly. In addition, these models must acknowledge that since desegregation, African American parents' concerns about the education of their children have not been embraced and addressed by educators and administrators who have maintained control of fiscal, material, and human resources (Fine, 1993). In this vein, teacher educators must develop activities and assignments that require critical examination of school districts and school cultures so that preservice teachers understand from a historical perspective how African American and other CLD parents have been treated in comparison with European American parents. These investigations should prompt preservice teachers to develop, at least hypothetically, parent and community involvement activities that lead to empowerment among African American parents and improved academic and social outcomes for their children. In addition, this focus should increase the chances of African American parents to provide prereadiness and readiness activities for their children and, potentially, reduce special education referrals.

CONCLUSION

In this chapter, I have presented my beliefs about preservice teacher preparation for African American learners and other CLD learners with exceptionalities through a cultural-historical lens. However, before claiming that implementation of these ideas will result in improved outcomes for teacher educators, preservice teachers, and the students they will teach, we must verify our hypotheses empirically and longitudinally. More specifically, teacher educators and researchers must document the learning and development of preservice teachers during their matriculation and early career experiences and examine how their preparation experience influences their reflection and practice. In addition, teacher educators and researchers must determine how prior experiences, coupled with preparation, influence social and academic outcomes for African American learners and other CLD learners with exceptionalities. Also, teacher educators and researchers must begin to study their practices longitudinally in efforts to identify conceptual frameworks and mediating artifacts that lead to preparation of significantly more teachers who can effectively meet the needs of African American learners and other CLD learners with exceptionalities. I believe teacher preparation programs that do not provide opportunities for preservice teachers to engage in critical reflection about the cultural-historical nature of schooling will only continue to perpetuate and reinforce concepts and practices that sustain and camouflage inequity. As teacher educators and researchers we must do better. The time for change is now.

REFERENCES

Artiles, A. J., & Trent, S. C. (2000). Culturally/linguistically diverse students, representation of. In C. R. Reynolds & E. Fletcher-Janzen (Eds.), *Encyclopedia of special education* (2nd ed., pp. 513-517). New York: Wiley.

Banks, J. A. (1998). *An introduction to multicultural education* (2nd ed.). Boston: Allyn & Bacon.

Cochran-Smith, M. (1995). Color blindness and basket making are not the answers: Confronting the dilemmas of race, culture, and language diversity in teacher education. *American Educational Research Journal, 32*(3), 493-522.

Edwards, P. A. (1990). Strategies and techniques for establishing home-school partnerships with minority parents. In A. Barona & E. E. Garcia (Eds.), *Children at risk: Poverty, minority status and other issues in educational equity* (pp. 217-263). Washington, DC: National Association of School Psychologists.

Engeström, Y. (1994). Teachers as collaborative thinkers: Activity-theoretical study of an innovative teacher team. In I. Carlgren, G. Handal, & S. Vaage (Eds.), *Teachers' minds and actions: Research on teachers' thinking and practice* (pp. 43-61). Washington, DC: Falmer.

Engeström, Y. (1999). Activity theory and individual and social transformation. In Y. Engeström, R. Miettinen, & R. Punamaki (Eds.), *Perspectives on activity theory* (pp. 19-36). New York: Cambridge University Press.

Englert, C. S., Tarrant, K. L., & Mariage, T. V. (1992). Defining and redefining instructional practice in special education. *Teacher Education and Special Education, 15*(2), 62-86.

Fine, M. (1993). Apparent involvement: Reflections on parents, power, and urban public schools. *Teachers College Record, 94*(4), 682-710.

Ford, D. Y. (1998). The under-representation of minority students in gifted education: Problems and promises in recruitment and retention. *Journal of Special Education, 32,* 4-14.

Kea, C. D., Trent, S. C., & Davis, C. P. (in press). African American student teachers' perceptions about preparedness to teach students from culturally and linguistically diverse backgrounds. *Multicultural Perspectives.*

Obiakor, F. E. (2001). *It even happens in "good" schools: Responding to cultural diversity in today's classrooms.* Thousand Oaks, CA: Corwin.

Trent, S. C. (1993). A case for multicultural teaching: "On the birth of a manchild—a grandfather's letter." *Holmes Group Forum, 7*(3), 19-22.

Trent, S. C., Artiles, A. J., Fitchett-Bazemore, K., McDaniel, L. L., & Coleman, A. (in press). Addressing ethics, power, and privilege in inclusive classrooms in urban schools: A cultural-historical approach. *Teacher Education and Special Education.*

Utley, C. A., & Obiakor, F. E. (2001). *Special education, multicultural education, and school reform: Components of quality education for learners with mild disabilities.* Springfield, IL: Charles C Thomas.

Walker, V. S. (1993). Caswell County Training School, 1933-1969: Relationships between community and school. *Harvard Educational Review,* 63-182.

Zeichner, K. M. (1994). Research on teacher thinking and different views of reflective practice in teaching and teacher education. In I. Carlgren, G. Handal, & S. Vaage (Eds.), *Teachers' minds and actions: Research on teachers' thinking and practice* (pp. 9-27). Washington, DC: Falmer.

Chapter Sixteen

Culturally Responsive Leadership for African Americans With Exceptionalities

Darrell L. Williams, Christlyn Frederick-Stanley,
and Adell Fair

In today's schools, principals are faced with myriad educational challenges. On a daily basis, principals are charged with the awesome responsibility of overseeing their educational program and ensuring a quality education for all students. However, in more recent years, there has been increased debate about the level of educational service received by students with special needs, particularly African Americans. In many large, urban school districts, African American students constitute the majority of students served in special education programs (e.g., programs for students with learning disabilities, emotional disturbances, and attention deficit disorder). While African American students are overrepresented in these programs, they are underrepresented in gifted and talented programs which may lead to advanced opportunities in the future. This overrepresentation contributes to the deferred dreams of many minority students, particularly African Americans, as they are denied the opportunity to maximize their potential in school and, ultimately, in life (Ford & Harris, 1994; Harris & Ford, 1999).

Despite concerns over the disproportion issue, the number of African American students placed in special education programs has continued to increase. Ideally, when African American students and White students enter school, their academic skills are quite similar. However, by fourth grade, there is a gap between the academic skills of African American and White students. Not only is there an increase in the achievement gap, but also, a substantial number of African American students are placed in lower-track special education programs while an increased number of Whites are placed into higher-track special education programs. These issues call for culturally responsive leadership in today's general and special education. It has become increasingly evident that African Americans are misidentified, misassessed, miscategorized, misplaced, and misinstructed (Obiakor, 2001). The hope for these students appears to be almost futile. In many instances, those placed in special education are viewed as helpless, hopeless, and future non-contributors to the society. Once students, particularly African Americans, are placed in special education programs, teacher expectations of them are lowered. Teachers tend to use more aggressive discipline with African American males. In fact, in some instances, they begin to feel sorry for them instead of helping them develop the necessary skills to succeed in school and in life. Thus these students rarely receive a quality, life-enhancing education in those special education programs in which they are often inappropriately placed (Patton, 1998). Despite educational reforms that have attempted to address these issues, inequities in education for African Americans with exceptionalities continue to be perpetuated (Daniels, 1998). The critical questions are, why are school principals and leaders silent while negative actions are taking place under their watch. Do they really understand their roles in the teaching and learning process of special education?

At the school level, the principal is the authority or overseer appointed to ensure that each student receives a quality education. The leadership and attitude of the school principal ultimately determine the effectiveness of a school's educational program. Goor and Schwenn (1997) asserted that educational leadership is the number one variable associated with effective schools. Principals produce the climate that makes learning possible and programs successful. Hence, school principals play a key role in providing culturally responsive leadership for African American students with special needs. However, because of increased duty demands, several principals are unaware of the extent of their responsibilities (Goor & Schwenn, 1997) as it relates to special education students. As a result, they delegate related tasks to the special education teacher, diagnostic teacher, or another designee. With the increased debate over various aspects of special education as it pertains to the overrepresentation of African Americans, quality of education received in special education programs, inappropriate placement, and miscategorization, staff development models have been developed to train principals to be more effective leaders of special education programs (Goor & Schwenn, 1997). For instance, many school districts, particularly Milwaukee Public Schools, engage principals in inservice training and professional development workshops that focus on the school's responsibility to provide a free and appropriate education (FAPE) for all students, particularly students with special needs. These trainings and workshops are not followed by awareness and appropriate action. In this chapter, we discuss ways of providing culturally responsive leadership for African American learners with exceptionalities. In addition, we present real examples in the form of cases that we have dealt with in our respective schools (the names of the children have been changed).

QUALITIES OF CULTURALLY RESPONSIVE LEADERSHIP IN SPECIAL EDUCATION

For several decades much attention has been given to the overrepresentation or the disproportionate representation of African Americans in special education (Artiles & Trent, 1994; Lara, 1994;

Patton, 1998; Serwatka & Deering, 1995). Lara described the disproportionate placement that occurs when the representation of a group in special education is disproportionately higher or lower than their numbers in the school district as a whole. Surely, such placements warrant a change in the leadership style exhibited by administrators and teachers in schools and districts where the percentage of African American students enrolled in special education programs is disproportionate to their overall district population. If positive change is to occur, there must be a change in the type of principal leadership in urban school districts.

Culturally responsive leaders focus on the differences of their teachers, students, and parent population (i.e., linguistic, ethnic, racial, socioeconomic, and learning differences). Such leadership does not view student differences as weaknesses or challenge areas but as qualities that make each individual unique and valuable. Culturally responsive leaders embrace individualities; effort is made to acknowledge individualities while sharing commonality. In fact, such leaders promote opportunities for differences to be recognized and provide opportunities to encourage growth and development (Sapon-Shevin, 2001). They realize recognizing and respecting students' cultural differences not only entails tolerance, as well, but also encouraging and allowing them to be themselves. Additionally, such leaders are aware of their personal strengths and weaknesses as they collaborate with, and empower, others around them to help provide students with support. They exhibit a sense of self-confidence that allows others to feel comfortable and does not prohibit others from being themselves. They trust and motivate others to work together to meet the academic and social needs of all students. Such leaders place importance on creating a family-like atmosphere within the school community where its stakeholders strive for collective success rather than for personal gratification. In the learning community, culturally responsive leaders establish a purpose and collaborate with students, teachers, parents, and community leaders to create a cohesive and cooperative environment that promotes student growth and development. To a large measure, they are team players who celebrate diversity and view students' cultural differences as assets rather than deficits.

Culturally responsive leaders allow all students to benefit and maximize their potential to learn, achieve, and succeed. They do not look for ways to categorize students; they encourage individualities and build on them to create a multifaceted, multicultural, multitalented learning community. This community works together to meet individual needs, value each member, and ensure higher learning through increased participation of various community members. Patton and Townsend (1997) noted that in an inclusive environment where educators plan to address the sociocultural and psychosocial needs of African American students, students, families, and communities are involved. Under the guidance of culturally responsive leaders, students would find a school community where their involvement has an identified role. Students know what to do and they know what is expected of them. Parents know how they can get involved in their children's education, and they feel accepted. In such learning communities, teachers go beyond the traditional responsibilities to ensure success for students outside the classroom. Members of the community know how they can benefit the school community, and they know how their efforts are directly correlated to the school vision and to student achievement.

PROBLEMS FACING SCHOOL LEADERS AND ADMINISTRATORS

Over the past 2 decades, there has been increased debate about African American students being placed in disproportionate numbers in special education classes (Singh & Ellis, 1997). The

---

BOX 16.1 CASE ONE

Ben was an African American third grader from the Cabrini Green Housing Project in Chicago. He had recently transferred to a new school in a suburban district. Prior to Ben's arrival at the new school, his teacher viewed his cumulative records from the previous school. Although Ben had not been a straight-A student at his previous school and had a few behavior concerns, he was a fairly good student who maintained B-average grades. However, upon discovering the environment where Ben came from, his teacher commented to the special education teacher, "I am getting another kid from the projects that most likely can't read and has a lot of behavior concerns. He may need to be tested early so we can help him in special education before it's too late during the school year."

---

identification of African Americans as candidates for special education programs is not a new phenomenon. During the civil rights movement, tension around racial issues and cultural diversity was common. Assessment of intelligence was often used to redefine racial and gender diversity as equivalent to being inferior. Such assessment gave birth to the deficit model of diversity. The deficit model viewed African Americans from a negative perspective and assumed that African Americans lacked intelligence before providing them with an opportunity to demonstrate their knowledge or skills.

Today, African Americans are still viewed from a deficit perspective. In many of our schools, African American students, especially those who come from homes with limited economic resources, are viewed through a negative lens when it comes to education. One of the major factors that contributes to this demise of African American student achievement by way of special education is teacher expectation (Obiakor, 2001). Many educators assume that poor African American students automatically need to be placed in special education programs to "right the wrong" or "recondition the mind" of students from the corruption in most urban environments. Although the realities of urban poverty are evident, the ability of these students cannot be misjudged based on their race and the environment from which they come. Consider Case One (see Box 16.1).

Such racist and discriminatory practices lie at the root of many social and academic achievement problems for African Americans (Ford & Harris, 1994). Despite awareness of such knowledge, the ability of African American students continues to be influenced by factors such as race and economic status. Unfortunately, many school leaders and administrators carry such beliefs into the classroom and then put them into practice. These beliefs and practices have proven to be detrimental to the quality of education that African American students receive in many schools. As Grossman (1991) pointed out,

> Those who believe there are ethnic and class differences in intelligence find it understandable that some groups are disproportionately placed in classes for the retarded and that Euro-American middle-class students are more likely to be assigned to courses of study (tracks) for "high potential" students in which teachers stress independent study and higher level cognitive skills. At the same time, Hispanic, Native American, African American, and working-class students are over represented in tracks for "low potential" students in which teachers stress instructional techniques that involve concrete, repetitive drill and practice. (p. 20)

BOX 16.2 CASE TWO

Jaron was a fifth-grade student who transferred into a new school. Upon enrolling in the new school, Jaron's behavior began to change. Jaron rarely participated in class discussions and rarely completed class work and homework assignments as he did prior to being transferred. After a month of his being at this new school, Jaron's first-year teacher referred him for placement in a learning disabilities program. The teacher never discussed this behavior with the student or his parents.

The biases teachers and administrators possess toward African American students also influence how they value their work. In many instances, they tend to view African American students' work to be of poorer quality than it actually is and their intellectual ability to be lower than what data would suggest (Grossman, 1991). When this occurs, teachers are very likely to consider placement in special education. Consider Case Two (see Box 16.2).

It appears that Jaron was referred for special education placement because he performed below teacher expectations in the classroom. However, several factors may have contributed to why he had not performed his best (e.g., school adjustment and change of home environment). During the assessment phase of the referral process, test data indicated that Jaron was not learning disabled but a gifted student who was not performing at his ability level. This scenario often occurs in many schools across the nation and must be addressed by school principals and administrators.

The role of principals and administrators in the identification process for special education is critical. Principals must ensure that students are not being conveniently referred into special education programs. They must help teachers find strategies to work with difficult students; they must empower and encourage teachers to try different techniques to maximize student achievement and minimize student placement in special education programs. Along with principal involvement, parents must be involved in the process as well. Before and when teachers make blanket referrals for students to be placed in special education programs, principals must work with the parents to be sensitive to the students' needs and seek alternatives in collaboration with teachers and parents, to reach and to motivate so-called "hard-to-reach students." According to Goor (1995), "Collaborative principals who promote educational excellence take an active approach in the process in which teachers request help with students before referring for special education evaluation" (pp. 137-138). Thus inservice and preservice training emerge as areas that need to be addressed. Graybill (1997) noted that lack of teacher training, poor learning environments, and poor self-esteem are associated more with students being placed in special education programs than their ability to learn. Hence improved teacher preparation regarding cultural learning styles may serve as a vehicle to address the number of referrals and placement of African American students in special education, and provide them with more opportunities to succeed.

LEADERSHIP PREPARATION IN TODAY'S SCHOOLS

One of the primary factors that contribute to African American placement in special education programs is lack of teacher training (Graybill, 1997). To provide a quality education for students with special needs, particularly African Americans, teacher preparation programs must be reformed to produce culturally responsive leaders. These programs must begin to prepare school leaders to implement programs for diverse groups of learners. As Ewing (1995) confirmed,

> Teacher education programs have failed to produce quality educators to improve school outcomes for African American students. In addition, traditional teacher education programs continue to prepare ethnocentric teachers and administrators who serve as barriers to improving school outcomes for African American children. (p. 191)

She added,

> It is the major responsibility of schools, colleges, and departments of education to ensure that knowledge and information applicable to culturally based learning and behavioral styles, teaching styles, culturally sensitive proactive educational practices, and family and community values be incorporated in teacher education programs. (p. 191)

In many cases, teachers and leaders enter urban settings with negative, preconceived notions about teaching urban children. They often label these children as failures before giving them a chance to be winners. Delpit (1992) noted that teacher preparation programs expose student teachers and future leaders to an education based on name-calling and labeling to conceal its flaws. In an informal conversation with a new teacher (European American female) who taught in an urban school composed of a majority of African American and Hispanic students, she commented, "I should have taken the job in the suburbs as my college advisor suggested, because these kids are too difficult for me to handle" (personal communication, May 10, 2001). Similarly, school leaders and administrators bring their own biases and values to schools and classrooms. When students, particularly African American students, behave, look, learn, and talk differently (Obiakor, 2001) from their teacher or other European American students, school teachers, with the support of their leaders, assume something is mentally wrong with them. Because African American males exhibit more lively behavior and are more outspoken, they are often targeted for placement in special education programs (e.g., for the emotionally disturbed). Instead of teachers and leaders viewing such student strengths as assets, they often view them as deficiencies (Dooley & Voltz, 1999). When college professors fail to provide balance in perspectives in leadership preparation programs, they indiscriminately encourage teachers to develop attitudes that prevent diverse learners from receiving a quality education (Dooley & Voltz, 1999). Such practice has been to the detriment of African American students. Teachers must be trained to use culturally relevant practices that meet the learning needs of a wide range of students.

Effective leaders encourage teachers to be effective. Grant and Gomez (1995) reported that effective teachers of students (a) have high expectations for their students and believe all students are capable of academic success; (b) communicate clearly, pace lessons appropriately, involve students in decisions, monitor students' progress, and provide frequent feedback; (c) use culturally relevant teaching approaches that integrate the students' native language and dialect, culture, and community into classroom activities to make input more relevant and comprehensible; and (d) use curricula in teaching strategies that promote coherence, relevance, progression, and continuity. Effective implementation of these strategies has yielded positive academic outcomes for students. Consider Case Three (see Box 16.3).

BOX 16.3 CASE THREE

Tim was an African American eighth grader who had been enrolled in special education classes since elementary school. During Tim's years in special education, he was taught by teachers who had high expectations of him. They assigned him culturally relevant and challenging work that contributed to his intellectual and social growth. In many cases, they assigned Tim more work to complete to strengthen his skills. These teachers used culturally relevant teaching strategies to meet his learning needs. In addition, they did not view Tim's learning disability as an excuse for lack of achievement but rather as a stumbling block that could be carved into a beautiful stepping stone to maximizing his potential. Tim graduated from middle school with honors.

As principals and administrators, we must be proactive in changing our own attitudes as well as changing the attitudes of teachers to embrace the cultural differences of the diverse student population we serve. In an informal conversation, an administrator in a large urban school district commented, "Many administrators and teachers do not want students with special needs in their schools because they may bring down test scores or prevent other students from learning due to requiring much of the teachers time" (personal communication, January 9, 2001). Preparing administrators and teachers to embrace the concept of cultural diversity will require professional development which examines content, methods of instruction, and teaching material (Dooley & Voltz, 1999). To facilitate this process, the principal must play a critical role. According to Guillaume, Zuniga-Hill, and Yee (1995), principals and administrators must help teachers do the following:

1. Develop a deep knowledge base about diverse ethnic groups and have multiple opportunities for teachers to examine personal attitudes toward students of color.

2. Develop culturally and linguistically supportive strategies and approaches that make learning available and equitable for all students.

3. Have ample exposure to students of diverse backgrounds and to teachers who can model appropriate instructional approaches.

4. Commit to professional growth regarding issues of diversity. (p. 70)

In addition, administrators and teachers must form meaningful and family-like relationships with students and parents. Creating such a family-like atmosphere in schools can develop caring attitudes toward students and cultivate sensitivity to students' needs, encourage understanding, and enhance teaching and learning. Effective implementation of such practices will lead to greater educational outcomes for diverse learners, especially African Americans.

To prepare leaders for today's schools, efforts must be made by principals and administrators to recruit teachers. To increase the quality of education received by African American students, especially students with special needs, greater recruitment of African American teachers must occur. As Ewing (1995) noted, the number of undergraduate special education majors in colleges, universities, and teacher education programs was 78% White and only 11% African American.

Recruitment of minority teachers, particularly African Americans, is the key to promoting a quality education for African American students. These percentages are staggering, considering that most of the students in special education are African American, yet they are being taught by a majority of White teachers. These percentages are also similar when compared to the racial demographics in many large urban school districts. During the 1998-1999 school year, Milwaukee Public Schools had a 79.8% minority student population compared to a 73% White teaching staff and 21% African American teaching staff (Public Policy Forum, 1999). To advocate for more African American teachers does not imply that White teachers cannot effectively teach African American students. However, to provide the best education possible to the masses of urban learners, who are composed of a majority of African American or other minority groups, it would be advantageous to equip our classrooms with culturally sensitive teachers and administrators who reflect their culture. Dooley and Voltz (1999) asserted that there is a need to diversify the pool of teachers in public schools to effectively teach and address the needs of all students as well as prepare teachers. There are several advantages to having a more culturally diverse teaching population that reflects the students being served, especially African American students with special needs. Ewing (1995) asserted that

1. African American teachers are less likely to mislabel culturally diverse students as disabled.

2. African American teachers can improve cross-cultural understanding and diverse cultural tolerance.

3. African American teachers can provide on-site collaboration for European American teachers.

4. African American teachers can encourage the development of a positive school climate that meets the academic, cultural, social, and emotional needs of African American learners. (p. 204)

We must begin to encourage more African Americans to pursue careers in teacher education. Only then will the missing link—the African American school leader or administrator—become the connecting chain.

CULTURALLY RESPONSIVE LEADERSHIP FOR LIFE

Culturally responsive leadership involves working with knowledge producers, parents, and community resources. Patton (1998) noted that there is a lack of African American knowledge producers in special education for African American learners. Patton (1998) called for a change to representatives who are culturally responsive and competent knowledge producers in the area of special education. These producers of knowledge must be responsive to their students and the community they serve. The voices of African American knowledge producers who recommend viable strategies for better education of these students is at a whisper. European American researchers have written the majority of literature pertaining to the education for African American students. To change this trend, a system must be developed by which the voices of African American knowledge producers can be heard, confirmed, and affirmed (Patton, 1998). As Patton pointed out, "It is paramount for minorities, especially African Americans, to write critical narratives about philosophy, theory, values, methodologies, systems and processes that undergird special education from their own ontological, epistemological, and anxioloigcal [*sic*] perspectives" (p. 31). Inclusion of these voices in the discussion of African American students would expand teacher knowledge of student learning styles and contribute to increased student achievement and decreased student placement in special education programs.

As indicated, culturally responsive leadership involves working with parents and community members. The role that parents play in their children's education has been underestimated and downplayed. However, to effectively address the needs of African American students with special needs, the important role of parents must be recognized. Parents are the first teachers of their children. Hence their participation with principals and administrators in discussions about their children is paramount, especially during the special education referral process. When a referral is made for possible special education consideration of students, principals and administrators must be sure that parents are invited for meetings and asked to sign the necessary forms. The multidisciplinary team (e.g., principal, teacher, psychologist, diagnostic teacher, speech pathologist, and social worker) will convene a meeting to share the results and make a determination of placement. In many instances, parents of many African American students do not show up for these important meetings. Principals and administrators must know that parents do not show up for meetings when

1. They assume they will hear a lot of negative comments regarding their children.

2. They cannot take off from work in the middle of the day to attend the meeting.

3. They assume that the teacher knows what is best for their child, since they went to school to learn how to work with children.

4. They assume their input is not needed, since school personnel already know what they want to do regarding their child.

Principals and administrators must maximize the opportunities for parents to participate on assessment teams by scheduling meetings at times convenient for parents, providing transportation, and providing child care accommodations if needed (Goor, 1995). Too often, scheduled assessment meetings occur without parents being present to voice their concerns. In addition, principals and administrators must ensure that information is being communicated in a language and at a level that all participants understand. Culturally responsive leaders empower parents to take a proactive stance on behalf of their children, because their voices are essential in helping to make a decision regarding educational services.

Culturally responsive leaders use community resources appropriately. The goal is to educate African American learners for life. Many opportunities that are present beyond school are limited for these learners because of what happens inside the school. In many instances, after graduation from high school, African American students with special needs have a difficult time obtaining meaningful, self-supporting, and family-supporting jobs. When employers are notified of the status of these students, they are at increased risk of not being hired or being hired in low-level positions. Principals and administrators must ensure that students with special needs are included in all aspects of the schooling that other students are. They must help other administrators, teachers, parents, and students to see that although students with special needs learn differently, they can learn. And students with special needs deserve to have the same opportunity to maximize their full potential in gaining and exploring community resources.

LEADERSHIP VISION FOR THIS CENTURY

Our collective vision is based on our collective experience. As principals and administrators of one of the largest school districts in this nation, we know that traditional methods do not work for African American learners, especially those with exceptionalities. In this century, we believe culturally responsive leaders must be (a) investors, (b) globally aware, (c) involved, and (d) spiritually connected.

Being an Investor

As culturally responsive leaders, we consistently invest in teachers, parents, related professionals, and our students. We understand that we must invest time to nurture, encourage, and educate teachers about culturally relevant teaching strategies. We should allow teachers to gain more expertise and knowledge about how to meet the learning needs of children from different cultures. As investors, our job is to help teachers to become more resourceful and gain confidence in their ability to work with the community to meet the needs of students in the classroom and beyond. As culturally responsive leaders, we have a vested interest in the professional development of our staff to better educate students.

Being Globally Aware

As leaders, we are globally aware to educate our students. We are aware of past and present challenges and stay abreast of future trends to better educate our students. As culturally responsive leaders, we know who we are, we honor our heritage and feel a sense of responsibility to our community. We are dedicated to providing teachers with information and materials necessary to improve the quality of life for all students. We are committed to the vision that the generation coming after us can have a higher quality of, and value for, life than we currently have. As culturally responsive leaders, we are personally committed to making this vision a reality.

Being Involved

Leaders must take time to be involved and build coalitions in the community. Our involvement in the community allows us to form relationships that help us to grow and learn. Building such coalitions and establishing such networks with community leaders promote sharing of resources that may enrich the school community and broaden learning opportunities for our students. We are in tune with what is going on in our school community. We not only listen to what students, parents, teachers, and community partners are saying but we also respond to their concerns and needs. We place a high level of importance on keeping the lines of communication open and clear. We make frantic efforts to communicate with all members in a variety of ways (e.g., written, verbal, nonverbal [gestures], telephone calls, e-mail) regarding student progress.

Being Spiritually Connected

As culturally responsive leaders, we endeavor to be mentally, physically, and spiritually strong. We know African Americans tend to be spiritual people. We are well respected, and we understand how reliable we are. Spiritual belief enables us to have faith in spite of the obstacles we encounter. Spiritual faith gives us the power to believe that what we are doing will make a difference not just for the present generation but for generations to come.

CONCLUSION

In this chapter, we have discussed several aspects of providing culturally responsive leadership for African American students. We incorporated a few of the cases that we have seen. The disproportionate number of African Americans placed in special education programs is a disturbing reality that we must address. Principals and administrators must be proactive in preventing the misassessment, miscategorization, and misplacement of students, particularly African Americans, in special education programs. It is important that we use our influence to gather resources to meet the learning needs of all students. No longer can meeting the academic needs of African American students be dismissed as a hopeless endeavor. We must provide culturally responsive leadership that ensures all students a high quality education. Our goal is to provide opportunities to succeed in school and in life.

From our perspective, to affect the future denial of quality educational opportunities for African American students, especially those with special needs, preservice and inservice training must be provided. We must recruit more African Americans and prepare them to work with a wide range of learners. Future leaders must be prepared to be aware of the cultural differences that are evident in today's schools. We must urge teachers and service providers to recognize, appreciate, and celebrate student diversity. As school leaders, we must help teachers develop and implement strategies used by effective, culturally relevant teachers to educate students. When all teachers begin to teach students using culturally relevant techniques, we will broaden students' knowledge base, expose them to new learning experiences, and provide them with greater opportunities to maximize their potential and succeed in life.

REFERENCES

Artiles, A. J., & Trent, S. C. (1994). Over representation of minority students in special education: A continuing debate. *Journal of Special Education, 27*(4), 410-428.

Daniels, V. I. (1998). Minority students in gifted and special education programs: The case for educational equity. *Journal of Special Education, 32*(1), 41-44.

Delpit, L. D. (1992). Education in a multicultural society: Our future's greatest challenge. *Journal of Negro Education, 61,* 237-249.

Dooley, E. A., & Voltz, D. L. (1999). Educating the African American exceptional learner. In F. E. Obiakor, J. O. Schwenn, & A. F. Rotatori (Eds.), *Advances in special education: Multicultural education for learners with exceptionalities* (pp. 15-33). Stamford, CT: JAI Press.

Ewing, N. (1995). Restructured teacher education for inclusiveness: A dream deferred for African Americans. In B. A. Ford, F. E. Obiakor, & J. Patton (Eds.), *Effective education of African American exceptional learners: New perspectives* (pp. 189-209). Austin, TX: Pro-Ed.

Ford, D. Y., & Harris, J. J., III. (1994). Promoting achievement among gifted black students. *Urban Education, 29*(2), 202-230.

Goor, M. B. (1995). *Leadership for special education administration: A case-based approach.* New York: Harcourt Brace.

Goor, M. B., & Schwenn, J. O. (1997). Preparing principals for leadership in special education. *Intervention in School & Clinic, 32*(3), 133-142.

Grant, C. A., & Gomez, M. L. (1995). *Making schooling multicultural: Campus and classroom.* Englewood Cliffs, NJ: Prentice Hall.

Graybill, S. W. (1997). Questions of race and culture: How they relate to the classroom for African American students. *Clearing House, 70*(6), 311-319.

Grossman, H. (1991). Special education in a diverse society. *Preventing School Failure, 36*(1), 19-28.

Guillaume, A. M., Zuniga-Hill, C., & Yee, I. (1995). Prospective teachers' use of diversity issues in a case study analysis. *Journal of Research and Development in Education, 28*, 69-78.

Harris, J. J., & Ford, D. Y. (1999). Hope deferred again. *Education and Urban Society, 31*(2), 225-238.

Lara, J. (1994). *State data collection and monitoring procedures regarding overrepresentation of minority students in special education* (Report No. 6-1-3). Alexandria, VA: National Association of State Directors of Special Education.

Obiakor, F. E. (2001). Multicultural education: Powerful tool for preparing future general and special educators. *Teacher Education and Special Education, 24*(3), 241-255.

Patton, J. M. (1998). The disproportionate representation of African Americans in special education: Looking behind the curtain for understanding and solutions. *Journal of Special Education, 32*(1), 25-32.

Patton, J. M., & Townsend, B. L. (1997). Creating inclusive environments for African American children and youth with gifts and talents. *Roeper Review, 20*(1), 13-15.

Public Policy Forum. (1999). *An annual report to area citizens: Public schooling in the Milwaukee metropolitan area: Enrollment, staffing, spending, taxes, performance, and ranking.* Milwaukee: Wisconsin Energy Corporation.

Sapon-Shevin, M. (2001). Schools fit for all. *Educational Leadership, 58*(4), 34-39.

Serwatka, T. S., & Deering, S. (1995). Disproportionate representation of African Americans in emotionally handicapped classes. *Journal of Black Studies, 25*(4), 492.

Singh, N. N., & Ellis, C. R. (1997). Value and diversity. *Journal of Emotional and Behavioral Disorders, 5*(1), 24-36.

Chapter Seventeen

Summary Comments: Race, Class, Gender, and Exceptionality of African American Learners

Edgar G. Epps

Schools are greatly influenced by, and cannot be analyzed apart from, the larger social, historical, and cultural contexts. Attempts to improve the quality of education available to African Americans must, therefore, consider how the education system is organized and how it functions. The quality of educational opportunities available to African Americans (and other language, social-class, and gender groups) is consistent with their relative prestige, wealth, and power in U.S. society. African American learners face barriers due to the historical, cultural, and social factors that have shaped the relationship between the African American community and the dominant power group, White Americans. Pervasive attitudes of racism (including racial stereotypes and prejudices) as well as differential access to power continue to limit educational opportunities for African Americans in the United States. "The distribution of power—and its expression in structures, ideologies, and practices at various institutional and individual levels— is significantly racialized in our society" (Omi, 2000, p. 244). Such inequities produce the achievement discrepancies in contemporary U.S. education.

Historically, academic writing about African American children and families has been based on the assumption that attitudes and patterns of behavior observed among European Americans are "normal," whereas those observed among other racial and ethnic populations are deviant. Similarly, the normal, White, middle-class male has been the standard against which women and lower-class children of all racial and ethnic groups, and children with disabilities, have been compared. It is important to understand that all such categorizations are social constructions, created and shaped by the society in which the individuals and groups reside. Societal definitions of appropriate behaviors and expectations for individuals in the various categories change over time (Omi, 2000), often in response to political and legal actions by advocates who perceive that certain groups or individuals are experiencing discrimination in education and other arenas (Higham, 1997).

In *Creating Successful Learning Environments for African American Learners With Exceptionalities*, Obiakor and Ford challenge us to put aside the traditional American assumptions about the capabilities of African American students. In order to create successful learning environments for African American learners with exceptionalities, we must first accept the challenge of shifting our paradigms and powers. While some progress has been made in recent years (Gay, 2001), African American students in Grades K-12, on average, score below the national average on most measures of academic achievement. Indeed, the Black-White test score gap (Jencks & Phillips, 1998) is the focus of considerable attention among researchers (e.g., Ferguson, 2000). While most scholars and educators reject the hereditary explanation (e.g., Kincheloe, Steinberg, & Gresson, 1996), there are still vestiges of other deficit conceptualizations influencing the way schools are organized and instructions are delivered (Carter & Goodwin, 1994). Perhaps the most persistent conceptual paradigm that influences educational outcomes is the deficit model. This model assumes that African American parents and communities, because of historical subjugation, institutional racism, and limited opportunities, do not provide children with the types of experiences required for success in American public schools. Compensatory education programs such as Head Start and Title I of the Elementary and Secondary Education Act (Gordon & Wilkerson, 1966) have been designed to compensate for these "deficiencies." Evaluations of these programs have yielded mixed results, but their impact has been modest at best (Borman, 2000). Where, then, shall we look for strategies that might maximize the potential of African American learners? Strategies that have been used in the past include (a) school desegregation, (b) inclusion by reducing tracking, (c) early childhood education, (d) studying effective schools to look for models, (e) searching for effective instructional strategies, (f) improving teacher quality, (g) reducing class size, and (h) restructuring schools. It is unfortunate that the major reform movements of the 1980s and 1990s have narrowly focused on higher academic standards, school-based management, and increasing multicultural content in the curriculum. Missing in these foci are approaches that have been tried, proven, or recommended. In this book, Obiakor and Ford call attention to the variety of ideas and programs that have been discussed or implemented by scholars and educators as they attempt to address the issue of improving African American students' opportunities for high-quality educational experiences. In addition to the ideas presented by this book's authors and contributors, I discuss a few model programs that appear to have promise for helping educators reconceptualize the role of schools in providing high-quality education for African American learners, especially those with exceptionalities.

THE TALENT DEVELOPMENT MODEL

The Talent Development Model is a focus of the Center for Research on the Education of Students Placed at Risk (CRESPAR) housed jointly at Johns Hopkins University and Howard University. It attempts to provide an alternative to the traditional sorting model of American education. In the words of Boykin (2000),

> As we seek to effectuate a new paradigm, we should recognize the consequences of the old through the practice of sorting out the vast majority of students who do not have access to a high-quality, challenging education. Student labeling results in such assignments as the "slow learner," the "underachiever," and the unmotivated student. As a consequence, when things go wrong at school, the student is blamed as the source of the problem and is thus in need of repair or remediation. Sorting leads to the waste of human talent that our society will need in the 21st century. The practice of sorting is all the more problematic when one considers that it all too often is done along race, class, and cultural lines (Parish & Aquila, 1996). As schools sort, they demoralize. As they sort, they alienate and embitter. They disenfranchise. As schools sort, they immobilize, disaffect, and restrict life opportunities. (pp. 6-7)

The Talent Development Model begins with the belief that all students can learn in an academic setting that is demanding and characterized by achievement expectations. According to Boykin (2000), this goal is reachable in schools "that are committed to providing the appropriate support and the appropriate structure, assistance, and conditions for learning" (p. 7) and in schools devoted to "maximizing every child's potential for academic development" (p. 7). Boykin explained that *talent*, as used in the model, "refers to high-level performance, skill, understanding, or knowledge that is predicated on an age-appropriate standard of excellence" (pp. 7-8). Development "refers to cultivating, fostering, and bringing talent to fruition." He expanded on this by emphasizing that the focus is on sustaining talent, enhancing talent, and promoting talent while "encouraging and motivating students to reach high standards of performance" (p. 8). Six themes contained in this framework are as follows:

1. *Focusing on assets.* Schools should capitalize on the adaptive assets children come to school with based on their home and community experiences.

2. *Transitional support.* Schooling should be designed to help students across key developmental transitions (e.g., from elementary school to middle school, or middle school to high school).

3. *Constructivist and activist learning.* While ensuring that children acquire the basic skills, the framework also focuses on the development of higher-order and critical thinking skills, as well as on creative problem solving, critical analysis, and self-reflection.

4. *Preparation for the 21st century.* Children must develop communication skills, creative writing and composition skills, higher-level numeracy skills, and conflict resolution skills. They must also develop computer skills and become multiculturally fluent. In addition, they must become producers of knowledge rather than consumers of knowledge.

5. *School as community.* The school should be a place to which students feel they belong. Students and staff members should feel that they are an integral part of this community and that they share a common purpose.

6. *Meaningful and connected learning.* What students learn should be relevant to their lives and future goals. Rather than acquiring knowledge in abstract and piecemeal terms, knowledge and learning should be thematically connected among various subjects and disciplines, and connected to the world of school in practical and meaningful ways so that education is centered proactively in children's lived experiences. (Boykin, 2000, p. 13)

The results of scholarly research on the Talent Development Model are summarized by Boykin (2000). The research includes studies of programs designed for students from preschool through high school that have been tested in some of the most challenging schools in cities such as Baltimore and Washington, D.C. While there are works that have demonstrated that "schools can achieve substantial and systematic improvements in both student learning and achievement and teacher support and performance," successful implementation of intervention programs requires "constant attention, energy, and hard work" (Balfanz & MacIver, 2000, p. 156). It remains to be seen whether such reforms can be implemented on a large scale, given the improvements in infrastructure and belief systems that would be required to make good on the promise to maximize every African American child's potential for academic development.

CHILD-PARENT CENTERS

Child-Parent Centers were developed in Chicago with Title I funds during the 1970s (Fuerst, 1977) and still exist in a few Chicago public schools. The centers take low-income children from the ages of 3 or 4 and work intensively with them and their parents. The original centers were 5-year programs for children up to the third grade or occasionally higher. Elements of the program include

1. Direct parent involvement in the center program and in activities designed to meet parent needs.

2. Elimination of social and health problems that may interfere with learning.

3. Use of a structured reading, language, and mathematics program.

4. A structured, consistent, long-term approach.

The staff of the Child-Parent Centers includes classroom teachers, teacher aides, home economists, adjustment teachers, teacher-nurses, assistant principals, head teachers, and speech therapists. Class sizes tend to be small (15 in preschool, 22 in primary grades). These centers have been extremely successful by traditional standards. That is, they have taken children from the most poverty-stricken areas of the city and provided them with an educational program that enabled them, by second grade, to score above the national average on a nationally standardized reading-achievement test, achieving a grade equivalent score of 3.1 compared to a national average of 2.8. In one school that continued the program through sixth grade, sixth graders performed at the national norm as well. Graduates who spent 5 years or more in Child-Parent Centers continued to perform near grade level in Grades 7 and 8 (Fuerst, 1977). This is a model that could be replicated widely if school districts were willing to allocate resources to a program that focuses on prevention of developmental delays in early reading and mathematics skills.

SUCCESS FOR ALL

Success for All was developed by Slavin and his colleagues at Johns Hopkins University and is now an integral part of the Talent Development Model. As Slavin and Madden (2000) pointed out,

> Success for All [is] a comprehensive program that focuses on reading, writing, and language arts in the elementary grades. Success for All provides well-structured curriculum materials and instructional strategies for prekindergarten, kindergarten, and Grades 1 through 6 reading, writing, and language arts, one-to-one tutoring for primary grades children struggling in reading, and extensive family support services. (p. 111)

This program is widely used in urban schools serving low-income African American and other Title I eligible children (Slavin & Madden, 2000). Independent evaluations of the program have consistently found that, where it is implemented effectively, student performance is superior to that in comparison schools.

OTHER POWERFUL INITIATIVES

There are other promising reform efforts, such as the Comer School Development Program (Comer, Haynes, Joyner, & BenAvie, 1996) and Roots and Wings (Slavin & Madden, 2000). In providing the brief descriptions of programs above, I have attempted to demonstrate that researchers and educators working together can devise strategies that hold promise for improving the academic performance of African American children and youth, especially those with exceptionalities. Researchers and educators have learned from experience that children perform best when their total ecology is supported at home and in school. Sustained intellectual growth depends on the quality of relationships established between parents, teachers, and children. For example, Slavin and Madden reiterated that

> Family Support and Integrated Services are designed to achieve three goals in Roots and Wings: (a) ensure success for every child; (b) empower parents through partnerships; and (c) integrate health, social, and educational services to children and families. Each school has a Family Support Team, a site-based team of school personnel who are concerned with four areas: attendance, school-based intervention, parent involvement, and creating and maintaining effective connections with community service providers. In addition, there is a network of community service providers who provide a broad range of necessary services for children and families. (p. 121)

An important feature of the philosophy of Roots and Wings is its "approach to special and remedial education called 'neverstreaming'" (Slavin & Madden, 2000, p. 124). In this approach, special education resources are directed toward prevention and early intervention. This approach is focused primarily on children who have not been identified for special education. However, children who have individualized education programs (IEPs) are mainstreamed to the maximum extent possible. This is consistent with other evidence that schools can create an inclusive environment for all students and that students with special needs can be educated in regular classes if they are provided with appropriate supports (Obiakor, 2001).

CONCLUSION

As we have seen, *Creating Successful Learning Environments for African American Learners With Exceptionalities* is a book for this century. It proactively suggests new ways of doing things. Clearly, the institutions of society are designed to maintain established patterns of dominance and subordination among competing groups. Since schools mirror the total society, is it reasonable to expect them to eliminate racial, ethnic, and social class inequality in access to high-quality education? Kohn (1998) made the argument that privileged parents undermine school reform to protect their children's advantages in the traditional sorting arrangements found in American schools. Who controls the schools may be more important in the long run than the quality of programs designed to provide excellence in education for African American children with and without exceptionalities. The continued reliance on standardized tests and the resistance to heterogeneous grouping arrangements in elementary classrooms, as well as the insistence on tracking in high schools, suggest that it will be extremely difficult to provide high-quality education for all children in this historically individualistic and competitive society. The lingering vestiges of racism and discrimination (neighborhood segregation, poor schools, limited access to higher education) are readily apparent to all observers. Just as Obiakor and Ford and their invited contributors indicated throughout this book, I agree that African American families and communities must mobilize all their political and economic resources to break the hold of tradition on our schools. It may be necessary to focus increasingly on community-based education programs that are not totally dependent on the political commitment of White Americans. Knowledge is power! I believe this book provides the kind of knowledge rarely visible in traditional texts today. Hopefully, it will be on the reading lists of undergraduate and graduate students, preservice and inservice trainers, general and special educators, community and national leaders, and local and national consultants. No doubt, we can all make a *big* difference in the educational success of African American learners, especially those with exceptionalities.

REFERENCES

Balfanz, R., & MacIver, D. (2000). Transforming high-poverty urban middle schools into strong learning institutions: Lessons from the first five years of the Talent Development Middle School. *Journal of Education for Students Placed at Risk, 5*(1&2), 137-158.

Borman, G. D. (2000). Title I: The evolving research base. *Journal of Education for Students Placed at Risk, 5*(1&2), 27-45.

Boykin, A. W. (2000). The Talent Development Model of schooling: Placing students at promise for academic success. *Journal of Education for Students Placed at Risk, 5*(1&2), 3-25.

Carter, R. T., & Goodwin, A. L. (1994). Racial identity and education. *Review of Research in Education, 20,* 291-336.

Comer, J. P., Haynes, N. M., Joyner, E. T., & BenAvie, M. (1996). *Rallying the whole village: The Comer process for reforming education.* New York: Teachers College Press.

Ferguson, R. F. (2000). Test-score trends along racial lines, 1971 to 1996: Popular culture and community academic standards. In N. J. Smelser, W. J. Wilson, & F. Mitchell

(Eds.), *American becoming: Racial trends and their consequences* (Vol. 1, pp. 348-390). Washington, DC: National Academy Press.

Fuerst, J. S. (1977, May-June). Child parent centers: An evaluation. *Integrated Education, 15*, 17-20.

Gay, G. (2001). Educational equality for students of color. In J. A. Banks and C. A. Banks (Eds.), *Multicultural education: Issues and perspectives* (6th ed., pp. 197-224). New York: John Wiley.

Gordon, E. W., & Wilkerson, D. A. (1966). *Compensatory education for the disadvantaged: Programs and practices.* New York: College Entrance Examination Board.

Higham, J. (1997). Introduction: A historical perspective. In J. Higham (Ed.), *Civil rights and civil wrongs: Black-White relations since World War II* (pp. 3-30). University Park: Pennsylvania State University Press.

Jencks, C., & Phillips, M. (1998). *The Black-White test score gap.* Washington, DC: Brookings Institution Press.

Kincheloe, J. L., Steinberg, S. R., & Gresson, A. D., III. (Eds.). (1996). *Measured lies: The bell curve examined.* New York: St. Martin's.

Kohn, A. (1998, April). Only for *my* kid: How privileged parents undermine school reform. *Phi Delta Kappan*, pp. 569-577.

Obiakor, F. E. (2001). *It even happens in "good" schools: Responding to cultural diversity in today's classrooms.* Thousand Oaks, CA: Corwin.

Omi, M. A. (2000). The changing meaning of race. In N. J. Smelser, W. J. Wilson, & F. Mitchell (Eds.), *America becoming: Racial trends and their consequences* (Vol. 1, pp. 243-263). Washington, DC: National Academy Press.

Slavin, R. E., & Madden, N. A. (2000). Roots and Wings: Effects of whole-school reform on student achievement. *Journal of Education for Students Placed at Risk, 5*(1&2), 109-136.

Index

**CORWIN
PRESS**

The Corwin Press logo—a raven striding across an open book—represents the happy union of courage and learning. We are a professional-level publisher of books and journals for K-12 educators, and we are committed to creating and providing resources that embody these qualities. Corwin's motto is "Success for All Learners."